Rails: Novice to Ninja

by Glenn Goodrich and Patrick Lenz

Copyright © 2016 SitePoint Pty. L

Product Manager: Simon Mackie
English Editor: Kelly Steele

Technical Editor: Enrique Gonzalez
Cover Designer: Alex Walker

Notice of Rights

Notice of Liability

The author and publisher have made every effort to ensure the accuracy of the information herein. However, the information contained in this book is sold without warranty, either express or implied. Neither the authors and SitePoint Pty. Ltd., nor its dealers or distributors will be held liable for any damages to be caused either directly or indirectly by the instructions contained in this book, or by the software or hardware products described herein.

Trademark Notice

Rather than indicating every occurrence of a trademarked name as such, this book uses the names only in an editorial fashion and to the benefit of the trademark owner with no intention of infringement of the trademark.

Published by SitePoint Pty. Ltd.

48 Cambridge Street Collingwood
VIC Australia 3066
Web: www.sitepoint.com
Email: business@sitepoint.com

ISBN 978-0-9943470-0-8 (print)

ISBN 978-0-9943470-6-0 (ebook)
Printed and bound in the United States of America

About Glenn Goodrich

Glenn Goodrich started programming when he was 12 and hasn't really stopped since. He has worked for large enterprises, startups, and everything in between. Glenn found Ruby in 2006 or so and (like so many other nerds) fell immediately in love. He can be found on the SitePoint Ruby channel, editing and writing and such. Glenn enjoys writing almost as much as coding, and he sincerely hopes this book helps at least one new Rubyist on their path.

About SitePoint

SitePoint specializes in publishing fun, practical, and easy-to-understand content for web professionals. Visit http://www.sitepoint.com/ to access our blogs, books, newsletters, articles, and community forums. You'll find a stack of information on JavaScript, PHP, Ruby, mobile development, design, and more.

I would like to dedicate this book my wife, who saw past the nerd and helps me see the life beyond the code every day.

Table of Contents

Chapter 5   Models, Views, and Controllers..139

Chapter 6   Helpers, Forms, and Layouts 175

Preface

When Simon Mackie approached me to update this book from Rails 2 to Rails 5, I didn't hesitate. For one, he said "Simon says 'UPDATE THIS BOOK'!" (groan). For two, I love writing and I love Rails, so this opportunity was a no-brainer. Throughout the process, I have remembered why Rails is such a paragon of productivity, and I've also discovered much I didn't know about the framework. I honestly believe there is no better way to be productive writing a web application than to write about the technology.

I'd be remiss if I didn't point out the truly excellent work done by Patrick Lenz on the first two editions of this book. Patrick has a gift for explaining technical things simply, something I leveraged over and over again in this update. Patrick's work shines through, into this version, and I learned much from both his content and his style.

Finally, I have always enjoyed writing. I have written many blog posts in my technical life, always with two goals: Firstly, to solidify my own understanding of the topic, and secondly, to share my knowledge with a community. The thought of someone getting better as a result of reading something I've penned is exhilarating. I sincerely hope that this book launches you on a career as rewarding as mine has been, and that you find the same joy in sharing your knowledge.

Who Should Read This Book

This book is for web developers who want to learn Ruby on Rails. You don't need any prior experience with Ruby, although some experience with another programming language will probably be useful.

Conventions Used

You'll notice that we've used certain typographic and layout styles throughout this book to signify different types of information. Look out for the following items.

Code Samples

Code in this book is displayed using a fixed-width font, like so:

```
<h1>A Perfect Summer's Day</h1>
 <p>It was a lovely day for a walk in the park. The
↪ birds were singing and the kids were all back at
↪ school.</p>
```

If the code is to be found in the book's code archive, the name of the file will appear at the top of the program listing, like this:

```
                                                      0-1. example.css
.footer {
  background-color: #CCC;
  border-top: 1px solid #333;
}
```

If only part of the file is displayed, this is indicated by the word *excerpt*:

```
                                              0-2. example.css (excerpt)
.footer {
  background-color: #CCC;
  border-top: 1px solid #333;
}
```

If additional code is to be inserted into an existing example, the new code will be displayed in bold:

```
function animate() {
  new_variable = "Hello";
}
```

Where existing code is required for context, rather than repeat all of it, ⋮ will be displayed:

```
function animate() {
  ⋮
  new_variable = "Hello";
}
```

Some lines of code should be entered on one line, but we've had to wrap them because of page constraints. An ↪ indicates a line break that exists for formatting purposes only, and should be ignored:

```
URL.open("http://www.sitepoint.com/responsive-web-design-real
↪ -user-testing/?responsive1");
```

Tips, Notes, and Warnings

 Hey, You!

Tips provide helpful little pointers.

 Ahem, Excuse Me ...

Notes are useful asides that are related—but not critical—to the topic at hand. Think of them as extra tidbits of information.

EXTRA CREDIT

EXTRA CREDIT notes contain additional homework exercises that you can do yourself to further your knowledge of Ruby on Rails. While you don't have to complete the extra credit exercises in order to follow the book, doing so will greatly enhance your understanding of Ruby, Rails, and the Rails ecosystem, so they are recommended.

Make Sure You Always ...

... pay attention to these important points.

Watch Out!

Warnings highlight any gotchas that are likely to trip you up along the way.

Supplementary Materials

- https://github.com/spbooks/rails3v5 has the downloadable code archive and example files for the book. Please note that each chapter has its own branch in the repository. If you're unfamiliar with Git and GitHub, you can simply download the code for each chapter as a Zip file. Go to https://github.com/spbooks/rails3v5/branches/all, select the branch that corresponds with the chapter that you're reading, and the click *Clone or download > Download ZIP*.
- https://www.sitepoint.com/community/ are SitePoint's forums, for help on any tricky web problems.
- **books@sitepoint.com** is our email address, should you need to contact us to report a problem, or for any other reason.

Chapter

Introducing Ruby on Rails

Since Ruby on Rails was first released, it has become a household name (well, in developers' households, anyway). Hundreds of thousands of developers the world over have adopted—and adored—this framework. I hope that, through the course of this book, you'll come to understand the reasons why. Before we jump into writing any code, let's take a stroll down memory lane and explore a little of the history of Ruby on Rails.

First, what exactly *is* Ruby on Rails?

The short-and fairly technical—answer is that Ruby on Rails (often abbreviated to "Rails") is a full-stack web application framework written in Ruby. That is a distinction worth emphasizing. Ruby is a **language** and Rails is a **framework**. Say that last sentence out loud a couple of times. Rails is often mentioned as if it is a language, so understanding that Ruby is the language and Rails is the framework is your first step on this journey of learning.

However, depending on your previous programming experience (and your mastery of tech-jargon, that answer might make little sense to you. Besides, the Ruby on Rails movement—the development principles it represents—really needs to be viewed in the context of web development in general if it is to be fully appreciated.

So, let's define a few of the terms in the definition above while taking in a brief history lesson along the way. Then we'll tackle the question of why learning Rails is one of the smartest moves you can make for your career as a web developer.

A **web application** is a software application that's accessed using a web browser over a network. In most cases, that network is the Internet, but it could also be a corporate intranet. The number of web applications being created has increased exponentially since Rails came into being, due mostly to the ubiquity of broadband internet access and the proliferation of mobile devices. We can only assume that you're interested in writing such a web application, given that you've bought this book!

A **framework** can be viewed as the foundation of a web application. It takes care of many of the low-level details that can become repetitive and boring to code, allowing the developer to focus on building the application's functionality.

A framework gives the developer classes that implement common functions used in *every* web application, including:

- database abstraction (ensuring that queries work regardless of whether the database is MySQL, PostgreSQL, MongoDB, SQLite, or [insert your favorite database here])

- templating (reusing presentational code throughout the application)

- management of user sessions

- generation of clean, search-engine-friendly URLs

Classes?

The reference to *classes* above can be taken to mean "collections of code." I'll cover more about classes later, so hang in there.

A framework also defines the architecture of an application; that is, how the application is physically laid out. This facility can be useful for those of us who fret over which file is best stored in which folder.

In a sense, a framework is an application that has been started for you, and a well-designed application at that. The structure—plus the code that takes care of the boring stuff—has already been written, and it's up to you to finish it off. You are truly standing on the shoulders of giants when you start building a Rails app.

Full-stack refers to the extent of the functionality that the Rails framework provides. You see, there are frameworks and then there are *frameworks*. Some provide great functionality on the server, but leave you high and dry on the client side; others are terrific at enhancing the user experience in the browser, but don't extend to the business logic and database interactions on the server. Rails, by the way, gives you both.

If you've ever used a framework before, chances are that you're familiar with the model-view-controller (MVC) architecture (if not, don't worry—we'll discuss it in <u>Chapter 4</u>. Rails covers *everything* in the MVC paradigm, from database abstraction to template rendering, and everything in between.

Ruby is an open-source object-oriented scripting language invented by Yukihiro Matsumoto (affectionately known as "Matz") in the early 1990s. We'll be learning both Ruby *and* Rails as we progress through the book (remember, Rails is written in Ruby).

Ruby makes programming flexible and intuitive, and with it we can write code that's readable by both humans and machines. Matz designed Ruby to make programmers happy, as you'll see as we move through this book.

What does Ruby syntax look like?

If you're experienced in programming with other languages, such as PHP or Java, you can probably make sense of the following Ruby code, although some parts of it may look new:

```
> "What does Ruby syntax look like?".reverse
=> "?ekil kool xatnys ybuR seod tahW"
> 8 * 5
=> 40
> 3.times { puts "cheer!" }
=> cheer!
=> cheer!
=> cheer!
> %w(one two three).each { |word| puts word.upcase }
=> ONE
=> TWO
=> THREE
```

Don't worry too much about the details of programming in Ruby for now—we'll cover all of the Ruby basics in Chapter 3.

History

Ruby on Rails originated as an application named Basecamp[1], a hosted project-management solution created by Danish web developer David Heinemeier Hansson (affectionately known as "DHH" to Rubyists) for former design shop 37signals. Due largely to Basecamp's success, 37signals has since moved into application development and production, and Heinemeier Hansson has become a partner in the company.

When I say "originated," I mean that Rails wasn't initially created as a stand-alone framework. It was extracted from an application already in use, so that it could be used to build other applications that 37signals had in mind. Heinemeier Hansson saw the potential to make his job (and life) easier by extracting common

---

[1]. http://www.basecamphq.com/

functionality such as database abstraction and templating into what later became the first public release of Ruby on Rails.

He decided to release Rails as open-source software to remake the way web applications are built. The first beta version of Rails was initially released in July 2004, with the 1.0 and 2.0 releases following in December, 2005 and 2007 respectively. A little over 2 years later, version 3.0 of Rails was released and the number of contributors had ballooned to approximately 1,600. Rails 4 came out in 2013, with minor releases continuing through to the end of 2014 with 4.2. Rails 5.0, which is the focus of this book, was released in mid-2016.

That the Rails framework was extracted from Basecamp (and is still the foundation of Basecamp today) is considered by the lively Rails community to represent one of the framework's inherent strengths: it was already solving *real* problems when it was released. Rails wasn't built in isolation, so its success wasn't a result of developers taking the framework, building applications with it, and then finding—and resolving—its shortcomings. Rails had already proven itself to be a useful, coherent, and comprehensive framework.

While Heinemeier Hansson pioneered Rails and still leads the Rails-related programming efforts, the framework has benefited greatly from being released as open-source software. Over time, many developers working with Rails have submitted thousands of extensions and bug fixes to the Rails development repository.[2] The repository is closely guarded by the Rails core team, which consists of about twelve highly skilled professional developers seen in figure 1-1, chosen from the crowd of contributors, and led by Heinemeier Hansson.

[2.] The Rails repository, located at https://github.com/rails/rails/, is used to track bugs and enhancement requests.

David
Since 2003
USA/Spain
Commits

Jeremy
Since 2005
USA
Commits

Santiago
Since 2010
Uruguay
Commits

Aaron
Since 2011
USA
Commits

Xavier
Since 2011
Spain
Commits

Rafael
Since 2012
Brazil
Commits

Andrew
Since 2012
UK
Commits

Guillermo
Since 2012
USA/Colombia
Commits

Carlos
Since 2012
Brazil
Commits

Yves
Since 2014
Switzerland
Commits

Godfrey
Since 2014
USA/Canada
Commits

Matthew
Since 2015
Australia
Commits

1-3. The Rails Core Team

There is also a "committer team" made up of eight or so individuals that can do everything except set policy and make final releases. On top of that, there is the community at large, the source of many patches and plugins. At present, Rails has accepted contributions from over 4,600 programmers!

Finally, a framework as mature as Rails should have some good documentation, and it does. The Rails Guides[3] are an excellent resource on understanding the many pieces of Rails. Bookmark these guides, as you'll likely return to them throughout your journey as a Rails programmer.

So, now you know what Rails is, how it came about, and who supports it. But why would you invest your precious time in learning how to use it?

I'm glad you asked.

Development Principles

Rails supports several software principles (a doctrine[4], if you will) that make it stand out from other web development frameworks. Those principles are:

- optimize for programmer happiness
- convention over configuration
- the menu is omakase
- no one paradigm
- exalt beautiful code
- value-integrated systems
- progress over stability
- push up a big tent

This doctrine has grown and changed as Rails has grown and changed in the last decade or so. The principles are not without controversy, and understanding them will help you understand how Rails became what it is.

Optimize for Programmer Happiness

I've mentioned that Matz designed Ruby to make programmers happy, and this tenet of the Rails doctrine is pulled directly from that sentiment. Just as Ruby replaces complexity with easy language and offers many ways to achieve a programmer's goal, so does Rails aim to make web application complexity more mundane. You'll see this immediately when we start coding the example application in this book. Using just two simple commands in the terminal, Rails is serving up a functional web application. The amount of complexity that is

---

[3.] http://guides.rubyonrails.org/
[4.] http://rubyonrails.org/doctrine/

abstracted away from the programmer is quite amazing, so that we can focus on building the desired application and not the niggling details of web development.

Still, if hiding complexity was all Rails did, programmer happiness would quickly cease. Not all web applications have the same requirements, which means Rails developers often have to get behind the curtain and tweak the magic of Rails. Do you want to change the database you're using? No problem. What about how user sessions are stored? Go for it. Rails hides the complex items until you need to alter them, then it makes changing complexity sensible. This aspect of Rails probably speeds up development of usable applications faster than anything else.

I should also mention that creating a Rails application is as good an experience as you can hope for in your development life. There is a Rails console that opens the guts of your web application, allowing you to poke around and find where the bugs are or test out code. Testing is built into Rails better than any other web development framework in the world, hands down. When I develop web apps in other languages or with other frameworks, I find myself pining for the tools and environment that Rails brings to the table.

Convention Over Configuration

The concept of convention over configuration refers to how Rails assumes a number of defaults for the way one should build a typical web application.

Many other frameworks require you to step through a lengthy configuration process before you can make a start with even the simplest of applications. The configuration information is usually stored in a handful of XML or JSON files, which can become quite large and cumbersome to maintain. In many cases, you're forced to repeat the entire configuration process whenever you start a new project.

While Rails was originally extracted from an existing application, extensive architectural work went into the framework later on. DHH purposely created Rails in such a way that there's no need for excessive configuration, as long as some standard conventions are followed. The result is that no lengthy configuration files are required. In fact, if you have no need to change these defaults, Rails really only requires a single (and short) configuration file in order to run your application.

Other conventions that are prescribed by Rails include the naming of database-related items and the process by which controllers find their corresponding models and views.

 MVC

The **model-view-controller (MVC)** architecture is a software architecture (also referred to as a design pattern) that separates an application's data model (model), user interface (view), and control logic (controller) into three distinct components.

Here's an example: when your browser requests a web page from an MVC-architected application, it's talking exclusively to the controller. The controller gathers the required data from one or more models and renders the response to your request through a view. This separation of components means that any change that's made to one component has minimal effect on the other two.

We'll talk at length about the MVC architecture and the benefits it yields to Rails applications in Chapter 4.

Rails is also considered to be **opinionated software**, a term coined to refer to software that isn't everything to everyone. DHH and his core team ruthlessly reject contributions to the framework that fail to comply with their vision of where Rails is headed, or aren't sufficiently applicable to be useful for the majority of Rails developers. This is a good way to fight a phenomenon known among software developers as **bloat**: the tendency for a software package to implement extraneous features just for the sake of including them.

The Menu is Omakase

This principle is similar to the goal of optimizing for programmer happiness. "Omakase" comes from the restaurant industry–sushi restaurants, to be more specific–and is the concept of letting the chef pick your meal based on his sophisticated palette. If you are new to ordering sushi, for example, using an omakase method can help you figure out what is good. As such, the Rails team will look at the practices and tools that most developers are using and evaluate whether they deserve inclusion in the core framework. This has resulted in tools such as CoffeeScript (which we'll discuss in <u>Chapter 7</u>) and Spring being included in the framework.

It's only fair to point out that this is probably the most controversial part of the Rails doctrine. While those new to Rails may like being served a stack of tools to use, experienced developers are different beasts altogether. Often, the selected tool is unpopular with a part of the community that is highly vocal about it. The good news is that these tools can be removed or swapped out for other tools without much ceremony.

No One Paradigm

Rails has been growing and changing for almost a decade. In that decade, the languages, tools, approaches, and design patterns have exploded. We know much more as an industry today than we did in 2007. As such, the design concepts and paradigms behind Rails that have been altered or refined are based on new understanding. This kind of change and continued learning will never stop, so Rails has to account for it.

When DHH describes Rails as a quilt, he means it's made up of several paradigms and ideas, instead of a single idea that permeates the framework. You'll hear about design patterns, such as Active Record, that is foundational to Rails models, but can be implemented differently or even completely removed (we'll discuss Active Record in <u>Chapter 4</u>). Rails is not pedantic in how it uses design patterns, always erring on the side of being practical. As you dive deeper into Rails, you'll be presented with more patterns and languages. Do you need to refine an SQL query? You can do that by writing the SQL yourself or leveraging the tools of Arel and Active Record. Does your client-side JavaScript need to perform some fancier stuff in the browser? You can add front-end libraries or write the code yourself. Do you think the Datamapper pattern is better than Active Record? Okay, swap it out.

The point is, not only is Rails a quilt, *each Rails application is a different quilt.* The paradigms presented are yours to use, or not. The downside is that you need to know a lot of design ideas and programming concepts to change these paradigms. But, don't worry, Rails will take you a long long way before you need to know about this stuff. Rails gets you excited about doing things fast, then it revs you up by supporting your education and growth as a programmer.

Exalt Beautiful Code

In my opinion, this is another concept that Rails has fully adopted from Ruby and its community. Ruby was designed for humans to read, not computers. As such, it is quite possible to write "beautiful" code. As with any beauty, it is in the eye of the beholder, but I'll bet we can agree that this code is beautiful:

```ruby
class Person
  belongs_to :family
  has_many :pets
  validates :name, presence: true
end
```

Without telling you anything about the application this code came from, you can still surmise much about what is happening. Ruby and Rails use the excellent design of Ruby's core libraries along with some Domain Specific Languages[5] (DSLs) to allow you, the happy developer, to write code that is expressive and concise. And that to me is beautiful.

One of the age-old adages that fits into this principle is called **Don't Repeat Yourself**, also known as the DRY principle. Being DRY in your code means you don't copy/paste the same code all over your codebase. Instead, you extract common code and reuse it where needed. This leads to a more maintainable and beautiful code base. I'll reference the DRY principle a few times throughout the book, and you'll see it in the wild.

So what? You might be asking. Well, when you are spending hours in a codebase that is poorly written or hard to read, it's exhausting. Your poor brain has to constantly translate the code and its abstractions. If the code is not expressive, this is a significant mental task. If the code lacks conciseness, it's tiring to read. Beautiful code is easier to share with your peers, making collaboration enjoyable and purposeful. As with anything in life, beauty in code is noble and meaningful.

[5.] https://en.wikipedia.org/wiki/Domain-specific_language

Value-integrated Systems

This particular principle is another of Rails' more controversial tenets. If you've read anything about web development recently, there's a lot of talk about splitting applications into many applications, creating **microservices**. These split-up applications are a reaction to large web apps, called **monoliths**. DHH and the Rails team believe in the value of keeping the application in a single codebase. They certainly believe that the app should start that way, rather than designing a suite of applications and services up front. There are benefits to both approaches, and what you do depends more on a particular use case than a Rails design principle.

Having said that, Rails is designed to build a complete and full-stack web application. In this book, that is what we will do.

Progress Over Stability

When talking about the history of Rails, I mentioned that the 3.0 release was a doozy. It took two years and had many, many breaking changes. This meant that applications on Rails 2.0 had a painful upgrade path. For a couple of years, it was impossible to swing a dead cat without hitting someone who had abandoned Rails rather than continue to try and upgrade. The core team felt that the changes made from 2.0 to 3.0 were necessary to avoid burdening Rails with the heavy baggage of the older framework. Rails 2.0 was cracking under its own weight. We had learned much about better design and new approaches to the problems Rails solves, and the changes had to be made. Looking back, it's hard to argue with the decisions made. Rails is better than ever, largely due to the decisions made for that 3.0 release.

If you stick around and become a Rails developer (and I sincerely hope you do), you'll hear about additions to Rails that rile parts—or even most—of the community. Tools such as Spring, Turbolinks, CoffeeScript, and Action Cable were all brought into the fold in the name of progress. Many breaking changes have been made to shave off the cruft of "old ways," ensuring that the future of Rails doesn't suffer as a result of its past.

Often these additions are the right thing to do, but they need the community to chime in before they are fully cooked. Hence, they are introduced to the framework as the approach or tool is honed and made better by the community and team. This is in the name of progress over stability, and it's likely a reason why Rails is as active as ever a decade after its birth.

Push Up a Big Tent

In the current programming environment, this tenet may be the most important. Rails is a big tent, and there are many, many folks under it with us. There's no entry admission charged; nor will we demand that you produce immediately. We will, however, expect you to value the community and its tools. We'll expect you to express your opinions, and be respectful and professional.

These are the member traits that build a strong foundation for the larger community. The people in the Rails tent are not a cult, they just want to build great things. They are people that want to learn from others. *Rubyists* are not all cut from the same cloth, and that's why this community is among the very best in the programming world.

DHH writes of his disdain for microservices or certain Ruby libraries that are very popular. Yet these libraries flourish, even without the endorsement of one of the most prominent community members. He loves that, and so do I. I want a tent full of diverse, intelligent, respectful, and fun individuals, and that is what the Rails community is today.

If your head is spinning from trying to digest these principles, don't worry—they'll be reinforced continually throughout this book, as we step through building our very own web application in Ruby on Rails.

Building the Example Web Application

As you read on, I expect you'll be itching to put the techniques we discuss into practice. For this reason, I've planned a fully functional web application that we'll build together throughout the ensuing chapters. The key concepts, approaches, and methodologies we'll discuss will have a role to play in the sample application, and we'll implement them progressively as your skills improve over the course of this book.

The application we'll build will be a functional clone of part of the popular link-sharing website, Reddit[6]: namely, the ability to share a link and vote on it. I've included all necessary files for this application in the book's code archive[7] (each chapter's code is located in its own branch of the repository).

Reddit describes its functionality as follows:

> The global Reddit community votes on which stories and discussions are important by casting upvotes or downvotes. The most interesting, funniest, impactful, or simply amazing stories rise to the top.

Basically, if you want to tell the world about that interesting article you found on the Internet—be it a blog post that's right up your street, or a news story from a major publication—you can submit its URL to Reddit, along with a short summary of the item. Your link will sit there, waiting for other users to "vote it up" (give your item a positive vote). As well as voting, users can comment on the story to create often lively discussions within Reddit.

Reddit was launched in 2005, and is consistently listed in the Alexa traffic rankings as one of the Internet's top 50 websites.[8]

This isn't the reason why you'll be developing your own Reddit clone, though; its feature set is not particularly complicated, and is sufficient to allow us to gain firsthand experience with the most important and useful facets of the Ruby on Rails framework.

And while your application might be unable to compete with the original site, reusing this sample project to share links within your family, company, or college class is perfectly conceivable. With any luck, you'll learn enough along the way to branch out and build other types of applications as well.

[6.] http://www.reddit.com/

[7.] https://github.com/spbooks/rails3v5

[8.] http://www.alexa.com/data/details/traffic_details/reddit.com

Features of the Example Application

As I mentioned, we want our application to accept user-submitted links to stories on the Web. We also want to allow other users to vote on the submitted items. In order to meet these objectives, we'll implement the following features as we work through this book:

- A database back end that permanently stores every story, user, vote, and so on. This way, nothing is lost when you close your browser and shut the application down.

- A link submission interface, which is a form that's available only to users who have registered and logged in.

- A simplistic, responsive layout as is typical for today's mobile-aware applications. We'll style it with Cascading Style Sheets (CSS) and enhance it with visual effects.

- Clean URLs for all the pages on our site. Clean URLs (also known as search-engine-friendly URLs) are usually brief and easily read when they appear in the browser status bar. An example of a clean URL is `http://del.icio.us/popular/software`, which I'm sure you'll agree is a lot nicer than `http://www.amazon.com/gp/homepage.html/103-0615814-1415024/`.

- A user registration system that allows users to log in with their usernames and passwords.

- The ability to check voting history on a per-user and per-story basis.

It's quite a list, and the result will be one slick web application! Some of the features rely upon others being in place, and we'll implement each feature as a practical example when we look at successive aspects of Rails.

Summary

Well, here we are; your first step towards Rails is complete. This chapter walked us through Rails' beginnings—a framework born as a way to solve real problems. There were mentions of Ruby, the language foundation of the Rails framework, along with some code snippets to whet your whistle. You learned that Ruby and Rails were created to make programmers happy and more productive. We looked at the founders and many contributors to Rails, along with the development principles that serve as its base.

These ambitious and sensible development principles drive Rails programmers, and you are about to be amongst their ilk. As we go through this book and build our application together, try to keep the principles in mind. You'll build habits that will influence your work for your entire career.

Finally, we created a brief specification for the web application we're going to build throughout this book. We described what our app will do, and identified the list of features that we're going to implement. We'll develop a lite clone of the link-sharing website Reddit iteratively, taking advantage of some of the Agile development practices that Rails supports.

In the next chapter, we'll install Ruby, Rails, and the SQLite database server software in order to set up a development environment for the upcoming development tasks.

Are you ready to join in the fun? If so, turn the page ...

Chapter

Getting Started

To get started with Ruby on Rails, we first must install some development software on our systems. The packages we'll be installing are:

The Ruby language The Ruby interpreter translates any Ruby code, including
interpreter   Rails itself, into a form the computer can understand and
execute. At the time of writing, Ruby 2.3.0 is recommended
for use with Rails, so that's what I've used here.

Found in Translation

There are many Ruby interpreters, but the most often used one is the Matz Ruby Interpreter, or MRI for short. You may also hear of other interpreters such as JRuby[1] or Rubinius[2]. Each has its pros and cons, but as it's beyond the scope of this book, you may want to take an hour or so and do some reading on the other interpreters and why they exist.

RubyGems package manager Many languages take advantage of package managers to help the community manage and install code libraries. Package managers allow developers to create libraries that can be shared easily and perform specific tasks. In fact, Rails itself comprises several RubyGems[3] (or **gems**, as they are called by Rubyists). RubyGems is, arguably, the best package manager for any language out there, and we'll use it to install gems as needed in the book. The RubyGems Guideshttp://guides.rubygems.org/ are worth perusing for an idea of how gems work.

The Ruby on Rails framework Once we've downloaded Ruby, we can install the Rails framework itself. As I mentioned in Chapter 1, Rails is written in Ruby. At the time of writing, version 5.0.0.1 was the most recent stable version of the framework.

The SQLite database engine The SQLite database engine is a self-contained software library that provides an SQL database without running a separate server process. While Rails supports plenty of other database servers (MySQL, PostgreSQL, Microsoft SQL Server, and MongoDB, to name a few), SQLite is easy to install, requires no configuration, and is the default database for which a new Rails application is configured straight out of the box. Oh, and it's free! At the time of writing, the most recent stable release of the SQLite database was version 3.14.1.

Instructions for installing Rails differ ever so slightly between operating systems. You may have to install some additional tools as part of the process, depending

---

[1.] http://jruby.org/

[2.] http://rubinius.com/

[3.] https://rubygems.org/

on the platform you use. Here, I'll provide installation instructions for Windows, Mac OS X, and Linux.

 New ≠ Tried + Tested

It's possible that by the time you read this, a more recent version of Ruby, SQLite, or another package mentioned here will have been released. Beware! Just because a package is newer, doesn't mean it can reliably be used for Rails development. While, in theory, every version should be compatible and these instructions should still apply, sometimes the latest is *not* the greatest. In fact, the Rails framework itself has a reputation for experiencing large changes between releases, such as specific methods or attributes being deprecated. While every effort has been made to ensure the code in this book is future-proof, there's no guarantee that changes included in forthcoming major releases of Rails won't require this code to be modified in some way for it to work. Such is the fast-paced world of web development!

Feel free to skip the sections on operating systems other than yours, and focus only on those that address your specific needs.

What does all this cost?

Everything we need is available for download from the Web, and licensed under free software licenses. This basically means that everything you install is free for you to use in both personal and commercial applications. If you're curious about the differences between each license, check out each package's individual license file, which is included in its download.

Installing Ruby and Rails can be tricky, which is why there are entire sites[4] devoted to it; however, it is *way* better than it used to be, and I don't think you'll have any issues.

Installing on Windows

Getting Rails up and running on Windows consists of three major steps:

1. Install Ruby

---

[4] http://installrails.com

2. Install the Ruby Development Kit
3. Install Rails
4. Install Git
5. Install NodeJS

Install Ruby

Ruby is a great community (you'll hear me say that a lot) comprised of people who support free tools to help others get started with the language. One such tool is the RubyInstaller for Windows[5].

2-1. RubyInstaller website

If you head over to the Downloads page, the current latest Ruby version is 2.3.1, but I would suggest you use Ruby 2.2.5:

[5.] http://rubyinstaller.org

for Windows

Downloads

RubyInstallers   ## Archives»

Not sure what version to download? Please read the right column for recommendations.

- Ruby 2.3.1
- Ruby 2.3.1 (x64)
- Ruby 2.2.5
- Ruby 2.2.5 (x64)
- Ruby 2.1.9
- Ruby 2.1.9 (x64)
- Ruby 2.0.0-p648
- Ruby 2.0.0-p648 (x64)

Other Useful Downloads

2-2. Ruby version

The 2.2 versions of Ruby are stable and gems have been built and tested against them. The download page itself recommends the 2.2.X versions for the same reason, and 2.2.5 will be fine for everything we do in this book.

Go ahead and click on the link for Ruby 2.2.5 and download that executable. You can use either 32 or 64-bit, depending on your needs. Double-click on that executable to start the installation process.

The install process is pretty normal. You can choose your language, and use the path the installer suggests (`C:\Ruby22`, in my case). However, I would recommend that you check the box that says *Add Ruby executables to your PATH*, shown here:

2-3. Add Ruby to Path

Click *Install* and the installation will complete. RubyInstaller adds an item to the *Start Menu* called *Start Command Prompt with Ruby* which, when clicked, will open a Windows command prompt with the Ruby environment variables all in place:

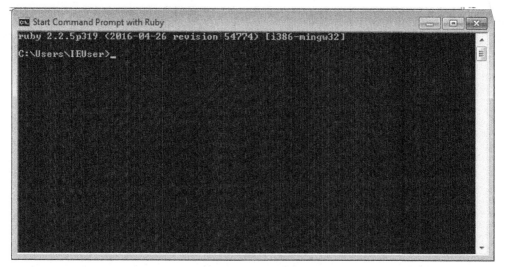

2-4. Ruby command prompt

Great. Ruby is installed. However, in order to install Rails (and other gems), we need some build tools to be installed. Thankfully, again, we can turn to the folks at RubyInstaller for help. The Ruby DevKit for Windows[6] installs these build tools for us.

The download for the DevKit is on the same *Downloads* page as the RubyInstaller:

---

6. http://rubyinstaller.org/add-ons/devkit/

Ruby 2.0.0-p40 documentation (CHM format)

DEVELOPMENT KIT

For use with Ruby 1.8.7 and 1.9.3:

 DevKit-tdm-32-4.5.2-20111229-1559-sfx.exe

For use with Ruby 2.0 and above (32bits version only):

 DevKit-mingw64-32-4.7.2-20130224-1151-sfx.exe

For use with Ruby 2.0 and above (x64 - 64bits only)

DevKit-mingw64-64-4.7.2-20130224-1432-sfx.exe

2-5. Getting the DevKit

Be sure to download the right one for the RubyInstaller you downloaded above. If
you're like me and you used the 32-bit 2.2.5 installer, you can download
`DevKit-mingw64-32-4.7.2-20130224-1151-sfx.exe`. Once downloaded, run the
executable and it will ask for a directory to install the DevKit. I choose
`C:\RubyDevKit`:

2-6. Installing the DevKit

Now, roll up your sleeves. Remember that new link the RubyInstaller added to
the Start menu? Click it to open a Ruby-savvy command prompt and `cd`

C:\RubyDevKit. You need to type a couple of commands to make the DevKit available to our newly installed Ruby. The first one is `ruby dk.rb init` and the second is `ruby dk.rb install`. The output is below:

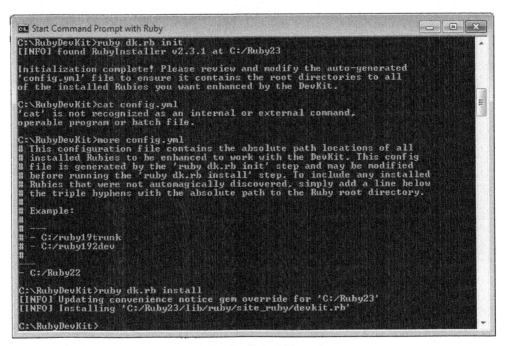

2-7. Making DevKit available to ruby

OK, now we can install Rails. At that same command prompt, change into our Ruby directory (`cd c:\Ruby22`) and type `gem install rails`. You will see many gems being built and installed:

2-8. Rails being installed

When the install is complete, you should see something like:

```
37 gems installed
c:\Ruby22>
```

Yay! Rails is installed. Enjoy this small, but significant, victory.

There are *still* a couple of things we still need to set up. First, we need to install Git, which is a version control system. If you're not sure what that is, don't worry about it right now. We'll cover some git basics later in the chapter. For now, let's just get it installed.

Open a browser and go to https://git-scm.com/downloads/win. This should kick off the download of the Git installer. If not, click on the *Download for Windows* button:

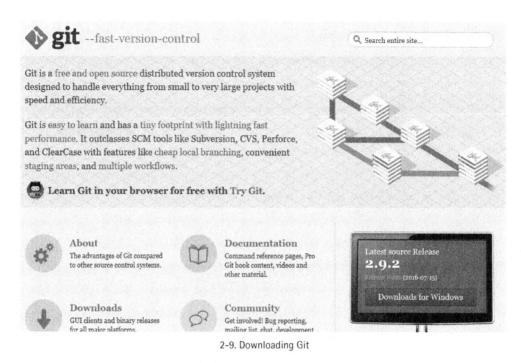

2-9. Downloading Git

Run the installer once the download completes. You can (and should) follow all the defaults offered by the installer. With the install complete, start a new Ruby Command Prompt (close and reopen it) and check the git version:

```
c:\Ruby22> git --version
git version 2.9.2.version.1
```

Next, we need to install SQLite3, which is the default database that Rails will use out of the box. Installing SQLite3 is a matter of going to the SQLite3 download page[7] and scrolling down to *Precompiled Binaries for Windows*. Select the first link, which is the SQLite3 DLL. Unzip the downloaded file and copy its contents to C:\Windows\System32.

Finally, the last thing we need to install is a JavaScript Runtime, as Rails expects one to exist. This is accomplished easily enough by installing NodeJS. So, head over to the NodeJS site[8], click on *Downloads*, and choose the Windows installer

---

7. http://www.sqlite.org/download.html
8. https://nodejs.org

that suits your needs (either 32 or 64-bit). Run the installer, accepting all the defaults:

2-10. Installing NodeJS

Once the Node installation completes, restart your Ruby Command Prompt and type node -v:

```
$ node -v
v4.4.7
```

You now have a working NodeJS install.

Congratulations! You have installed Ruby, Rails, and all the supporting characters! Feel free to take a break and high-five yourself. Oh, and you can skip the instructions for Mac and Linux.

Installing on Mac OS X

While Mac OS X isn't usually a tricky platform to manage, installing Rails is just a tad harder than installing a regular Mac application.

Your first task is to install Xcode from the Mac App Store, as shown below.

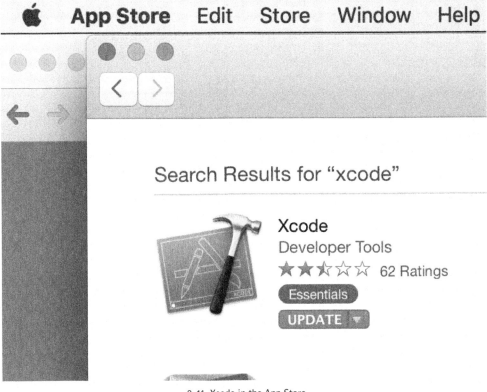

2-11. Xcode in the App Store

The good news is Xcode is free. The bad news is it's huge and takes a while to install. Use this time to thumb through the Rails Guides and get coffee.

Done? Excellent. Now, open a terminal, which can be found in *Applications =>* *Utilities => Terminal*, as shown in Figue 2-12.

2-12. Terminal App

This will launch a window that looks a bit like what can be seen below.

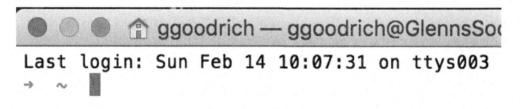

2-13. A terminal window

You're now in your home directory.

Taking Command

Much of working with Ruby and Rails is done at the command line in a terminal. Being comfortable with basic terminal commands[9], such as `cd`, `dir`, and `ls` is all but required to be an effective Ruby and Rails developer. If necessary, take some time to research and practice using the terminal to navigate around your Mac. You'll be glad you did.

Installing Homebrew

I previously mentioned RubyGems, a package manager for Ruby. Well, there are package managers for operating systems, too, and Mac OS X has a good one called Homebrew[10]. It is open source and has a bit of an odd installation, but it's an excellent package manager and used by most Mac developers to install the items they need.

To install Homebrew, go to your terminal and type (or paste) in the following:

```
/usr/bin/ruby -e "$(curl -fsSL
↳ https://raw.githubusercontent.com/Homebrew/install/master/
install)"
```

Homebrew's installation will be confirmed by a `brew` command becoming available in the terminal, as depicted in Figure 2-14.

```
●  ●  ●  ⌂ ggoodrich — ggoodrich@GlennsSookumMac — ~ — -zsh — 80×24
Last login: Sun Feb 14 10:07:31 on ttys003
[→  ~  brew -v
Homebrew 0.9.5 (git revision 29509c; last commit 2015-10-16)
 →  ~  █
```

2-14. The brew terminal command

---

[9] http://mally.stanford.edu/~sr/computing/basic-unix.html
[10] http://brew.sh

With Homebrew in place, installing Ruby becomes very, very easy; however, I need to explain the sate of affairs first. I've noted the somewhat volatile nature of Ruby and Rails. With several new releases every year for each, when you're developing using particular versions of Ruby and Rails, it can become complicated to install new versions without breaking your environment and applications. Rubyists, being the problem-solving pragmatists that they are, solved this problem by creating a "version manager" for Ruby. In fact, there are a couple of version managers out there. The idea behind a **version manager** is that you can switch between versions of Ruby without breaking your environment. Now, it's easy to try a new version with your application and be assured that it won't break your work. It is an elegant solution to a sticky problem.

Version Managers: Good for Developing Developers!

While it is possible to install Ruby without using package managers and avoid jumping through these small hoops to set up our environment, it is not recommended. All of the Ruby developers I know and work with use version managers, so if you're going to become a real Ruby dev, you need to understand the how and why of version managers. If I were a parent, I'd say "this builds character" or "you'll thank me later".

So, we're going to install a package manager called RVM[11], which stands for Ruby Version Manager. At your command prompt, type:

```
\curl -sSL https://get.rvm.io | bash -s stable
```

When the script completes, close your terminal window and open a new one. Then type:

```
rvm | head -n 1
```

This should respond with =rvm, as shown in figure 2-15.

---

[11] https://rvm.io

2-15. RVM is installed

Great! Your Ruby Version Manager is installed and ready to go. Time to install Ruby.

With RVM, installing a new version of Ruby is a walk in the park. In your terminal, type:

```
rvm install 2.3.0
```

This tells RVM to install Ruby 2.3.0. Oh, and it will take a while, so it's time for another break. Go for a walk around the block. It's good for you.

Okay, Ruby is now installed, but we're not quite done yet. With version managers, you have to specify which version of Ruby you want to use. With RVM, that's done by typing:

```
rvm use 2.3.0 --default
```

Figure 2-16 reveals what that should look like.

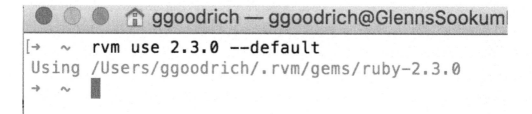

2-16. Telling RVM which Ruby to use

 Why default?

The `--default` option in the aforementioned command tells RVM to use 2.3.0 as the default Ruby for your computer. Every time you open a new terminal window, Ruby 2.3.0 will be the current version of Ruby. Without the default, you'll have to type `rvm use 2.3.0` every time you open a terminal. It's your choice.

Boom, now we're done with Ruby.

With Ruby in place, installing Rails is just a matter of asking our awesome package manager, RubyGems, to do the deed:

```
gem install rails
```

This will crank out a ton of text in the terminal, a snippet of which is seen below.

```
[→  ~ gem install rails
Fetching: i18n-0.7.0.gem (100%)
Successfully installed i18n-0.7.0
Fetching: thread_safe-0.3.5.gem (100%)
Successfully installed thread_safe-0.3.5
Fetching: tzinfo-1.2.2.gem (100%)
Successfully installed tzinfo-1.2.2
Fetching: concurrent-ruby-1.0.2.gem (100%)
Successfully installed concurrent-ruby-1.0.2
Fetching: activesupport-5.0.0.1.gem (100%)
Successfully installed activesupport-5.0.0.1
Fetching: rack-2.0.1.gem (100%)
```
:o resize this window and retake to

2-17. Installing Rails

Now, just to make sure Rails is ready, type:

```
rails --version
=> Rails 5.0.0.1
```

Excellent. Now we just need to install SQLite3, which can be done with Homebrew:

```
brew install sqlite
```

When that completes, check your SQLite version to make sure it's there:

```
sqlite3 --version
 => 3.8.10.2 2015-05-20 18:17:19
 ↳ 2ef4f3a5b1d1d0c4338f8243d40a2452cc1f7fe4
```

And now we're ready to go.

Help on Hand

Remember—if you get really stuck, you can always try asking for help on SitePoint's Ruby forum.[12]

Installing on Linux (Ubuntu)

Thanks to the hard work of people in the incredible Ruby and Rails communities, installing Ruby and Rails on Linux is as straightforward as can be. I have copied a script from the Rails Girls guides[13] to a SitePoint Github repository, which enables you to run a single command line to install Ruby, Rails, Sqlite3, and Git. This is a far cry from how it used to be, and I am *soooo* thankful that Rails Girls put this together.

About Rails Girls

Rails Girls[14] is a group whose aim is to "give tools and (create) a community for women to understand technology and to build their ideas." It is one example of the groups that have formed to increase diversity and make people feel comfortable learning Ruby and Rails. There are others with similar aims sprinkled throughout the community and I think it's great. If you think you'd benefit from being involved with Rails Girls, check them out.

The script you need to run is located on GitHub[15]. The following command will pull down that script and run it in your terminal. Open up a terminal and paste in the following:

```
bash < <(curl -sL
↪ https://raw.githubusercontent.com/spbooks/rails3v5/master/
scripts/install_linux.sh)
```

[12.] https://www.sitepoint.com/community/c/ruby
[13.] http://guides.railsgirls.com/install#setup_for_linux
[14.] http://railsgirls.com
[15.] https://raw.githubusercontent.com/spbooks/rails3v5/master/scripts/install_linux.sh

You will be prompted for your password and you'll require an account with sudo level access. The script will then run through installing Ruby, RVM, Sqlite3, git, and Rails, as seen in Figure 2-18.

2-18. Installing on Linux

When the script completes, type in the following to validate the install:

```
source ~/.rvm/scripts/rvm
rails -v
=> Rails 5.0.0
```

Congratulations! You have successfully installed Ruby and Rails on Linux.

Additional Installation Options

If, for some reason, none of the previous installation options fit your bill, there are more possible solutions to have you up and running with Rails. I am, of course, speaking of *The Cloud*. Some companies offer a full Ruby and Rails environment that you access solely with your browser. A good example is Nitrous.IO[16].

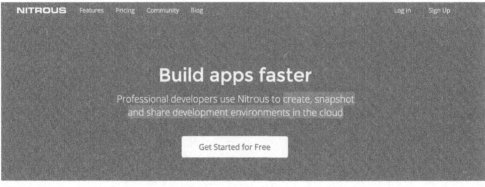

2-19. Nitrous.IO

As the screenshot declares, Nitrous.io allows you to "create, snapshot, and share development environments in the cloud". When you sign up for Nitrous, you have options of which kind of application you want to create, one of which is Rails. Figure 2-20 shows what a Rails application looks like in the browser on Nitrous.

2-20. Creating a Rails app in Nitrous

---

16. http://nitrous.io

A wizard then guides you through the process, and your first application is free.

If you're more advanced and know what a virtual machine is, companies such as Amazon Web Services[17] or Digital Ocean[18] provide **Infrastructure as a Service** (**IaaS**). With an **IaaS**, you basically create an entire computer in the cloud and then run through one of the previous sets of instructions to install Ruby and Rails.

And Now the Fun Begins

Okay, is everyone here? Windows? Check. Mac? Check. Linux? Check. Great! It's time to set the foundation for the application we're going to build throughout the remainder of this book.

One Directory Structure to Rule Them All

If you remember from the section on the Rails doctrine, one of the tenets was "Convention over configuration". One of the conventions of Rails is its directory structure, where a Rails application always has the same base structure on disc. By gently forcing this directory structure upon developers, Rails ensures that your work is organized in the Rails way.

Figure 2-21 shows what the structure looks like. We'll create this directory structure for our application in just a moment.

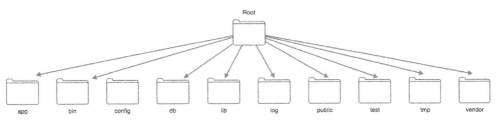

2-21. The conventional Rails application directory structure

As you can see, this standard directory structure consists of quite a few subdirectories (and I'm yet to even show *their* subdirectories!). This wealth of

---

17. http://aws.amazon.com

18. http://digitalocean.com

subdirectories can be overwhelming at first, but we'll explore them one by one. A lot of thought has gone into establishing the folders and naming them, and the result is an application with a well-structured file system.

Before you go and manually create all these directories yourself, let me show you how to set up that pretty directory structure using just one command—I told you that Rails allows us to do *less* typing!

Creating the Standard Directory Structure

It's easy to generate the default directory structure for a new Rails application using the `rails` command.

Before we start, I'd like to introduce you to the secret under-the-hood project name we'll give our Reddit-lite project clone: *Readit*. It's exactly this kind of creativity that has companies begging me to run their marketing departments. Not.

Now, let's go ahead and create the directory structure to hold our application.

The `rails` command takes various secondary commands, new being one of them. As you've probably guessed, the `rails new` command creates the directory where you'd like to store your application, along with all the files required. You can, and are encouraged to, execute it from the parent directory in which you want your new Rails application to live. I'll do this in my home directory. If you're on Windows, you may want to do this inside `C:\Ruby22`:

```
$ rails new readit
create
create   README.rdoc
create   Rakefile
create   config.ru
create   .gitignore
create   Gemfile
create   app
create   app/assets/javascripts/application.js
create   app/assets/stylesheets/application.css
create   app/controllers/application_controller.rb
```

```
create  app/helpers/application_helper.rb
create  app/views/layouts/application.html.erb
...
```

Congratulations, your directory structure has been created! You'll need to use `cd readit` to ensure the active directory is the root of our new application. We will run all our Rails commands from inside the application root.

Starting Our Application

Even before we write any code, it's possible to start up our application environment to check that our setup is working correctly. This exercise should give us a nice boost of confidence before we progress any further.

Rails wants you to be productive as soon as possible, and if you can't look at your web application in a web browser, you can't be productive. So, Rails includes a development web server, called Puma, that you can fire up with the single command: `rails server`, as shown in Figure 2-22. Oh, and because Rails is obsessed with making you efficient, you can also type `rails s` for the same result.

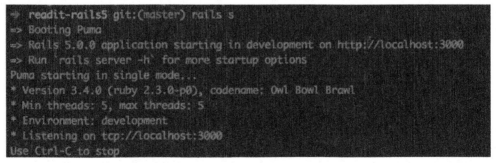

2-22. Firing up the Rails server

Choice Gems: A Plethora of Web Servers

It's worth noting that it is very easy to change the development web server, as the Ruby community has created many web server gems; however, we will stick with good ol' Puma, as it is well-suited to our needs. We will, however, discuss some other options in Chapter 12, on deployment.

Well done: you just started up your application for the first time. Okay, so there's little it can do at this stage—we're yet to write any lines of code, after all—but you can now connect to your application by entering `http://localhost:3000/` into your web browser's address bar. You should see a similar sight to Figure 2-23.

2-23. Rails' default page

The default page shows the versions of Ruby and Rails, along with providing a link to http://rubyonrails.org.

So, you're up and running on Rails. Feels good, eh? Before we keep going with Rails, we need to take a quick tangent.

Version Control and Git

Writing code is a delicate undertaking. No matter how experienced you are as a programmer, you will make mistakes. Lots of them. And some of these mistakes may only be discovered after days, weeks, or months. Once discovered, undoing the mistake can be troublesome, especially if it's been buried by months of accumulated code. It would be nice if you could store versions of the code as you go, in case you need to return to an old version to fix code, or see what's changed between versions.

Turns out, you *can* do this with version control software. Version control has been around a long time, evolving over decades. In the current software landscape, the most popular version control software is Git[19].

Git is an open source, distributed version control software. If you do any development in open source, you'll need to learn how to use Git. Space only permits me to cover the basics here, but you should definitely spend some time getting comfortable with Git. The learning curve is steep at first, but you'll conquer that soon enough and Git will become one of your most-used tools.

EXTRA CREDIT: Get Learning Git

Seriously, jump on the Internet and run through some basic Git tutorials or buy a book. There's a good article from SitePoint to get you started[20].

Git Basics

To use Git, you need to create a Git repository for your code. This is done by typing the following in the directory of the code you wish to manage:

[19.] https://git-scm.com
[20.] http://www.sitepoint.com/git-for-beginners/

```
$ git init .
Initialized empty Git repository in /current/path/.git/
```

Once you have a Git repository, add files to it. You can add these one by one, or add all files in a directory as shown here:

```
git add .
```

`git add` provides no feedback, so to see if it did anything, type:

```
$ git status
On branch master

Initial commit

Changes to be committed:
  (use "git rm --cached <file>..." to unstage)

    new file:   .gitignore
    new file:   .ruby-gemset
    new file:   .ruby-version
    new file:   Gemfile
... lots more files, maybe...
```

As you can see, Git has added the files "to be committed". So we need to commit them:

```
git commit -m "My first git commit"
[master (root-commit) 057e21f] My first git commit
 92 files changed, 1410 insertions(+)
 create mode 100644 .gitignore
 create mode 100644 .ruby-gemset
 create mode 100644 .ruby-version
 create mode 100644 Gemfile
```

```
... lots more creates ...
```

And there you have it. Our files are now being tracked by Git. Not so bad, eh?

To check the status of your Git managed files, type:

```
$ git status
nothing to commit, working directory clean
```

At this point, you can happily start coding. Git will keep an eye on what's happening. Here's the output of `git status` after I change a file:

```
$ git status
On branch master
Changes not staged for commit:
  (use "git add <file>..." to update what will be
↳ committed)
  (use "git checkout -- <file>..." to discard changes in
↳ working directory)

    modified:   app/models/blorgh/article.rb
 no changes added to commit (use "git add" and/or "git commit
↳ -a")
```

Git tells me that I have made a change but not committed it. It will also show me the change:

```
$ git diff
 diff --git a/app/models/blorgh/article.rb
↳ b/app/models/blorgh/article.rb
index 79a6664..9f936ae 100644
--- a/app/models/blorgh/article.rb
+++ b/app/models/blorgh/article.rb
@@ -1,5 +1,6 @@
 module Blorgh
```

```
  class Article < ActiveRecord::Base
    has_many :comments
+   has_many :likes
  end
 end
```

The + sign shows the line I added. If I had deleted lines, they would be shown with a - sign.

I now follow the same process I did with the initial commit: add the files to be committed and then commit them with a message:

```
$ git add .
$ git commit -m "Changed article"
[master bf8b89d] Changed article
1 file changed, 1 insertion(+)
```

The "code, add, commit" sequence is used to commit your changes to Git. Again, not so bad, eh?

One last point to cover about Git are its "remotes". Git is a **distributed** version control system, which means there is no central server to hold the source master. Every clone of a Git repository is the *entire* repository, including all history, branches, and so on. I can add a reference to another user's Git repository and push or pull code to or from that repository. The other coder's repository is called a *remote*.

We will use remotes without creating one explicitly when we deploy the site in chapter 12.

There is so much more to Git: branching, partial commits, working with other developers on Github, and so on, but that's all beyond our scope. We need to move on.

So now you're finally ready to write some code. But wait! Which text editor will you be using?

Which Text Editor?

The question of which text editor is best for web development has spawned arguments that border on religious fanaticism. While it's certainly possible to develop Rails applications using the default text editor that comes bundled with your operating system, I'd stop short of recommending it. The benefits provided by a specifically designed programmer's editor can prevent typing errors and increase your productivity immeasurably. In this section, I've suggested a couple of alternatives for each operating system, enabling you to make a choice that suits your personal preferences and budget.

Windows and Cross-platform Text Editors

The best editors for Windows are all cross-platform, in my opinion. You'll notice that any editor worth its salt has some kind of plugin-type framework, allowing the community to write plugins. These plugins are almost always the best features of an editor, as they're focused on making specific editing tasks simple.

Sublime Text

One of the most popular cross-platform editors is Sublime Text, currently on version 3, seen in Figure 2-24. It can be downloaded for free, but requires a license for continued use. The current price for a Sublime Text license is US$70. Sublime Text comes with a ton of impressive core features, including a Plugin API resulting in a slew of plugins that make development more efficient and enjoyable.

2-24. Sublime Text

Atom

Atom[21], seen in figure 2-25, is another cross-platform editor with a robust plugin framework. It is built on Electron, a framework for building cross-platform apps using web technologies. Atom was developed by the great folks at GitHub and is open-sourced, meaning it is 100% free of charge. I know many developers that use Atom and they say nothing but great things about it.

[21.] https://atom.io

2-25. Atom editor

Visual Studio Code

The folk behind Visual Studio have created a very nice cross-platform editor that supports 30+ languages and is extensible. Before too long, someone will have built some Rails plugins for this editor. I'm yet to use it, but as you can see in Figure 2-26, it does look awesome.

2-26. Visual Studio Code editor

Linux and Mac OS X Editors

A number of development-centric text editors that run on a variety of platforms are available to download for free. The following editors have loyal followings, and all run equally well on Linux and Mac OS X. Emacs and Vim are probably the two editors with the most fervent followings. For the record, I happen to be a Vim user.

Both of these editors have a steeper learning curve than the Windows/cross-platform editors, but the long-term benefits are substantial. Mastering an editor that runs in the terminal is invaluable for a programmer, but it is also something one grows into. If you choose one of these editors, you'll need to spend time getting comfortable with them.

Emacs

Emacs is an editor created in the 1970s by the GNU Project, and can be seen in Figure 2-27. It claims to be an "extensible, customizable text editor" with an active, robust set of extensions developed by the community. Several prominent Rubyists use and love Emacs. The Emacs Wiki[22]

2-27. By Emacs development team - Ferk (user who took this screenshot), CC BY-SA 3.0, https://commons.wikimedia.org/w/index.php?curid=6412319

---

[22]. http://www.emacswiki.org/ is the ideal place to start learning about Emacs.

Vim

Vim[23]–or "VI Improved"–is the evolution of a core Unix editor called "vi". Vim also has an enormous set of community-developed extensions that allow you to make Vim do just about anything you can imagine. The best place to start learning about Vim is on the Vim wiki[24], or take one of the many online tutorials, such as OpenVim[25].

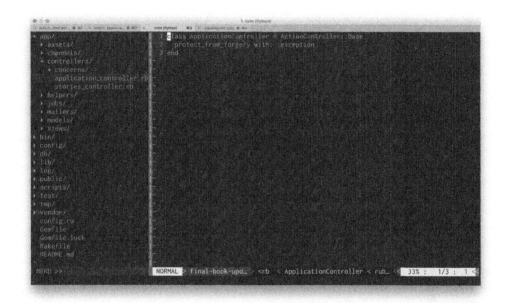

2-28. Vim

IDEs

Some Ruby programmers choose to use an **Integrated Development Environment**, or **IDE**. IDEs, which usually come with a price tag, are complex applications that try to do it all for the programmer. A good IDE makes your application code easy to navigate, runs basic tasks with simple keystrokes, automates code refactoring and tests, and offers up an integrated console. As you might imagine, some perform these tasks better than others. If you're interested in the IDE approach,

---

[23.] http://www.vim.org/
[24.] http://vim.wikia.com/wiki/Tutorial
[25.] http://www.openvim.com/

check out the SitePoint Ruby channel for articles[26] on which IDEs are favored by Rubyists.

Summary

In this chapter, I showed you how to install all the necessary software to develop a web application in Ruby on Rails.

We installed Ruby, Rails, and SQLite, and set up the standard directory structure for our application, which we've named "ReadIt." Then we launched the application for the first time, enabling us to check which versions we were running of the components involved. And finally, we looked at some of the text editors that are available to help you build the application.

All this work has been in preparation for Chapter 4, where we'll start to write our first lines of application code. But first, there's some theory we have to tackle. Hold on tight, we'll be coding soon enough!

[26.] http://www.sitepoint.com/ides-rubyists-use/

Chapter

Introducing Ruby

While this chapter makes no attempt to constitute a complete guide to the Ruby
language, it will introduce you to some of its basics. We'll power through a crash
course in object-oriented programming that covers the more common features of
the language, leaving the more obscure aspects of Ruby for a dedicated reference
guide.[1] I'll also point out some of the advantages that Ruby has over other
languages when it comes to developing applications for the Web.

There used to be a longstanding axiom (previously known as "The Rails Newbie
Axiom") that one could learn Rails without first learning Ruby. This axiom has
been challenged and, rightly so, proven less true than originally thought. I came
to Ruby through Rails many moons ago, and my lack of Ruby knowledge caught
up with me in a hurry. As I mentioned over and over again in Chapter 1, Rails is a

---

[1] http://www.ruby-doc.org/stdlib/

framework written in Ruby, the *language*. The more you know about the language, the better you'll be using the framework.

However, this is not a book on Ruby, and teaching you all of Ruby and then Rails is too much. As such, I'm going to modify the Axiom to:

> You can learn just enough Ruby to be productive in Rails.

This fits with the Rails aim of making you productive in a hurry. But you have to promise me that you'll keep learning Ruby as you continue your journey with Rails, okay? Pinky promise? Done. Learning Ruby will not only make you a better Rails programmer, it will make you a better overall programmer.

Ruby is a Scripting Language

In general, programming languages fall into one of two categories: they're either compiled languages, or scripting languages. Let's explore what each of those terms means, and understand the differences between them.

Compiled Languages

The language in which you write an application is not actually a language understood by your computer. Your code needs to be translated into bits and bytes that can be executed by your computer. This process of translation is called **compilation**, and any language that requires compilation is referred to as a **compiled language**. Examples of compiled languages include C, C#, and Java.

For a compiled language, the actual compilation is the final step in the development process. You invoke a compiler—the software program that translates your final handwritten, human-readable code into machine-readable code—and the compiler creates an executable file. This final product is then able to execute independently of the original source code.

Thus, if you make changes to your code and you want those changes to be incorporated into the application, you must stop the running application, recompile it, then start the application again.

Scripting Languages

On the other hand, a **scripting language** such as Ruby, Javascript, or Python relies upon an application's source code all the time. Scripting languages have no compiler or compilation phase per se; instead, they use an **interpreter**—a program that runs on the web server—to translate handwritten code into machine-executable code on the fly. The link between the running application and your handcrafted code is never severed, because that scripting code is translated every time it's invoked; in other words, for every web page that your application renders.

As you might have gathered from the name, the use of an interpreter rather than a compiler is the major difference between a scripting language and a compiled language.

The Great Performance Debate

If you've come from a compiled-language background, you might be concerned by all this talk of translating code on the fly—how does it affect the application's performance?

These concerns are valid. Translating code on the web server every time it's needed is certainly more expensive performance-wise than executing precompiled code, as it requires more effort on the part of your machine's processor. The good news is that there are ways to speed up scripted languages, including techniques such as **code caching**—caching the output of a script for reuse rather than executing the script every time—and **persistent interpreters**—loading the interpreter once and keeping it running instead of having to load it for every request. However, performance topics are beyond the scope of this book.

There's also an upside to scripted languages in terms of performance—namely, *your* performance while developing an application.

Imagine that you've just compiled a shiny new Java application and launched it for the first time, and then you notice an embarrassing typo on the welcome screen. To fix it you have to stop your application, go back to the source code, fix the typo, wait for the code to recompile, and restart your application to confirm that it's fixed. And if you find another typo, you'll need to repeat that process *again*. Lather, rinse, repeat.

In a scripting language, you can fix the typo and just reload the page in your browser—no restart, no recompile, no nothing. It's as simple as that.

Choose What Works

The landscape of languages today, both compiled and scripting, is virtually endless with more coming out every week. In the last decade, being an effective programmer has become less about completely mastering one language and more about knowing when to choose the right language. In other words, languages are tools, each with their own strengths and weaknesses. Your job is to know when to use and—maybe more importantly—when *not* to use a language.

But that's all academic for what we're here to do, which is to learn Rails. Rails is written in Ruby, so let's choose Ruby. See? You're already learning how to choose the right tool.

Ruby is an Object Oriented Language

Ruby, from its very beginnings, was built as a programming language that adheres to the principles of object-oriented programming (OOP). Before discussing Ruby specifics, let's unpack some fundamental concepts of OOP. The theory can be a bit dry when you're itching to start coding, but we'll cover a lot of ground in this short section. It will hold you in good stead, so don't skip it.

OOP is a programming paradigm that first surfaced in the 1960s, but didn't gain traction until the 1980s with C++. Its core idea is that programs should be composed of individual entities, or objects, each of which has the ability to communicate with other objects around it by passing messages. Additionally, each object may have the facility to store data internally (called **state**), as depicted in Figure 3-1.

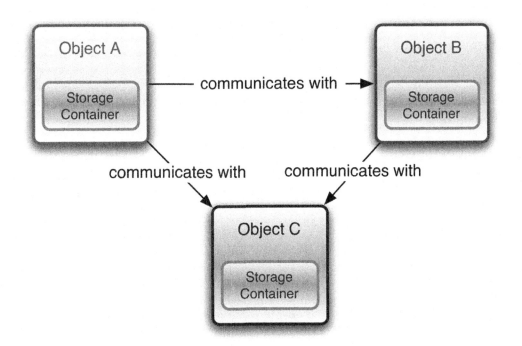

3-1. Object interaction in Ruby

Objects in an OOP application are often modeled on real-world objects, so even non-programmers can usually recognize the basic role that an object plays.

And, just like the real world, OOP defines objects and classes with similar characteristics belonging to the same classes and objects. A **class** is a construct for defining properties for objects that are alike and equipping them with functionality. For example, a class named `Car` might define the attributes *color* and *mileage* for its objects, and assign them functionality: actions such as *open the trunk*, *start the engine*, and *change gears*. These different actions are known as **methods**, although you'll often see Rails enthusiasts refer to the methods of a controller (a kind of object used in Rails with which you'll become very familiar) as **actions**; you can safely consider the two terms to be interchangeable.

Understanding the relationship between a class and its objects is integral to understanding how OOP works. For instance, one object can invoke functionality on another object, and can do so without affecting other objects of the same class. So, if one car object was instructed to open its trunk, its trunk would open, but the trunk of other cars would remain closed—think of KITT, the talking car from the television show *Knight Rider*, if it helps with the metaphor.[2] Similarly, if our high-tech talking car were instructed to change color to red, it would do so, but other cars would not.

When we create a new object in OOP, we base it on an existing class. The process of creating new objects from a class is called **instantiation**. Figure 3-2 illustrates this concept.

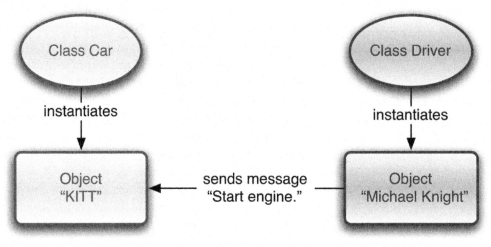

3-2. Instantiation in Ruby

As I've mentioned, objects can communicate with each other via messages, invoking functionality (methods) on other objects. Invoking an object's methods can be thought of as asking the object a question and getting an answer in return.

Consider the example of our famous talking car again. Let's say we ask the talking car object to report its current mileage. This question is not ambiguous: the answer that the object gives is called a return value, and is shown in Figure 3-3.

[2.] Knight Rider was a popular 1980s series that featured modern-day cowboy Michael Knight (played by David Hasselhoff) and his opinionated black Pontiac Firebird named KITT. If you missed it in the '80s, you may be more familiar with the Ford Mustang voiced by Val Kilmer in the 2008 remake. Don't worry, having seen the show isn't a prerequisite to understanding object-oriented programming!

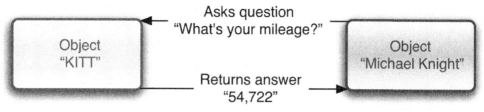

3-3. Asking a simple question in OOP

In some cases, the question-and-answer analogy seems ill-fitting. In these situations, we might rephrase the analogy to consider the question to be an instruction, and the answer a status report indicating whether or not the instruction was executed successfully. This process might look like the diagram in Figure 3-4.

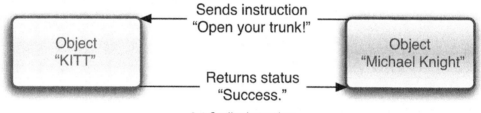

3-4. Sending instructions

Sometimes we need more flexibility with our instructions. For example, if we wanted to tell our car to change gear, we tell it not only to change gear, but also which gear to change to. The process of asking these kinds of questions is referred to as passing an argument to the method.

An **argument** (also called a "parameter") is an input value that's provided to a method. An argument can be used to influence:

- how a method operates

- on which object a method operates

An example is shown in Figure 3-5 below, where the method is "change gear," and the number of the gear to which the car must change (two) is the argument.

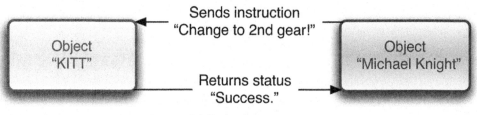

3-5. Passing arguments

A more general view of all these different types of communication between objects is this: invoking an object's methods is accomplished by sending messages to it. As one might expect, the object sending the message is called the *sender*, and the object receiving the message is called the *receiver*.

Armed with this basic knowledge about object-oriented programming, let's look at some Ruby specifics.

Reading and Writing Ruby Code

Learning the syntax of a new language has the potential to induce the occasional yawn. So, to make things more interesting, I'll present it to you in a practical way that lets you play along at home. We'll use the interactive Ruby shell.

The Interactive Ruby Shell (irb)

You can fire up the interactive Ruby shell by entering irb into a terminal window:

```
$ irb
irb>
```

Windows Users

Windows users, remember to use the *Ruby > Start Command Prompt with Ruby* option from the Ruby 2.3.1 menu to ensure that the environment you're using contains the right settings.

irb allows you to issue Ruby commands interactively, one line at a time. This ability is great for playing with the language, and it's also handy for debugging, as we'll see in Chapter 11.

A couple of points about the irb output you'll see in this chapter are that lines beginning with:

▨ the Ruby shell prompt (irb>) are typed in by the user

▨ the => show the return value of the command that has been entered

We'll start with a *really* brief example:

```
irb> 1
=> 1
```

Here, I've simply thrown the number 1 at the Ruby shell and received back what appears to be the very same number.

Looks can be deceiving, though. It's actually *not* the very same number. What has been handed back is actually a fully-featured Ruby object.

Remember our discussion about object-oriented programming in the previous section? Well, in Ruby, absolutely everything is treated as an object with which we can interact; each object belongs to a certain class, therefore each object is able to store data and functionality in the form of methods.

To find the class to which our number belongs, we call the number's **class** method:

```
irb> 1.class
=> Fixnum
```

We touched on senders and receivers earlier. In this example, we've sent the **class** message to the 1 object, so the 1 object is the receiver (there's no sender, as we're sending the message from the interactive command line rather than from another object). The value that's returned by the method we've invoked is `Fixnum`, which is the Ruby class that represents integer values.

Since everything in Ruby is an object (*including* a class), we can actually send the very same message to the `Fixnum` class. The result is different, as we'd expect:

```
irb> Fixnum.class
=> Class
```

This time, the return value is `Class`, which is reassuring—we did invoke it on a class name, after all.

Note that the `class` method is all lowercase, yet the return value, `Class`, begins with a capital letter. A method in Ruby is always written in lowercase, whereas the first letter of a class is always capitalized.

 Constants, Classes, and Capitals

Class names start with a capital letter because they are constants. In programming-speak, a constant is a value that, once set, does not change throughout the lifetime of the program. Classes are considered constants, so they are capitalized. You'll see other constants in ALL_CAPS, which is a Ruby convention that says "this value is a constant, but it is not a class." I'll talk more about this soon.

Interacting with Ruby Objects

Being accustomed to thinking in terms of objects can take some time. Let's look at a few types of objects, and see how we can interact with them.

Literal Objects

Literal objects are character strings or numbers that appear directly in the code, such as the number 1 returned in the previous section. We've seen numbers in action, so let's now look at a string literal.

A **string literal** is an object that contains a string of characters, such as a name, an address, or an especially witty phrase. In the same way that we created the 1 literal object in the previous example, we can easily create a new string literal object, then send it a message. A string literal is created by enclosing the characters that make up the string in single or double quotes:

```
irb> "The quick brown fox"
=> "The quick brown fox"
```

First, we'll confirm that our string literal indeed belongs to class String:

```
irb> "The quick brown fox".class
=> String
```

This String object has a wealth of embedded functionality. For example, we can ascertain the number of characters that our string literal comprises by sending it the length message:

```
irb> "The quick brown fox".length
=> 19
```

Easy stuff, eh?

Variables and Constants

Every application needs a way to store information. Enter our variables and constants. As their names imply, these two data containers have unique roles to play.

A **constant** (which I mentioned earlier) is an object that's assigned a value once, and once only—usually when the application starts up. Constants are therefore used to store information that won't change within a running application. As an example, a constant might be used to store the version number for an application. Constants in Ruby are always written using uppercase letters, as shown below:

```
irb> CONSTANT = "The quick brown fox in a constant"
=> "The quick brown fox in a constant"
irb> APP_VERSION = 5.04
=> 5.04
```

The one exception to the ALL_CAPS convention is class constants, but you already knew that, didn't you?

Variables, in contrast, are objects that are able to change at any time. They can even be reset to nothing, freeing up the memory space that they previously occupied. Variables in Ruby always start with a lowercase character:

```
irb> variable = "The quick brown fox in a variable"
=> "The quick brown fox in a variable"
```

There's one more special (and, you might say, *evil*) side to a variable: scope. The scope of a variable is the part of the program to which a variable is visible. If you try to access a variable from outside its scope (for example, from a part of an application to which that variable is not visible), your attempts will generally fail.

 Scoping Scope

Scope is a big concept in most programming languages, and understanding it is a true way to hone your craft. I wish I could spend more time on scope, but since I can't, check out *Understanding Scope in Ruby* [3] on SitePoint in your spare time.

The notable exception to the rules defining a variable's scope are **global variables**. As the name implies, a global variable is accessible from any part of the program. While this might sound convenient, using global variables is discouraged—that they can be written to and read from any part of the program introduces security concerns.

[3.] http://www.sitepoint.com/understanding-scope-in-ruby/

Watching Your G's and Q's

In programming, there are many things, like globals, whose use are "discouraged." What this really means is that you should only use them when you really understand how they work and what they mean. Think of them like swear or curse words: when you're young in your Ruby life, you aren't supposed to use them, yet you hear adults using them all the time. As you grow up, you'll misuse them plenty of times, but eventually you'll know when to drop a G-bomb and when to think better of it.

Let's return to the string literal example we just saw. Assigning a `String` to a variable allows us to invoke on that variable the same methods we invoked on the string literal earlier:

```
irb> fox = "The quick brown fox"
=> "The quick brown fox"
irb> fox.class
=> String
irb> fox.length
=> 19
irb> fox.reverse
=> "xof nworb kciuq ehT"
```

See? Just more messages and return values, but now on our variable. And isn't the `reverse` method cool? I love that one.

Basic Punctuation in Ruby

Punctuation in Ruby code differs greatly from other languages such as Perl and PHP, so it can seem confusing at first if you're used to programming in those languages; however, once you have a few basics under your belt, punctuation in Ruby becomes quite intuitive, greatly enhancing the readability of your code.

Dot Notation

One of the most common punctuation characters in Ruby is the period (.). As we've seen, Ruby uses the period to separate the receiver from the message that's being sent to it in the form *Object.receiver.*

 EXTRA CREDIT: Dot Notation

There are other uses for a period in Ruby, but they are much rarer. One example is in ranges; for example, (1..10). I'd suggest you Google "Ruby ranges" and figure out what they do.

You can "comment" a line, either to temporarily take a line of code out of the program flow or for documentation purposes, by using a hash mark (#). Comments in a line of code may start at the beginning of a line, or they may appear further along after some Ruby code:

```
irb> # This is a comment. It doesn't actually do
↳ anything.
irb> 1 # So is this, but this one comes after a
↳ statement.
=> 1
irb> fox = "The quick brown fox"      # Assign to a
↳ variable
=> "The quick brown fox"
irb> fox.class                        # Display a
↳ variable's class
=> String
irb> fox.length                       # Display a
↳ variable's length
=> 19
```

Chaining Statements Together

Using characters to separate commands in Ruby is unnecessary, unless we want to chain multiple statements together on a single line. In this case, a semicolon (;)

is used as the separator. However, if you put every statement on its own line (as we've been doing until now), the semicolon is completely optional.

If you chain multiple statements together in the interactive shell, only the output of the last command that was executed will be displayed to the screen:

```
irb> fox.class; fox.length; fox.upcase
=> "THE QUICK BROWN FOX"
```

Don't be confused. All the messages were sent and methods executed, but irb only shows us the last one.

Use of Parentheses

If you ever delved into the source code of one of the many JavaScript libraries out there, you might have run screaming from your computer when you saw all the parentheses that are involved in the passing of arguments to methods.

In Ruby, the use of parentheses for method calls is optional in cases where no arguments are passed to the method. The following statements are therefore equal:

```
irb> fox.class()
=> String
irb> fox.class
=> String
```

It's common practice (and encouraged) to include parentheses for method calls with multiple arguments, such as the insert method of the String class:

```
 irb> "jumps over the lazy dog".insert(0, 'The quick brown
↪ fox ')
=> "The quick brown fox jumps over the lazy dog"
```

This call inserts the second argument passed to the `insert` object (`"The quick brown fox "`) at position 0 of the receiving `String` object (`"jumps over the lazy dog"`). Position 0 refers to the very beginning of the string.

Method Notation

Until now, we've looked at cases where Ruby uses *less* punctuation than its competitors. Yet, in fact, Ruby makes heavy use of expressive punctuation when it comes to the naming of methods.

A regular method name, as we've seen, is a simple alphanumeric string of characters. If a method has a potentially destructive nature (for example, it directly modifies the receiving object rather than changing a copy of it), it's commonly suffixed with an exclamation point (`!`).

The following example uses the `upcase` method to illustrate this point:

```
irb> fox.upcase
=> "THE QUICK BROWN FOX"
irb> fox
=> "The quick brown fox"
irb> fox.upcase!
=> "THE QUICK BROWN FOX"
irb> fox
=> "THE QUICK BROWN FOX"
```

Here, the contents of the `fox` variable have been modified by the `upcase!` method.

Punctuation is also used in the names of methods that return Boolean values. A **Boolean value** is one that's either `true` or `false`; these are commonly used as return values for methods that ask yes/no questions. Such methods end in a question mark, which nicely reflects that they have yes/no answers:

```
irb> fox.empty?
=> false
irb> fox.is_a? String
```

```
=> true
```

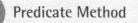 **Predicate Method**

A method that returns only `true` or `false` is also known as a predicate method.

These naming conventions make it easy to recognize methods that are destructive and those that return Boolean values, making your Ruby code more readable.

Object-oriented Programming in Ruby

Let's build on the theory covered at the start of this chapter as we take a look at Ruby's implementation of OOP.

As we already know, the structure of an application based on OOP principles is focused on interaction with objects. These objects are often representations of real-world objects; for example, a `Car`. Interaction with an object occurs when we send it a message or ask it a question. If we really did have a `Car` object called `kitt`, starting the car might be as simple as doing this:

```
irb> kitt.start
```

This short line of Ruby code sends the message `start` to the object `kitt`. Using OOP terminology, we would say that this code statement calls the `start` method of the `kitt` object.

As I've mentioned, in contrast to other object-oriented programming languages such as Python and PHP, *everything* is an object in Ruby. Especially when compared with PHP, Ruby's OOP feels far from being like a tacked-on afterthought—it was clearly intended to be a core feature of the language from the beginning, which makes using the OOP features in Ruby a real pleasure.

As we've seen, even the simplest of elements in Ruby (such as literal strings and numbers) are objects to which you can send messages.

Classes and Objects

As in any other OOP language, each object belongs to a certain class in Ruby (for example, `pontiac_firebird` might be an object of class `Car`). We know that a class can group objects of a certain kind, and equip those objects with common functionality. This functionality comes in the form of methods, and in the object's ability to store information. For example, a `pontiac_firebird` object might need to store its mileage, as might any other object of the class `Car`.

In Ruby, the **instantiation** of a new object that's based on an existing class is accomplished by sending that class the new message. The result is a new object of that class. The following few lines of code show an extremely basic class definition in Ruby; the third line is where we create an instance of the class that we just defined:

```
irb> class Car
irb> end
=> nil
irb> kitt = Car.new
=> #<Car:0x75e54>
```

Another basic principle in OOP is **encapsulation**. According to this principle, objects should be treated as independent entities, each taking care of its own internal data and functionality. If we need to access an object's information—its internal variables, for instance—we make use of the object's interface, which is the subset of the object's methods that are made available for other objects to call.

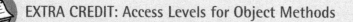 **EXTRA CREDIT: Access Levels for Object Methods**

> Object methods can have different access levels, meaning, some are accessible *publicly*, while others are accessible only by the object itself. A method can have one of three access levels within an object: public, protected, or private. Go and ask Google what these mean.

Ruby provides objects with functionality at two levels—object level and class level—and adheres to the principle of encapsulation while it's at it! Let's dig deeper.

Object-level Functionality

At the object level, data storage (state) is handled by instance variables (a name that's derived from the instantiation process mentioned). Think of instance variables as storage containers that are attached to the object, but to which other objects do not have direct access.

To store or retrieve data from these variables, another object must call an accessor method defined on the object. An accessor method has the ability to set (and get) the value of the object's instance variables.

Let's look at how instance variables and accessor methods relate to each other, and how they're implemented in Ruby.

Instance Variables

Instance variables are bound to an object, and contain values for that object only.

Revisiting our car example, the mileage values for a number of different `Car` objects are likely to differ, as each car will have a different mileage. Therefore, mileage is held in an instance variable.

An instance variable can be recognized by its prefix: a single "at" (`@`) sign. What's more, instance variables don't even need to be declared! There's only one issue: we don't have any way to retrieve or change them from outside the object once they do exist. This is where instance methods come into play.

A Link to Social Media

I like to think of instance variables as the inspiration for mentions on Twitter and social media. I have no idea if this is true, but Twitter did start life in Ruby.

Instance Methods

Data storage and retrieval is not the only capability that can be bound to a specific object; functionality can also be bound to objects. We achieve this binding through the use of **instance methods** that are specific to an object. Invoking an instance method (in other words, sending a message that contains the method name to an object) will invoke that functionality on the receiving object only.

Instance methods are defined using the `def` keyword, and end with the `end` keyword. Enter the following example into a new Ruby shell:

```
$ irb
irb> class Car
irb>   def open_trunk
irb>     # code to open trunk goes here
irb>   end
irb> end
=> nil
irb> kitt = Car.new
=> #<Car:0x75e54>
```

What you've done is define a class called `Car`, which has an instance method with the name `open_trunk`. A `Car` object instantiated from this class will—possibly using some fancy robotics connected to our Ruby program—open its trunk when its `open_trunk` method is called. Ignore that `nil` return value for the moment; we'll look at `nil` values in the next section.

Indentation in Ruby

While the indentation of code is a key element of the syntax of languages such as Python, in Ruby, indentation is purely cosmetic: it aids readability without affecting the code in any way. In fact, while we're experimenting with the Ruby shell, don't worry too much about indenting any of the code; however, when we're saving files that will be edited later, you'll want the readability benefits that come from indenting nested lines.

The Ruby community has agreed upon two spaces being optimum for indenting blocks of code such as class or method definitions. We'll adhere to this indentation scheme throughout this book.

With our class in place, we can make use of this method:

```
irb> kitt.open_trunk
=> nil
```

Since we want to avoid having the trunks of all our cars to open at once, we've made this functionality available as an instance method.

I know, I know—we *still* haven't modified any data. We'll use accessor methods for this task.

Accessor Methods

An **accessor method** is a special type of instance method, used to read or write to an instance variable. There are two types: readers (sometimes called "getters") and writers (or "setters").

A **reader method** will look inside the object, fetch the value of an instance variable, and hand this value back to us. **A writer method**, on the other hand, will look inside the object, find an instance variable, and assign the variable the value that it was passed.

Let's add some methods for getting and setting the @mileage attribute of our Car objects. Once again, exit from the Ruby shell so that we can create an entirely new Car class definition. Our class definition is a bit longer now, so enter each line carefully. If you make a typing mistake, exit the shell, and start over:

```
$ irb
irb> class Car
irb>    def set_mileage(x)
irb>       @mileage = x
irb>    end
irb>    def get_mileage
irb>       @mileage
irb>    end
irb> end
=> nil
irb> kitt = Car.new
```

```
=> #<Car:0x75e54>
```

Now, we can finally modify and retrieve the mileage of our `Car` objects:

```
irb> kitt.set_mileage(5667)
=> 5667
irb> kitt.get_mileage
=> 5667
```

This is still a bit awkward. Wouldn't it be nice if we could give our accessor methods the same names as the attributes that read and control? Luckily, Ruby contains shorthand notation for this very task. We can rewrite our class definition as follows:

```
$ irb
irb> class Car
irb>    def mileage=(x)
irb>       @mileage = x
irb>    end
irb>    def mileage
irb>       @mileage
irb>    end
irb> end
=> nil
irb> kitt = Car.new
=> #<Car:0x75e54>
```

With these accessor methods in place, we can read to and write from our instance variable as if it were available from outside the object:

```
irb> kitt.mileage = 6032
=> 6032
irb> kitt.mileage
```

```
=> 6032
```

These accessor methods form part of the object's interface. By the way, since Ruby is all about programmer productivity and happiness, the standard library supplies shortcut methods to define accessor methods. Check it out:

```
irb> class Car
irb>    attr_accessor :mileage
irb> end
=> nil
irb> kitt = Car.new
=> #<Car:0x75e54>
irb> kitt.mileage = 6032
=> 6032
irb> kitt.mileage
=> 6032
```

Pretty neat, eh?

Class-level Functionality

At the class level, **class variables** handle data storage. They're commonly used to store state information, or as a means of configuring default values for new objects. Class variables are typically set in the body of a class, and can be recognized by their prefix: a double "at" sign (@@).

First, enter the following class definition into a new Ruby shell:

```
$ irb
irb> class Car
irb>    @@number_of_cars = 0
irb>    def initialize
irb>       @@number_of_cars = @@number_of_cars + 1
irb>    end
irb> end
```

```
=> nil
```

In the code, the class definition for the class `Car` has an internal counter for the total number of `Car` objects that have been created. Using the special instance method `initialize`, which is invoked automatically every time an object is instantiated, this counter is incremented for each new `Car` object.

By the way, we've already used a class method; I snuck it in there. The `new` method is an example of a class method that ships with Ruby and is available to all classes, whether they're defined by you or form part of the Ruby Standard Library.[4]

Custom class methods are commonly used to create objects with special properties (such as a default color for our `Car` objects—called **factory methods**), or to gather statistics about the class's usage.

Extending the earlier example, we could use a class method called `count` to return the value of the `@@number_of_cars` class variable. Remember that this is a variable that's incremented for every new `Car` object created. Class methods are defined identically to instance methods: using the `def` and `end` keywords. The only difference is that class method names are prefixed with `self`. Enter this code into a new Ruby shell:

```
$ irb
irb> class Car
irb>    @@number_of_cars = 0
irb>    def self.count
irb>       @@number_of_cars
irb>    end
irb>    def initialize
irb>       @@number_of_cars += 1
irb>    end
irb> end
```

[4.] The Ruby Standard Library is a large collection of classes that's included with every Ruby installation. The classes facilitate a wide range of common functionality, such as accessing websites, date calculations, file operations, and more.

```
=> nil
```

The following code instantiates some new `Car` objects, then makes use of our new class method:

```
 irb> kitt = Car.new          # Michael Knight's talking
↪ car
=> #<0xba8c>
 irb> herbie = Car.new        # The famous Volkswagen love
↪ bug!
=> #<0x8cd20>
irb> batmobile = Car.new     # Batman's sleek automobile
=> #<0x872e4>
irb> Car.count
=> 3
```

The method tells us that three instances of the `Car` class have been created. Note that we can't call a class method on an object:[5]

```
irb> kitt.count
 NoMethodError: undefined method 'count' for
↪ #<Car:0x89da0>
```

As implied by the name, the `count` class method is available only to the `Car` class, not to any objects instantiated from that class.

Avoid the CV Word

Class variables are treated in much the same way as global variables in that they are discouraged. Think of them as the "CV" word and avoid them.

[5.] Ruby actually does provide a way to invoke *some* class methods on an object using the `::` operator, but we won't worry about that for now. We'll see the `::` operator in use in Chapter 4.

I sneakily introduced another operator in there. In many languages, including PHP and Java, the ++ and -- operators are used to increment a variable by one, but Ruby doesn't support this notation; instead, we use the += operator. Therefore, the shorthand notation for incrementing our counter in the class definition is:

```
irb> @@number_of_cars += 1
```

This code is identical to:

```
irb> @@number_of_cars = @@number of cars + 1
```

Both of these lines can be read as "my_variable becomes equal to my_variable plus one."

Inheritance

If your application deals with more than the flat hierarchy we've explored so far, you may want to construct a scenario whereby some classes inherit from other classes. **Inheritance** is a tenet of object-oriented programming where one class can be used as a parent (or *super*) class of another. This means that the methods and variables defined on the super class are available on the child class. You use inheritance when one class *is a* kind of another class. The example code will make this more clear.

Continuing with the car analogy, let's suppose that we have a green limousine named Larry (this assignment of names to cars may seem a little strange, but it's important for this example, so bear with me). In Ruby, the larry object would probably descend from a StretchLimo class, which could in turn descend from the class Car (a StretchLimo *is a* Car). Let's implement that class relationship to see how it works:

```
$ irb
irb> class Car
```

```
irb>    WHEELS = 4
irb> end
=> nil
irb> class StretchLimo < Car
irb>    WHEELS = 6
irb>    def turn_on_television
irb>       # Invoke code for switching on on-board TV here
irb>    end
irb> end
=> nil
```

Now, if we were to instantiate an object of class StretchLimo, we'd end up with a different kind of car. Instead of the regular four wheels that standard Car objects have, this one would have six wheels (stored in the class constant WHEELS). It would also have extra functionality, made possible by the presence of the extra method turn_on_television, which could be called by other objects.

However, if we were to instantiate a regular Car object, the car would have only four wheels, and there would be no instance method for turning on an on-board television. Think of inheritance as a way for a class's functionality to become more specialized the further we move down the inheritance path.

Don't worry if you're struggling to wrap your head around all the aspects of OOP. You'll become accustomed to them as you work through this book. It may be useful to come back to this section, though, especially if you need a reminder about a certain term later on.

Modules and Composition

Another foundational concept is **composition**, which is basically reusing functionality across objects by including them in the class definition. In other words, the behavior of a class is *composed of* defined functional sets. These functional sets are not a part of the base class definition, but are *included* in any class desiring that functionality. I like to think that if inheritance defines "is a", then composition defines "has a".

Ruby allows the definition of sets of functionality in **modules**. A module looks a lot like a class except that it has no `new` method, which means it can't be instantiated. Here is an example module:

```
irb> module Nitrous
irb>    def push_the_red_button
irb>       # Invoke code kicking on the nitrous here! ZOOM!
irb>       "ZOOM!"
irb>    end
irb> end
```

Not all cars have nitrous installed, but for cars that are fast and, possibly, furious, nitrous is a must. Now that we have a module, how do we include it in the class definition of our race cars? By using `include`.

Modules are included in a class using the `include` keyword. Let's look at an example:

```
irb> class Racer < Car
irb>   include Nitrous
irb> end
=> nil
irb> race_car = Racer.new
irb> race_car.push_the_red_button
=> ZOOM!
irb> limo = StretchLimo.new
irb> limo.push_the_red_button
 => NoMethodError: undefined method `push_the_red_button'
↳ for #<StretchLimo:0x007f89760c9188>
```

As we've included the `Nitrous` module in our `Racer` class, the `push_the_red_button` method is available to instances of `Racer`. The limo, however, doesn't have nitrous.

One more quick point. You'll notice that `include`ing a module in a class creates instance methods. What if we want to define class methods? I'm glad you asked.

There is another keyword, `extend`, that adds the methods defined in a module as class methods like so:

```
irb> module Lemon
irb>   def recalls
irb>     "The engine explodes if you switch into reverse"
irb>   end
irb> end
irb> class Pinto < Car
irb>   extend Lemon
irb> end
=> nil
irb> pos = Pinto.new
irb> pos.recalls
=> NoMethodError
irb> Pinto.recalls
=> "The engine explodes if you switch into reverse"
```

Modules are used extensively in Ruby and Rails, and learning how to use them effectively can make your code much more maintainable.

Support for Methods

What if you wanted to add some methods from a module as instance methods, and other methods in that module as class methods? Googling "ActiveSupport Concern" will reward you with the answer you seek.

Much of the core Rails functionality is implemented via modules, so we've covered enough to ensure there are no surprises.

Return Values

It's always great to receive feedback. Remember our talk about passing arguments to methods? Well, regardless of whether or not a method accepts arguments, invoking a method in Ruby *always* results in feedback. It comes in the form of a return value, which is returned either explicitly or implicitly.

To return a value explicitly, use the `return` statement in the body of a method:

```
irb> def toot_horn
irb>    return "toooot!"
irb> end
=> nil
```

Calling the `toot_horn` method in this case would produce the following:

```
irb> toot_horn
=> "toooot!"
```

However, if no return statement is used, the result of the last statement that was executed is used as the return value. This behavior is quite unique to Ruby:

```
irb> def toot_loud_horn
irb>    "toooot!".upcase
irb> end
=> nil
```

Calling the `toot_loud_horn` method in this case would produce:

```
irb> toot_loud_horn
=> "TOOOOT!"
```

Standard Output

When you need to show output to the users of your application, use the `print` and `puts` statements. Both methods will display the arguments passed to them as a `String`; `puts` also inserts a carriage return at the end of its output. Therefore, in a Ruby program the following lines:

```
print "The quick "
print "brown fox"
```

... would produce this output:

```
The quick brown fox
```

Yet, using puts like so:

```
puts "jumps over"
puts "the lazy dog"
```

... results in:

```
jumps over
the lazy dog
```

You might be wondering why *all* of the trial-and-error code snippets that we typed into the Ruby shell actually produced output, given that there's been no use of the print or puts methods up to this point. It's because irb automatically writes the return value of the last statement it executes to the screen before displaying the irb prompt. This means that using print or puts from within the Ruby shell might in fact produce two lines of output: the output that you specify should be displayed, and the return value of the last command that was executed, as in this example:

```
irb> puts "The quick brown fox"
"The quick brown fox"
=> nil
```

Here, `nil` is actually the return value of the `puts` statement. Looking back at previous examples, you will have encountered `nil` as the return value for class and method definitions, and you'll have received a hexadecimal address such as `#<Car:0x89da0>` as the return value for object definitions. This hexadecimal value showed the location in memory that the object we instantiated occupied. Luckily we can forget about bothering with such geeky details any further.

Having met the `print` and `puts` statements, you should be aware that a Rails application has a completely different approach to displaying output, called templates. We'll look at templates in Chapter 4.

 Put It There

For what it's worth, 99.99998% of the times you want to write to standard output, use `puts`. It's what all the cool kids do.

Ruby Core Classes

We've already talked briefly about the `String` and `Fixnum` classes in the previous sections, but Ruby has a lot more under its hood. Let's explore!

Strings

The typical Ruby `String` object—yep, that very same object we've already been using—holds and manipulates sequences of characters. Most of the time, new `String` objects are created using string literals that are enclosed in single or double quotes. The string literal can then be stored in a variable for later use:

```
irb> a_phrase = "The quick brown fox"
=> "The quick brown fox"
irb> a_phrase.class
=> String
```

If the string literal includes the quote character used to enclose the string itself, it must be escaped with a backslash character (\):

```
irb> 'I\'m a quick brown fox'
=> "I'm a quick brown fox"
irb> "Arnie said, \"I'm back!\""
=> "Arnie said, \"I'm back!\""
```

An easier way to specify string literals that contain quotes is to use the %Q shortcut, like this:

```
irb> %Q(Arnie said, "I'm back!")
=> "Arnie said, \"I'm back!\""
```

String additionally supports the substitution of Ruby code into a string literal via the Ruby expression #{}:

```
irb> "The current time is: #{Time.now}"
=> "The current time is: Wed Aug 02 21:15:19 CEST 2006"
```

The String class methods also have rich embedded functionality for modifying String objects. Here are some of the most useful methods:

▨ gsub substitutes a given pattern within a String:

```
irb> "The quick brown fox".gsub('fox', 'dog')
=> "The quick brown dog"
```

▨ include? returns true if a String contains another specific String:

```
irb> "The quick brown fox".include?('fox')
=> true
```

▨ length returns the length of a String in characters:

```
irb> "The quick brown fox".length
=> 19
```

■ slice returns a portion of a String:

```
irb> "The quick brown fox".slice(0, 3)
=> "The"
```

The complete list of class methods and instance methods provided by the String class is available via the Ruby reference documentation, which you can access by entering the ri command into the terminal window (for your operating system, *not* the Ruby shell), followed by the class name you'd like to look up:

```
$ ri String
```

Oh, and ri stands for ruby interactive, in case you're wondering. Don't confuse it with irb.

Ruby Interactive Documentation

If ri returns nothing or errors, or says Nothing known about String, you need to install the ri documentation. If you are using RVM, you can type rvm docs generate-ri. If you are on Windows, try this:

```
$ gem install rdoc-data
$ rdoc-data --install
```

That should do the trick.

Numerics

Since there are so many different types of numbers, Ruby has a separate class for each—the popular `Float`, `Fixnum`, and `Bignum` classes among them. They're actually all subclasses of `Numeric`, which provides the basic functionality.

Just like `Strings`, numbers are usually created from literals:

```
irb> 123.class
=> Fixnum
irb> 12.5.class
=> Float
```

Each of the specific `Numeric` subclasses comes with features that are relevant to the type of number it's designed to deal with; however, the following functionality is shared between all `Numeric` functionality:

- `integer?` returns `true` if the object is a whole integer:

  ```
  irb> 123.integer?
  => true
  irb> 12.5.integer?
  => false
  ```

- `round` rounds a number to the nearest integer:

  ```
  irb> 12.3.round
  => 12
  irb> 38.8.round
  => 39
  ```

- `zero?` returns `true` if the number is equal to zero:

```
irb> 0.zero?
=> true
irb> 8.zero?
=> false
```

Additionally, there are ways to convert numbers between the `Numeric` subclasses. `to_f` converts a value to a `Float`, and `to_i` converts a value to an `Integer`:

```
irb> 12.to_f
=> 12.0
irb> 11.3.to_i
=> 11
```

Symbols

In Ruby, a `Symbol` is a simple textual identifier. Like a `String`, a `Symbol` is created using literals; the difference is that a `Symbol` is prefixed with a colon (:) like so:

```
irb> :fox
=> :fox
irb> :fox.class
=> Symbol
```

The main benefit of using a `Symbol` over a `String` is that a `Symbol` is *immutable*, meaning it doesn't change. This is different from `Strings`, which can be changed. Immutability is a big subject, so let's focus on the biggest benefit: memory. Each string you created is different from all other strings, even if the strings have the same characters. Check it out:

```
irb> "fox".object_id
=> 70114175443000
irb> "fox".object_id
70114175426920
irb> :fox.object_id
```

```
544488
irb> :fox.object_id
544488
```

In Ruby, every object has an `object_id`, which is, in essence, where that object sits in memory. As you can see from the example, every time you type `"fox"`, you get a new `object_id`, a new object; however, when you type `:fox`, it's the same object every time.

This can be an advantage in certain situations when we want to ensure we have the same object. For example, when we store values in a `Hash` (which we'll cover in a sec), a unique key is important. Otherwise, we could store several values with the same key value, but that would be confusing.

Objects of class `String` can be converted to class `Symbol`, and vice versa:

```
irb> "fox".to_sym
=> :fox
irb> :fox.to_s
=> "fox"
```

We'll be using `Symbol` frequently as we deal with Rails functionality in successive chapters of this book.

Arrays

We use Ruby's `Array` to store collections of objects. Each individual object that's stored in an `Array` has a unique numeric key, which we can use to reference it. As with many languages, the first element in an `Array` is stored at position 0 (zero).

To create a new `Array`, simply instantiate a new object of class `Array` using the `Array.new` construct. You can (and should) also use a shortcut approach, which is to enclose the objects you want to place inside the `Array` in square brackets.

For example, an `Array` containing the mileage at which a car is due for its regular service might look similar to this:

```
irb> service_mileage = [5000, 15000, 30000, 60000,
↪ 100000]
=> [5000, 15000, 30000, 60000, 100000]
```

To retrieve individual elements from an Array, we specify the numeric key in square brackets:

```
irb> service_mileage[0]
=> 5000
irb> service_mileage[2]
=> 30000
```

Ruby has more shortcuts that allow us to create an Array from a list of Strings: the %w( ) and %i() syntaxes. Using these shortcuts saves us from typing a lot of double-quote characters. The former (%w) creates an array of strings, while the latter (%i) creates an array of symbols:

```
irb> string_colors = %w( red green blue black )
=> ["red", "green", "blue", "black"]
irb> string_colors[0]
=> "red"
irb> string_colors[3]
=> "black"
irb> symbol_colors = %i( red green blue black )
=> [:red, :green, :blue, :black]
irb> symbol_colors[0]
=> :red
```

In addition to facilitating simple element retrieval, Array comes with a set of class methods and instance methods that ease data management tasks tremendously.

▨ empty? returns true if the receiving Array contains no elements:

```
irb> available_colors.empty?
=> false
```

size returns the number of elements in an Array:

```
irb> available_colors.size
=> 4
```

The complete list of class methods and instance methods provided by the Array class is available via the Ruby reference documentation:

```
$ ri Array
```

Hashes

A Hash is another kind of data storage container that is similar conceptually to a dictionary: it maps one object (the key; for example, a word) to another (the value; a word's definition) in a one-to-one relationship.

A new Hash can be created either by instantiating a new object of class Hash (using the Hash.new construct) or by using the curly brace shortcut shown in the code that follows. When defining a Hash, we must specify each entry using one of two syntaxes: either key: value or key => value. The former is newer and, in this writer's opinion, preferred but either way works.

In the following example, the Hash maps car names to a color:

```
irb> car_colors = {
irb>   kitt: 'black',
irb>   herbie: 'white',
irb>   batmobile: 'black',
irb>   larry: 'green'
irb> }
 => {"kitt"=>"black", "herbie"=>"white",
```

```
↳ "batmobile"=>"black", "larry"=>"green"}
```

To query this newly built `Hash`, we pass the key of the entry we want to look up in square brackets as a symbol:

```
irb> car_colors[:kitt]
=> "black"
```

All sorts of useful functionality is built into a `Hash`, including the following methods:

▨ `empty?` returns `true` if the receiving `Hash` doesn't contain any elements:

```
irb> car_colors.empty?
=> false
```

▨ `size` returns the number of elements in a `Hash`:

```
irb> car_colors.size
=> 4
```

▨ `keys` returns all keys of a `Hash` as an `Array`:

```
irb> car_colors.keys
=> ["kitt", "herbie", "batmobile", "larry"]
```

▨ `values` returns all values of a `Hash` as an `Array` in the order they were added to the `Hash`:

```
irb> car_colors.values
=> ["black", "white", "black", "green"]
```

There are lots more class methods and instance methods provided by the Hash class. For a complete list, consult the Ruby reference documentation by typing:

```
ri Hash
```

nil Values

I promised earlier that I'd explain nil values—now's the time!

All programming languages have a value they can use when they actually mean *nothing*. Some use undef; others use NULL. Ruby uses nil. A nil value, like everything in Ruby, is also an object. It therefore has its own class: NilClass.

Basically, if a method returns nothing, it is returning the value nil. And if you assign nil to a variable, you effectively make it empty. nil shows up in a couple of other places, but we'll cross those bridges when we come to them.

Running Ruby Files

For the simple Ruby basics that we've experimented with so far, the interactive Ruby shell (irb) has been our tool of choice. I'm sure you'll agree that experimenting in a shell-like environment where we can see immediate results is a great way to learn the language.

Now we're going to be talking about control structures, and for tasks of such complexity you'll want to work in a text editor. This environment will allow you to run a chunk of code several times without having to retype it.

In general, Ruby scripts are simple text files containing Ruby code and a .rb extension. These files are passed to the Ruby interpreter, which executes your code:

```
$ ruby myscript.rb
```

To work with the examples that follow, I'd recommend that you open a new text file in your favorite text editor (which might be one of those I recommended back in Chapter 2) and type the code out as you go—this really is the best way to learn.

As has been demonstrated, to run the files from the command line you simply need to type ruby, followed by the filename.

Control Structures

Ruby has a rich set of features for controlling the flow of your application. **Conditionals** are keywords that are used to decide whether or not certain statements are executed based on the evaluation of one or more conditions; **loops** are constructs that execute statements more than once; and **blocks** are a means of encapsulating functionality (for example, so as to be executed in a loop).

To demonstrate these control structures, let's utilize some of the Car classes that we defined earlier. Type out the following class definition and save the file; we'll build on it in this section as we explore some control structures:

```
class Car
  WHEELS = 4                  # class constant
  @@number_of_cars = 0        # class variable
  def initialize
    @@number_of_cars = @@number_of_cars + 1
  end
  def self.count
    @@number_of_cars
  end
  def mileage=(x)             # instance variable writer
    @mileage = x
  end
  def mileage                 # instance variable reader
    @mileage
  end
```

```
end

class StretchLimo < Car
  WHEELS = 6                   # class constant
  @@televisions = 1            # class variable
  def turn_on_television
    # Invoke code for switching on on-board TV here
  end
end

class PontiacFirebird < Car
end

class VolksWagen < Car
end
```

Conditionals

There are two basic conditional constructs in Ruby: `if` and `unless`. Each can be used to execute a group of statements on the basis of a given condition.

The `if` Construct

An `if` construct wraps statements that are to be executed only if a certain condition is met. The keyword `end` defines the end of the `if` construct. The statements that are contained between the condition and the `end` keyword are executed only if the condition is met:

```
if Car.count.zero?
  puts "No cars have been produced yet."
end
```

You can provide a second condition by adding an `else` block. When the condition is met the first block is executed; otherwise, the `else` block is executed. This kind of control flow will probably be familiar to you. Here it is in action:

```
if Car.count.zero?
  puts "No cars have been produced yet."
else
  puts "New cars can still be produced."
end
```

The most complicated example involves an alternative condition. If the first condition is not met, a second condition is evaluated. If neither conditions are met, the else block is executed:

```
if Car.count.zero?
  puts "No cars have been produced yet."
elsif Car.count >= 10
  puts "Production capacity has been reached."
else
  puts "New cars can still be produced."
end
```

If the count method returned 5, this code would produce the following output:

```
New cars can still be produced.
```

An alternative to the traditional if condition is the if statement modifier. A **statement modifier** does just that: it modifies the statement of which it is part. The if statement modifier works exactly like a regular if condition, but it sits at the *end* of the line that's affected, rather than before a block of code:

```
puts "No cars have been produced yet." if Car.count.zero?
```

This version of the if condition is often used when the code that's to be executed conditionally comprises just a single line. Having the ability to create conditions such as this results in code that's a lot more like English than other programming languages with more rigid structures.

The unless Construct

The unless condition is a negative version of the if condition. It's useful for situations in which you want to execute a group of statements when a certain condition is *not* met.

Let's create a few instances to work with:[6]

```
kitt = PontiacFirebird.new
kitt.mileage = 5667

herbie = VolksWagen.new
herbie.mileage = 33014

batmobile = PontiacFirebird.new
batmobile.mileage = 4623

larry = StretchLimo.new
larry.mileage = 20140
```

Now if we wanted to find out how many Knight Rider fans KITT could take for a joyride, we could check the class of the kitt object. As with the if expression, the end keyword defines the end of the statement:

```
unless kitt.is_a?(StretchLimo)
  puts "This car is only licensed to seat two people."
end
```

Like the if condition, the unless condition may have an optional else block of statements, which is executed when the condition is met:

[6.] Aficionados of comics will notice that I've visualized the Batmobile as a Pontiac Firebird. In fact, the caped crusader's choice of transport has varied over the years, taking in many of the automobile industry's less common innovations, and including everything from a 1966 Lincoln Futura to an amphibious tank. But we'll stick with a Pontiac for this example.

```
unless kitt.is_a?(StretchLimo)
  puts "This car is only licensed to seat two people."
end
```

Since KITT is definitely *not* a stretch limousine, this code would return:

```
This car only has room for two people.
```

Unlike `if` conditions, `unless` conditions do *not* support a second condition; however, like the `if` condition, the `unless` condition is also available as a statement modifier. The following code shows an example of this. Here, the message will not display if KITT's mileage is less than 25,000:

```
puts "Service due!" unless kitt.mileage < 25000
```

Loops

Ruby provides the `while` and `for` constructs for looping through code (that is, executing a group of statements a specified number of times, or until a certain condition is met). A number of instance methods are also available for looping over the elements of an `Array` or `Hash`; we'll cover these in the next section.

`while` and `until` Loops

A `while` loop executes the statements that it encloses repeatedly, as long as the specified condition is met:

```
while Car.count < 10
  Car.new
  puts "A new car instance was created."
end
```

This simple `while` loop executes the `Car.new` statement repeatedly, as long as the total number of cars is below 10. It exits the loop when the number reaches ten.

Like the relationship between `if` and `unless`, the `while` loop also has a complement: the `until` construct. If we use `until`, the code within the loop is executed *until* the condition is met. We could rewrite the prevous loop using `until` like so:

```
until Car.count == 10
  Car.new
  puts "A new car instance was created."
end
```

 ## Assignment and Equation Operators

It's important to note the difference between the assignment operator (=), a single equal sign, and the equation operator (==), a double equal sign, when using them within a condition.

If you're comparing two values, use the equation operator:

```
if Car.count == 10
  ⋮
end
```

If you're assigning a value to a variable, use the assignment operator:

```
my_new_car = Car.new
```

If you confuse the two, you might modify a value that you were hoping only to inspect—with potentially disastrous consequences!

`for` Loops

`for` loops allow us to iterate over the elements of a collection, such as an `Array`, and execute a group of statements once for each element. Here's an example:

```
for car in [ kitt, herbie, batmobile, larry ]
  puts car.mileage
end
```

This code would produce the following output:

```
5667
33014
4623
20140
```

This simple `for` loop iterates over an `Array` of `Car` objects and outputs the mileage for each car. In each iteration, the `car` variable is set to the current element of the `Array`. The first iteration has `car` set to the equivalent of `kitt`; the second iteration has it set to `herbie`, and so forth.

In practise, the traditional `while` and `for` loops covered here are used rarely. Instead, most people use the instance methods provided by the `Array` and `Hash` classes, which we'll cover next.

Blocks, Procs, and Lambdas. Oh my!

Blocks are probably the single most attractive feature of Ruby; however, they also tend to take a while to drop into place for Ruby newcomers. Before we dig deeper into creating blocks, let's take a look at some of the core features of Ruby that use blocks.

We looked at some loop constructs in the previous section, which was a useful way to explore the tools that are available to us. Yet you'll probably only come across very few of these constructs in your work with other Ruby scripts, simply because it's almost always easier to use a block to perform the same task. A block, in conjunction with the `each` method provided by the `Array` and `Hash` classes, is a very powerful way to loop through your data.

Let me illustrate this point with an example. Consider the `for` loop we used a moment ago. We could rewrite that code to use the `each` method, which is an instance method of the `Array`, and a block:

```
[ kitt, herbie, batmobile, larry ].each do |car_name|
  puts car_name.mileage
end
```

Let's analyze this: the block comprises the code between the `do` and `end` keywords. A block is able to receive parameters, which are placed between vertical bars (|) after the `do` keyword. Multiple parameters are separated by commas. Therefore, this code performs an identical operation to the `for` loop we saw before, but in a much more succinct manner.

Let's take another example. To loop through the elements of a `Hash`, we use the `each` method and pass two parameters to the block: the key (`car_name`) and the value (`color`):

```
car_colors = {
  kitt:  'black',
  herbie: 'white',
  batmobile: 'black',
  larry: 'green'
}
car_colors.each do |car_name, color|
  puts "#{car_name} is #{color}"
end
```

This produces the following output:

```
kitt is black
herbie is white
batmobile is black
larry is green
```

The `Integer` class also sports a number of methods that use blocks. The `times` method of an `Integer` object, for example, executes a block exactly *n* times, where *n* is the value of the object:

```
10.times { Car.new }
puts "#{Car.count} cars have been produced."
```

Here's the resultant output:

```
10 cars have been produced.
```

One final point to note here is the alternative block syntax of curly braces. Instead of the do…end keywords that we've been using, curly braces are the preferred syntax for blocks that are very short, as in the previous example.

Here's another method of the `Integer` class. In the spirit of times, the `upto` method of an `Integer` object counts from the value of the object up to the argument passed to the method:

```
5.upto(7) { |i| puts i }
```

And here's the output:

```
5
6
7
```

In Ruby parlance, the object i is a parameter of the block. Parameters for blocks are enclosed in vertical bars, and are usually only available from within the block. If we have more than one parameter we separate them using commas, like so: |parameter1, parameter2|. In the previous example, we would no longer have access to i once the block had finished executing.

It's worth mentioning that there are a couple of other constructs in Ruby that are very similar to blocks: procs and lambdas. The difference between these three items is subtle, especially for the needs of this book. For what we'll cover, it's really only important that you are aware of the syntactical differences. Here are some examples:

```
10.times { Car.new } => Makes 10 cars
car_maker = Proc.new { Car.new }
10.times(&car_maker)   => Makes 10 cars
competitor = lambda { |i| Car.new }
10.times(&competitor) => Makes 10 cars
another_competitor = ->(i){ Car.new } => Makes 10 cars
```

The first example is a block. The second example (`Proc.new`) creates a `Proc` object. Procs and blocks are almost identical, except a proc is an object and a block is not. The last two examples (with `lambda` and the odd-looking "stabby lambda" `->()` create lambdas which are types of procs with a couple of behavioral differences. These differences are around **arity** (the number of arguments) and how the lambda returns when it completes. Again, it's more than you need to know right now, so you know what that means, right? It's time for some ...

EXTRA CREDIT: Ruby Rites

Learning the difference between procs, blocks, and lambdas is a Ruby rite of passage. To help you take yours, go check out the *Blocks, Procs and Lambdas*[7] video on SitePoint Premium. It's a great little video ... I recommend you make popcorn first.

As we work through this book, we'll explore many more uses of blocks, procs, and lambdas in combination with the Rails core classes.

[7.] https://www.sitepoint.com/premium/tutorials/blocks-procs-and-lambdas

Summary

Wow, we covered a lot in this chapter! First, we swept through a stack of object-oriented programming theory—probably the equivalent of an introductory computer science course! This gave us a good grounding for exploring the basics of the Ruby programming language, and the Interactive Ruby Shell (`irb`) was a fun way to conduct this exploration.

We also investigated many of the Ruby core classes from within the Ruby shell, such as `String`, `Symbol`, `Array`, and `Hash`. We then moved from the shell to create and save proper Ruby files, where we experimented with control structures such as conditionals, loops, and blocks.

In the next chapter, we'll look at the major cornerstones that make up the Rails framework.

Chapter

Rails Revealed

As we've already covered in Chapter 1, quite a bit of thought has been put into the codebase that makes up the Rails framework. Over time, many of the internals have been rewritten, items have been added and removed, and conventions have changed. All of this change has improved speed and efficiency, allowing the implementation of additional features, but the original architecture remains largely unchanged. This chapter will shed some light on the inner workings of Rails.

Three Environments

Rails encourages the use of a different environment for each stage in an application's life cycle development, testing, and production. If you've been developing web applications for a while, this is probably how you operate anyway; Rails simply formalizes these environments.

In the development environment, changes to an application's source code are immediately visible; we just reload the corresponding page in a web browser. Speed is not a critical factor in this environment. Instead, the focus is on providing the developer with as much insight as possible into the components responsible for displaying each page. When an error occurs in the development environment, we are able to tell at a glance which line of code is responsible for the error and how that particular line was invoked. This capability is provided by the **stack trace**—a comprehensive list of all the method calls leading up to the error—which is displayed when an unexpected error occurs.

In testing, we usually refresh the database with a baseline of dummy data each time a test is repeated. This step ensures that the results of the tests are consistent and behavior is reproducible. Unit and functional testing procedures are fully automated in Rails. When we test a Rails application, we don't view it using a traditional web browser. Instead, tests are invoked from the command line, and can be run as background processes. The testing environment provides a dedicated space in which these processes can operate.

By the time your application finally goes live, it should be sufficiently tested that all—or at least most—of the bugs have been eliminated. As a result, updates to the codebase should be infrequent, enabling the production environments to be optimized to focus on performance. Tasks such as writing extensive logs for debugging purposes should be unnecessary at this stage. Besides, if an error does occur, you want to avoid scaring your visitors away with a cryptic stack trace; that's best kept for the development environment.

As the requirements for each of the three environments are quite different, Rails stores the configuration for each environment separately. The dependencies for each environment will be different; the data for each environment will be different. You'll likely want to have more detailed logs in development than production. Rails makes handling the configuration of all these items simple.

Application Dependencies

One of the great aspects of Rails is its community and all the gems it has created that we, as Rails developers, can use in our apps. Each gem you use in your application becomes a **dependency**, meaning that your app depends on it. It's likely that your apps will have a lot of dependencies. In fact, it's such a common occurrence that Rubyists created a tool to make managing dependencies easy.

Bundler

Rails manages application dependencies using a Ruby gem called Bundler[1]. As its homepage states, Bundler:

> "provides a consistent environment for Ruby projects by tracking and installing the exact gems and versions that are needed."

These dependencies are listed in the application `Gemfile`, which is found in the root of the application structure. Gems are listed by name and version. Here is part of the `Gemfile` that Rails created with our application:

```
source 'https://rubygems.org'

 # Bundle edge Rails instead: gem 'rails', github:
↪ 'rails/rails'
gem 'rails', '~> 5.0.0'
# Use sqlite3 as the database for Active Record
gem 'sqlite3'
# Use SCSS for stylesheets
gem 'sass-rails', '~> 5.0'
...
group :development, :test do
 # Call 'byebug' anywhere in the code to stop execution and
↪ get a debugger console
  gem 'byebug', platform: mri
end
```

[1.] http://bundler.io/

```
group :development do
 # Access an IRB console on exception pages or by using
↳ <%= console %> in views
  gem 'web-console', '~> 2.0'
end
```

As you can see, everything is a gem, including Rails itself! The first line (`source 'https://rubygems.org'`) tells Bundler to look for gems on the RubyGems website, where the community happens to publish gems. Did you notice that Bundler lets you define dependencies in each environment?

```
group :development do
 # Access an IRB console on exception pages or by using
↳ <%= console %> in views
  gem 'web-console'
end
```

The `group :development` block declaration tells Bundler to only load these gems in the development environment. Neat, huh?

Once the `Gemfile` includes all the app dependencies, running `bundle install` will make Bundler retrieve all the gems and pull them into the current environment:

```
$ bundle install
Fetching gem metadata from https://rubygems.org/.........
Fetching additional metadata from https://rubygems.org/...
Resolving dependencies...
Using rake 10.3.1
Using json 1.8.1
Installing minitest 5.3.3
Installing i18n 0.6.9
Installing thread_safe 0.3.3
...
```

Bundler is smart. Really smart. It checks all the gems, ensuring that their dependencies are met and there are no version clashes. A version clash is when two gems require different versions of a third gem, and that can be a nightmare to handle. Thankfully, Bundler does that for you.

A successful `bundle install` creates another file called `Gemfile.lock`, which lists the exact gems and versions used in the last successful "bundle." When Rails starts up, it checks this file to load all the gem dependencies so that your app is ready to go. Any change to the `Gemfile` (meaning, dependencies added or removed) requires another `bundle install`. Don't worry, though; Bundler is smart and will just load (or remove) the changes, check that everything is okay, and reuse gems from previous bundles. Bundler is like your Dependency Compliance Officer ensuring everyone gets along.

Finally, Bundler is not a Rails-only tool. It can be (and is) used in other Ruby projects, so you'll see it all over the Ruby landscape.

 EXTRA CREDIT: Bundler's Brass Tacks

> There are a lot of details around using Bundler that are outside the scope of this book. It behooves you, as an aspiring Ruby developer, to read up on all the things Bundler can do and the ways it can do them on the Bundler site[2].

Database Configuration

By default, Rails creates a distinct database for each environment. At any given time, you might have:

- live data with which real users are interacting in the production environment

- a partial copy of this live data to debug an error or develop new features in the development environment

- a set of testing data that's constantly being reloaded into the testing environment

---

[2.] http://bundler.io

Configuring the database for a Rails application is incredibly easy. All the critical information is contained in just one file: `config/database.yml`. We'll take a close look at this database configuration file, then create some databases for our application to use.

The Database Configuration File

The separation of environments is reflected in the Rails database configuration file `database.yml`. An example of this was created when we used the `rails` command to create the application. Go take a look—it lives in the `config` subdirectory of our Readit application.

 Yo YAML!

The format of many configuration files in Ruby frameworks, such as Rails, is "YAML Ain't Markup Language" or YAML. YAML defines data structures and object trees in a very human-readable fashion. The `database.yml` file that follows is a YAML file, and you can see that it defines keys and their values using colons (`:`) and whitespace (the environment values are indented under the environment name.) You will see YAML a lot in your Ruby travels.

With the comments removed, the file should look like this:

```
default: &default
  adapter: sqlite3
  pool: 5
  timeout: 5000

development:
  <<: *default
  database: db/development.sqlite3

test:
  <<: *default
  database: db/test.sqlite3

production:
  <<: *default
```

```
database: db/production.sqlite3
```

This file lists the minimum amount of information required in order to connect to the database server for each environment (development, test, and production). With the default setup of SQLite that we installed in Chapter 2, every environment is allocated its own physically separate database file, which calls the db subdirectory home. Notice how YAML allows us to define defaults and pull those into each environment configuration.

The parameter database sets the name of the database that is to be used in each environment. As the configuration file suggests, Rails can support multiple databases (and even different types of database engines, such as PostgreSQL for production and SQLite for development) in parallel. Note that we're talking about different *databases* here, not just different tables—each database can host an arbitrary number of different tables in parallel. Figure 4-1 shows a graphical representation of this architecture.

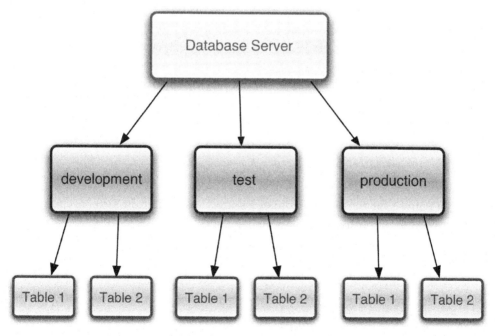

4-1. The database architecture we'll use

Yet there's one startling aspect missing from our current configuration: looking at the db subdirectory, the databases referenced in our configuration file are yet to exist! Fear not, Rails will magically create them as soon as they're required. There's nothing we need to do as far as they are concerned.

 EXTRA CREDIT: Database Engines

There are lots of database engines in the world; for example, SQLite and PostgreSQL. Rails uses SQLite by default because it's the easiest to set up to get you going; however, almost no one uses SQLite as their production database. The reasons for eschewing SQLite in production have to do with the way it stores data and how it only allows a single writer at a time. Because installing another database is beyond the scope of this book, however, we will be using it. Your extra credit? Investigate other database engines, install one, and hook it up to your Rails app.

The Model-View-Controller Architecture

The model-view-controller (MVC) architecture that we first encountered in Chapter 1 is not unique to Rails. In fact, it predates both Rails and the Ruby language by many years. Rails, however, really takes the idea of separating an application's data, user interface, and control logic to a whole new level.

Let's take a look at the concepts behind building an application using the MVC architecture. Once we have the theory in place, we'll see how it translates to our Rails code.

MVC in Theory

MVC is a pattern for the architecture of a software application. It separates an application into the following components:

- **Models** for handling data and business logic
- **Controllers** for handling the user interface and application
- **Views** for handling graphical user interface objects and presentation

This separation results in user requests being processed as follows:

1. The browser (on the client) sends a request for a page to the controller on the server.
2. The controller retrieves the data it needs from the model in order to respond to the request.
3. The controller gives the retrieved data to the view.
4. The view is rendered and sent back to the client for the browser to display.

This process is illustrated in Figure 4-2 below.

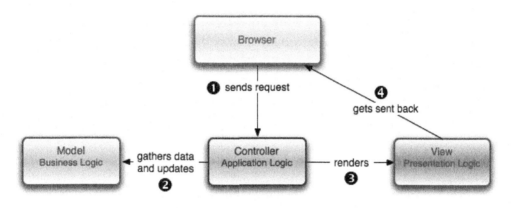

4-2. User requests being processed

Separating a software application into these three distinct components is a good idea for a number of reasons, including:

▪ *improved scalability* (the ability for an application to grow)–for example, if your application begins experiencing performance issues because database access is slow, you can upgrade the hardware running the database without other components being affected

▪ *ease of maintenance*—as the components have a low dependency on each other, making changes to one (to fix bugs or change functionality) does not affect another

▪ *reusability*—a model may be reused by multiple views

If you're struggling to get your head around the concept of MVC, don't worry. For now, what's important to remember is that your Rails application is separated into three distinct components. Jump back to the MVC diagram if you need to refer to it later on.

MVC the Rails Way

Rails promotes the concept that models, views, and controllers should be kept separate by storing the code for each element as separate files in separate directories.

This is where the Rails directory structure that we created back in Chapter 2 comes into play. It's time to poke around a bit within that structure. If you take a look inside the app directory, depicted in Figure 4-3, you'll see some folders whose names might start to sound familiar.

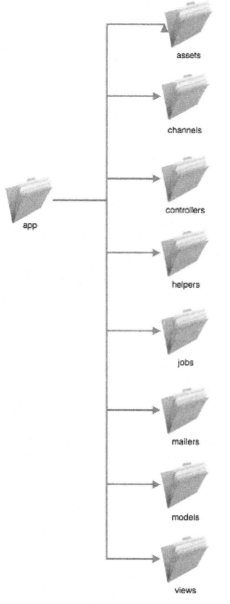

4-3. The app subdirectory

As you can see, each component of the model-view-controller architecture has its place within the app subdirectory—the models, views, and controllers subdirectories respectively. (We'll talk about assets in <u>Chapter 7</u>, helpers in <u>Chapter 6</u>, and mailers <u>later on in this chapter</u>. jobs and channels are beyond the scope of this book.)

This separation continues within the code that comprises the framework itself. The classes that form the core functionality of Rails reside within the following modules:

ActiveRecord   ActiveRecord is the module for handling business logic and database communication. It plays the role of model in our MVC architecture.[3]

ActionController ActionController is the component that handles browser requests and facilitates communication between the model and the view. Your controllers will inherit from this class. It forms part of the ActionPack library, a collection of Rails components that we'll explore in depth in <u>Chapter 5</u>.

ActionView   code>ActionView is the component that handles the presentation of pages returned to the client. Views inherit from this class, which is also part of the ActionPack library.

Let's take a closer look at each of these components in turn.

The ActiveRecord Module

ActiveRecord is designed to handle all of an application's tasks that relate to the database, including:

- establishing a connection to the database server
- retrieving data from a table
- storing new data in the database

ActiveRecord has a few other neat tricks up its sleeve. Let's look at some of them now.

[3.] While it might seem odd that ActiveRecord doesn't have the word "model" in its name, there is a reason for this: Active Record is also the name of a famous design pattern—one that this component implements in order to perform its role in the MVC world. Besides, if it had been called ActionModel, it would have sounded more like an overpaid Hollywood star than a software component ...

Database Abstraction

`ActiveRecord` ships with database adapters to connect to SQLite, MySQL, and PostgreSQL. A large number of adapters are available for other popular database server packages, such as Oracle, MongoDB, and Microsoft SQL Server, via RubyGems.

The `ActiveRecord` module is based on the concept of database abstraction. As a refresher from Chapter 1, database abstraction is a way of coding an application so that it isn't dependent upon any one database. Code that's specific to a particular database server is hidden safely in `ActiveRecord`, and invoked as needed. The result is that a Rails application is not bound to any specific database server software. Should you need to change the underlying database server at a later time, no changes to your application code are required.

The Jury's Out on ActiveRecord

As I said, `ActiveRecord` is an implementation of the Active Record pattern. There are those that disagree with the approach taken by `ActiveRecord`, so you'll hear a lot about that, too. For now, I suggest you learn the way `ActiveRecord` works, then form your judgement of the implementation as you learn.

Some examples of code that differ greatly between vendors, and which `ActiveRecord` abstracts, include:

- the process of logging into the database server
- date calculations
- handling of Boolean (`true`/`false`) data
- evolution of your database structure

Before I can show you the magic of `ActiveRecord` in action, though, a little housekeeping is necessary.

Database Tables

Tables are the containers within a relational database that store our data in a structured manner, and they're made up of rows and columns. The rows map to individual objects, and the columns map to the attributes of those objects. The collection of all the tables in a database, and the relationships between those tables, is called the **database schema**. An example of a table is shown in Figure 4-4.

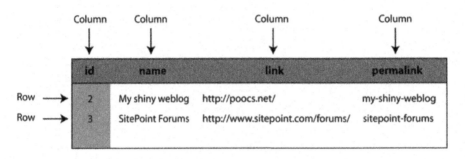

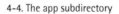

4-4. The app subdirectory

In Rails, the naming of Ruby classes and database tables follows an intuitive pattern: if we have a table called `stories` that consists of five rows, this table will store the data for five `Story` objects. What's nice about the mapping between classes and tables is that there's no need to write code to achieve it; the mapping just happens, because `ActiveRecord` infers the name of the table from the name of the class.

Object Relational Mapper

The Active Record pattern is a way of mapping the *rows* of a database table to the *objects* of our object-oriented application. The term for this is "Object Relational Mapper", or ORM. You'll hear the term "ORM" a lot when discussing `ActiveRecord`, so I thought I'd mention it.

Note that the name of our class in Ruby is a singular noun (`Story`), but the name of the table is plural (`stories`). This relationship makes sense if you think about it: when we refer to a `Story` object in Ruby, we're dealing with a single story. But the SQL table holds a multitude of stories, so its name should be plural. While you can override these conventions—as is sometimes necessary when dealing with legacy databases—it's much easier to adhere to them.

The close relationship between objects and tables extends even further. If our `stories` table were to have a `link` column, as our example in Figure 4-4 does, the data in this column would automatically be mapped to the `link` attribute in a

`Story` object. And adding a new column to a table would cause an attribute of the same name to become available in all of that table's corresponding objects.

So, let's create some tables to hold the stories we create.

For the time being, we'll create a table using the old-fashioned approach of entering SQL into the SQLite console. You could type out the following SQL commands, although typing out SQL is no fun. Instead, I encourage you to download the following script from the code archive, and copy and paste it straight into your SQLite console that you invoked via the following command in the application directory:

```
$ sqlite3 db/development.sqlite3
```

Once your SQLite console is up, paste in the following:

```
CREATE TABLE stories (
  "id" INTEGER PRIMARY KEY AUTOINCREMENT NOT NULL,
  "name" varchar(255) DEFAULT NULL,
  "link" varchar(255) DEFAULT NULL,
  "created_at" datetime DEFAULT NULL,
  "updated_at" datetime DEFAULT NULL
);
```

You don't have to worry about remembering these SQL commands to use in your own projects; instead, take heart in knowing that in <u>Chapter 5</u> we'll look at migrations. Migrations are special Ruby classes that we can write to create database tables for our application without using any SQL at all.

 ### Seek some SQL Smarts

Even though Rails abstracts away the SQL required to create tables and database objects, you'd be doing yourself a favor if you become familiar with SQL and its syntax. SitePoint has published *Simply SQL*[4], a book on learning SQL, so check that one out.

---

[4] https://www.sitepoint.com/premium/books/simply-sql

Using the Rails Console

Now that we have our `stories` table in place, let's exit the SQLite console (simply type `.quit`) and open up a Rails console. A Rails console is just like the interactive Ruby console (`irb`) that we used in Chapter 3, but with one key difference. In a Rails console, you have access to all the environment variables and classes that are available to your application while it's running. These are not available from within a standard `irb` console.

To enter a Rails console, change to your `readit` folder, and enter the command `rails console` or `rails c`, as shown in the code that follows. The `>>` prompt is ready to accept your commands:

```
$ cd readit
$ rails console
Loading development environment (Rails 5.0.0)
>>
```

Saving an Object

To start using `ActiveRecord`, simply define a class that inherits from the `ActiveRecord::Base`. We touched on the `::` operator very briefly in Chapter 3, where we mentioned that it was a way to invoke class methods on an object. It can also be used to refer to classes that exist within a module, which is what we're doing here. Flip back to the section on object-oriented programming (OOP) in Chapter 3 if you need a refresher on inheritance.

Consider the following code snippet:

```
class Story < ActiveRecord::Base
end
```

These two lines of code define a seemingly empty class called `Story`; however, this class is far from empty, as we'll soon see.

From the Rails console, let's create this `Story` class and an instance of the class called `story` by entering these commands:

```
>> class Story < ActiveRecord::Base; end
=> nil
>> story = Story.new
 => #<Story id: nil, name: nil, url: nil, created_at:
↪ nil,
  updated_at: nil>
>> story.class
=> Story(id: integer, name: string, link: string,
  created_at: datetime, updated_at: datetime)
```

As you can see, the syntax for creating a new `ActiveRecord` object is identical to the syntax we used to create other Ruby objects in Chapter 3. At this point, we've created a new `Story` object; however, this object exists in memory only—we're yet to store it in our database.

We can confirm that our `Story` object hasn't been saved by checking the return value of the `new_record?` method:

```
>> story.new_record?
=> true
```

Since the object is yet to be saved, it will be lost when we exit the Rails console. To save it to the database, we invoke the object's save method:

```
>> story.save
=> true
```

Now that we've saved our object (a return value of `true` indicates that the save method was successful), our story is no longer a new record. It's even been assigned a unique ID:

```
>> story.new_record?
=> false
>> story.id
=> 1
```

Defining Relationships between Objects

As well as the basic functionality that we've just seen, `ActiveRecord` makes the process of defining relationships (or associations) between objects as easy as it can be. Of course, it's possible with some database servers to define such relationships entirely within the database schema. In order to put `ActiveRecord` through its paces, let's look at the way it defines these relationships within Rails instead.

Object relationships can be defined in a variety of ways; the main difference between these relationships is the number of records that are specified in the relationship. The primary types of database association are:

- one-to-one associations
- one-to-many associations
- many-to-many associations

Let's look at some examples of each of these associations. Feel free to type them into the Rails console if you like, for the sake of practice. Remember that your class definitions won't be saved, though—I'll show you how to define associations in a file later.

Suppose our application has the following associations:

- An `Author` can have one `Blog`:

```
class Author < ActiveRecord::Base
  has_one :weblog
end
```

- An `Author` can submit many `Stories`:

```
class Author < ActiveRecord::Base
  has_many :stories
end
```

A `Story` belongs to an `Author`:

```
class Story < ActiveRecord::Base
  belongs_to :author
end
```

A `Story` has, and belongs to, many different `Topics`:

```
class Story < ActiveRecord::Base
  has_and_belongs_to_many :topics
end
class Topic < ActiveRecord::Base
  has_and_belongs_to_many :stories
end
```

You're no doubt growing tired of typing class definitions into a console, only to have them disappear the moment you exit the console. For this reason, we won't go any further with the associations between our objects for now—instead we'll delve into the Rails `ActiveRecord` module in more detail in Chapter 5.

The `ActionPack` Library

`ActionPack` is the name of the library that contains the view and controller parts of the MVC architecture. Unlike the `ActiveRecord` module, these modules are more intuitively named: `ActionController` and `ActionView`.

Exploring application logic and presentation logic on the command line makes little sense; views and controllers *are* designed to interact with a web browser, after all! Instead, I'll provide a brief overview of the `ActionPack` components, and we'll cover the hands-on stuff in Chapter 5.

`ActionController` (the Controller)

The **controller** handles the application logic of your program, acting as glue between the application's data, the presentation layer, and the web browser. In this role, a controller performs a number of tasks including:

- deciding how to handle a particular request (for example, whether to render a full page or just one part of it)
- retrieving data from the model to be passed to the view
- gathering information from a browser request and using it to create or update data in the model

When we introduced the MVC diagram in Figure 4-2 earlier in this chapter, it might not have occurred to you that a Rails application can consist of a number of different controllers. Well, it can! Each controller is responsible for a specific part of the application.

For our Readit application, we'll create:

- one controller for displaying story links, which we'll name `StoriesController`
- another controller for handling user authentication, called `SessionsController`
- a controller to display user pages, named `UsersController`
- a controller to display comment pages, named `CommentsController`
- a final controller to handle story voting, called `VotesController`

Every Rails application comes with an `ApplicationController` (which lives in `app/controllers/application_controller.rb`) that inherits from `ActionController::Base`. All our controllers will inherit from the `ApplicationController`,[5] but they'll have different functionality that is implemented as instance methods. Here's a sample class definition for the `StoriesController` class:

[5.] There will actually be an intermediate class between this class and the `ActionController::Base` class; however, this doesn't change the fact that `ActionController::Base` is the base class from which every controller inherits. We'll cover the creation of the `StoriesController` class in more detail in Chapter 5.

```
class StoriesController < ApplicationController
  def index
  end

  def show
  end
end
```

This simple class definition sets up our `StoriesController` with two empty methods: the `index` method, and the `show` method. We'll expand upon these methods in later chapters.

Each controller resides in its own Ruby file (with a `.rb` extension), which lives within the `app/controllers` directory. The `StoriesController` class that we just defined, for example, would inhabit the file `app/controllers/stories_controller.rb`.

Naming Conventions for Classes and Files

You'll have noticed by now that the names of classes and files follow different conventions:

- Class names are written in CamelCase (each word beginning with a capital letter, with no spaces between words).[6]

- Filenames are written in lowercase, with underscores separating each word.

This is an important detail. If this convention is *not* followed, Rails will have a hard time locating your files. Luckily, you won't need to name your files manually very often, if ever, as you'll see when we look at generated code in Chapter 5.

`ActionView` (the View)

As discussed earlier, one of the principles of MVC is that a view should contain presentation logic only. This principle holds that the code in a view should only perform actions that relate to displaying pages in the application; none of the

---

[6.] There are actually two variations of CamelCase: one with an uppercase first letter (also known as PascalCase), and one with a lowercase first letter. The Ruby convention for class names requires an uppercase first letter.

code in a view should perform any complicated application logic, nor store or retrieve any data from the database. In Rails, everything that is sent to the web browser is handled by a view.

Predictably, views are stored in the app/views folder of our application.

A view need not actually contain any Ruby code at all—it may be the case that one of your views is a simple HTML file; however, it's more likely that your views will contain a combination of HTML and Ruby code, making the page more dynamic. The Ruby code is embedded in HTML using embedded Ruby (ERb) syntax.

ERb allows server-side code to be scattered throughout an HTML file by wrapping that code in special tags. For example:

```
<strong><%= 'Hello World from Ruby!'
↳ %></strong>
```

There are two forms of the ERb tags pair: one that includes the equals sign, and one without it:

`<%= … %>`	This tag pair is for regular output. The output of a Ruby expression between these tags will be displayed in the browser.
`<% … %>`	This tag pair is for execution. The output of a Ruby expression between these tags will not be displayed in the browser.

Here's an example of each ERb tag:

```
<%= 'This line is displayed in the browser' %>
 <% 'This line executes silently, without displaying any
↳ output' %>
```

You can place any Ruby code—be it simple or complex—between these tags.

Creating an instance of a view is a little different to that of a model or controller. While ActionView::Base (the parent class for all views) is one of the base classes for views in Rails, the instantiation of a view is handled completely by the ActionView module. The only file a Rails developer needs to modify is the template, which is the file that contains the presentation code for the view. As you might have guessed, these templates are stored in the app/views folder.

As with everything else Rails, a strict convention applies to the naming and storage of template files:

- A template has one-to-one mapping to the action (method) of a controller. The name of the template file matches the name of the action to which it maps.
- The folder that stores the template is named after the controller.

- The extension of the template file is twofold and varies depending on the template's type and the actual language in which a template is written. By default, there are three types of extensions in Rails:

  html.erb   This is the extension for standard HTML templates that are sprinkled with ERb tags.

  xml.builder   This extension is used for templates that output XML (for example, to generate RSS feeds for your application).

  json.builder   This extension is used for templates that output JSON, which is a common data integration for APIs. We'll talk more about JSON in <u>Chapter 9</u> on advanced topics.

This convention may sound complicated, but it's actually quite intuitive. For example, consider the StoriesController class defined earlier. Invoking the show method for this controller would, by default, attempt to display the ActionView template that lived in the app/views/stories directory. Assuming the page was a standard HTML page (containing some ERb code), the name of this template would be show.html.erb.

Rails also comes with special templates such as layouts and partials. **Layouts** are templates that control the global layout of an application, such as structures that remain unchanged between pages (the primary navigation menu, for instance). **Partials** are special subtemplates (the result of a template being split into separate files, such as a secondary navigation menu or a form) that can be used multiple times within the application. We'll cover both layouts and partials in Chapter 7.

Communication between controllers and views occurs via instance variables that are populated from within the controller's action. Let's expand upon our sample `StoriesController` class to illustrate this point (no need to type any of this out just yet):

```
class StoriesController < ActionController::Base
  def index
    @variable = 'Value being passed to a view'
  end
end
```

As you can see, the instance variable `@variable` is being assigned a string value within the controller's action. Through the magic of `ActionView`, this variable can now be referenced directly from the corresponding view, as shown in this code:

```
<p>The instance variable @variable contains: <%=
↪ @variable %></p>
```

This approach allows more complex computations to be performed outside the view—remember, it should only contain presentational logic—and allow the view to display just the end result of the computation.

Rails also provides access to special containers, such as the `params` and `session` hashes. These contain such information as the current page request and the user's session. We'll make use of these hashes in the chapters that follow.

RESTful-style

In Chapter 1, I listed common development principles and best practices that the Rails team advises you to adopt in your own projects. One that I kept under my hat until now was RESTful-style development, or resource-centric development. REST will make much more sense with your fresh knowledge about models and controllers as the principal building blocks of a Rails application.

In Theory

REST stands for *Re*presentational *S*tate *T*ransfer and originates from the doctoral dissertation of Roy Fielding[7], a co-founder of the Apache Software Foundation and one of the authors of the HTTP specification.

REST, according to the theory, is not restricted to the World Wide Web. The basis of the resource-centric approach is derived from the fact that most of the time spent using network-based applications can be characterized as a client or user interacting with distinct resources. For example, in an ecommerce application, a book and a shopping cart are separate resources with which the customer interacts.

Every resource in an application needs to be addressed by a unique and uniform identifier. In the world of web applications, the unique identifier would be the URL by which a resource can be accessed. In our Readit application, each submitted link is able to be viewed at a unique URL.

The potential interactions within an application are defined as a set of operations (or verbs) that can be performed with a given resource. The most common are *c*reate, *r*ead, *u*pdate, and *d*elete, which are often collectively referred to as "**CRUD** operations." If you relate this to our Readit application, you'll see that it covers most of the interactions possible with the Readit links: a user will create a link; another user will read the link; and the link can also be updated or deleted.

The client and server have to communicate via the same language (or protocol) in order to implement the REST architecture style successfully. This protocol in resource-centric applications is also required to be stateless, cacheable, and layered.

[7.] http://www.ics.uci.edu/~fielding/pubs/dissertation/top.htm

Here, **stateless** means that each request for information from the client to the server needs to be completely independent of prior or future requests. Each request needs to contain everything necessary for the server to understand the request and provide an appropriate answer.

Cacheable and layered are architectural attributes that improve the communication between client and server without affecting the communication protocol.

REST and the Web

As stated in the previous section, REST as an architecture pattern can be used in any application domain; however, the Web is probably the domain that implements REST most often. Since this is a book that deals with building web applications, we'd better take a look at the implementation details of RESTful style development for web applications.

HTTP (Hypertext Transfer Protocol: the communication protocol used on the Web), as the astute reader will know, also makes heavy use of verbs in its day-to-day operations. When your browser requests a web page from any given web server, it will issue a so-called GET request. If you submit a web page form, your browser will do so using a POST request (not always, to be honest, but 99% of the time).

In addition to GET and POST, HTTP defines three additional verbs that are less commonly used by web browsers. (Many of the browsers in widespread use actually implement them.) These verbs are PUT, PATCH, and DELETE. If you compare the list of HTTP verbs with the verbs of CRUD, they line up fairly nicely, as you can see below.

4.1. HTTP Verbs versus CRUD Verbs

CRUD	HTTP
CREATE	POST
READ	GET
UPDATE	PUT, PATCH
DELETE	DELETE

EXTRA CREDIT: Verbalicious

There are even more HTTP verbs that we won't discuss here, such as OPTIONS and HEAD. Sounds like a good homework assignment, eh?

The language in which client (the browser) and server (the web server) talk to each other is obviously HTTP. HTTP is, by definition, stateless. This means that as soon as a browser downloads all the information the server offered as a reply to the browser's request, the connection is closed and the two might never ever talk again. Or the browser could send another request just milliseconds later asking for additional information. Each request contains all the necessary information for the server to respond appropriately, including potential cookies, the format, and the language in which the browser expects the server to reply.

HTTP is also layered and cacheable, both of which are attributes the REST definition expects of the spoken protocol. Routers, proxy servers, and firewalls are only three (very common) examples of architectural components that implement layering and caching on top of HTTP.

REST in Rails

REST and Rails not only both start with the letter R, they have a fairly deep relationship. Rails comes with a generator for resources (see Code Generation below for a primer on this topic) and provides all sorts of assistance to easily construct the uniform addresses by which resources can be accessed. In fact,

Rails encourages the RESTful style in much the same way a ski resort encourages you to use the chairlifts. Sure, you can reach the top of the mountain without them, but you better bring your own tools and know what you're doing.

Rails' focus on the MVC architecture (which we'll be getting our hands on shortly, in <u>Chapter 5</u>) is also a perfect companion for RESTful style development. Models resemble the resources themselves, while controllers provide access to the resource and allow interaction based on the interaction verbs listed earlier.

I've mentioned that some verbs aren't implemented in the majority of browsers on the market. To support the verbs `PUT`, `PATCH`, and `DELETE`, Rails uses `POST` requests with a little tacked-on magic to simulate those verbs transparently for both the user and the Rails application developer. Nifty, isn't it?

We will gradually start implementing and interacting with resources for our Readit application over the course of the next chapters, which are more "hands on", so let's now talk about yet another batch of components that make up the Rails framework.

Code Generation

Rather than having us create our application code from scratch, Rails gives us the facility to generate an application's basic structure with considerable ease. In the same way that we created our application's entire directory structure, we can create new models, controllers, and views using a single command.

To generate code in Rails, we use the `rails generate` command. Give it a try now: type `rails generate` (or `rails g`) without any command parameters. Rails displays an overview of the available parameters for the command, and lists the generators from which we can choose, as shown here:

```
$ rails generate
Usage: rails generate GENERATOR [args] [options]

General options:
```

```
  -h, [--help]      # Print generator's options and usage
  -p, [--pretend]   # Run but do not make any changes
  -f, [--force]     # Overwrite files that already exist
  -s, [--skip]      # Skip files that already exist
  -q, [--quiet]     # Suppress status output

Please choose a generator below.

Rails:
  assets
  controller
  generator
  helper
  integration_test
  jbuilder
  job
  mailer
  migration
  model
  resource
  scaffold
  scaffold_controller
  task
  [...content elided...]
```

There are many core Rails generators, and some gems will add generators, as well.

Rails can generate code of varying complexity. At its simplest, creating a new controller causes a template file to be placed in the appropriate subdirectory of your application. The template itself consists of a mainly empty class definition, similar to the Story and Author classes that we looked at earlier in this chapter.

Code generation, however, can also be a very powerful tool for automating complex, repetitive tasks; for instance, you might generate a foundation for handling user authentication. We'll launch straight into generating code in Chapter 5, when we begin to generate our models and controllers.

Another example is the generation of a basic web-based interface to a model, referred to as scaffolding. We'll also look at scaffolding in Chapter 5, as we make a start on building our views.

The `ActionMailer` Component

While not strictly part of the Web, email is a big part of our online experience, and Rails' integrated support for email is worth a mention. Web applications frequently make use of email for tasks such as sending sign-up confirmations to new users and resetting a user's password.

`ActionMailer` is the Rails component that makes it easy to incorporate the sending and receiving of email into your application. `ActionMailer` is structured in a similar way to `ActionPack` in that it consists of mailers (instead of controllers) and actions with views.

While the creation of emails and the processing of incoming email are complex tasks, `ActionMailer` hides these complexities and handles the tasks for you. As a result, creating an outgoing email is simply a matter of supplying the subject, body, and recipients of the email using templates and a little Ruby code. Likewise, `ActionMailer` processes incoming email for you, providing you with a Ruby object that encapsulates the entire message in a way that's easy to access.

Adding email functionality to a web application is beyond the scope of this book, but you can read more about `ActionMailer` in the Ruby on Rails guides[8].

Testing and Debugging

As mentioned back in Chapter 1, a unit-testing framework is already built into Ruby on Rails. It also, rather helpfully, supplies a full stack trace for errors to assist with debugging.

[8.] http://wiki.rubyonrails.com/rails/pages/ActionMailer/

Testing

A number of different types of testing are supported by Rails, including unit and integration testing.

Unit Testing

The concept of unit testing isn't new to the world of traditional software development, and this is certainly the case in web application development. Having a comprehensive set of unit tests can help you sleep easier in the knowledge that some simple error won't bring your site down. Additionally, developing unit tests can help you figure out if your objects are designed well; however, not everyone sees the value of unit testing. Although performing unit tests is optional, developers may decide against this option for reasons ranging from the complexity of the task to time constraints.

We touched on this briefly in Chapter 1, but it's worth stressing again: the fact that comprehensive unit testing is built into Rails and is dead easy to implement means there's no longer a question about whether or not you should test your apps. *Just do it!*

The `rails generate` command that we introduced a moment ago will automatically create testing templates that you can use with your controllers, views, and models. (Note that Rails just assists you in doing your job; it's not replacing you—yet!)

The extent to which you want to implement unit testing is up to you. It may suit your needs to wait until something breaks, then write a test that proves the problem exists. Once you've fixed the problem and the test no longer fails, you'll never again receive a bug report for that particular problem.

If, on the other hand, you'd like to embrace unit testing completely, you can even write tests to ensure that a specific HTML tag exists at a precise position within a page's hierarchy.[9] Yes, automated tests *can* be that exact.

---

[9]. The hierarchy referred to here is the Document Object Model (DOM), a W3C standard for describing the hierarchy of an (X)HTML page.

You've probably heard of **test-driven development (TDD)** as a way to build an application. When you build an app using TDD, you actually write the tests *before* you write the code. This serves a couple of purposes in that it:

- creates tests for your application that can be used for regression so you know your app works
- forces you to think about the design of the classes in your application from the outside in, which can lead to a better design

The vast majority of Rails developers are TDD fans, but we won't be using TDD for Readit. However, you should look into it, which means ...

EXTRA CREDIT: Test Driving TDD

Do some research on TDD and how it works. Learn what "red-green-refactor" means and how that cadence can help you build an app with a good design and strong foundation. A great book to investigate is *Test Driven Development: By Example*[10] by Kent Beck. TDD is as much art as science, so it requires a commitment to learning how to do it right.

Integration Testing

Rails' testing capabilities also include integration testing.

Integration testing refers to the testing of several website components in succession. Typically, the order of components resembles the path that a user would follow when using the application. You could, for example, construct an integration test that reconstructs the actions of a user clicking on a link, registering for a user account, confirming the registration email you send, and visiting a page that's restricted to registered users.

We'll look at both unit testing and integration testing in more detail as we progress through the development of our application.

---

10. http://www.amazon.com/Test-Driven-Development-By-Example/dp/0321146530

Debugging

When you're fixing problems, the first step is to identify the source of the problem. Like many languages, Ruby assists this process by providing the developer (that's you!) with a full stack trace of the code. We mentioned earlier in Three Environments that a stack trace is a list of all the methods that were called up to the point at which an exception was raised. The list includes not only the name of each method but also the classes those methods belong to, and the names of the files they reside within.

Using the information contained in the stack trace, you can go back to your code to determine the problem. There are several ways to tackle this, depending on the nature of the problem itself:

- If you have a rough idea of what the problem might be, and are able to isolate it to your application's model (either a particular class or aspect of your data), your best bet is to use the Rails console that we looked at earlier in this chapter. Type `rails c` to launch the console. Once inside, you can load the particular model that you're interested in, and poke at it to reproduce and fix the problem.

- If the problem leans more towards being related to the user's browser or session, you can add a `debugger` statement around the spot at which the problem occurs. With this in place, you can reload the browser and step through your application's code using the ruby-debug tool to explore variable content or to execute Ruby statements manually.

- In the last few years, Rails has added some shiny, new tools to make debugging even easier. We'll explore them later as problems arise.

We'll be covering all the gory details of debugging in Chapter 11.

Summary

In this chapter, we peeled back some of the layers that comprise the Ruby on Rails framework. By now you should have a good understanding of which parts of Rails perform particular roles in the context of an MVC architecture.

We also discussed how a request that's made by a web browser is processed by a Rails application.

We looked at the different environments that Rails provides to address the different stages in the life cycle of an application, and we configured databases to support these environments. We also provided Rails with the necessary details to connect to our database.

We also had our first contact with real code, as we looked at the `ActiveRecord` models, `ActionController` controllers, and `ActionView` templates for our Readit application. We explored the REST style of application architecture, code generation, testing, as well as debugging.

In the next chapter, we'll build on all this knowledge as we use the code-generation tools to create actual models, controllers, and views for our Readit application. It's going to be a big one!

Chapter

Models, Views, and Controllers

In Chapter 4, we introduced the principles behind the model-view-controller architectural pattern, and saw how each of the components is implemented within the Rails framework. Now we'll put this knowledge to good use as we use Rails' code generation techniques to create these components for our own Readit application.

Generating a Model

As our application will be used to share links to stories on the Web, a Story is the fundamental object around which our application will evolve. Here, we'll use the Rails model generator to create a Story model, then build everything else around it.

The Model Generator

The model generator is actually driven by a command line script that we encountered back in <u>Chapter 4</u>: the `rails generate` command. This makes our generation of a `Story` model very simple.

Running the `generate` Command

`rails generate`, which can be shortened to `rails g`, can be called from the command line and takes several parameters. The first parameter is the type of component that's to be generated. You can probably guess which value I'm going to suggest you use for this parameter: we're creating a model, so the parameter to pass is simply `model`. Let's take a look at what happens when we pass that to the script:

```
$ cd readit
$ rails g model
```

Figure 5-1 below shows the resulting output.

5-1. the output from the rails g command

We can deduce from this output that using `rails g` to create a new model for our application in its simplest form won't actually do very much—some **stubs** (empty files) will be created in the appropriate directories, but that's about all.

The various examples in the aforementioned figure show the slightly more advanced versions. To give our model a jump-start, we'll add everything necessary to start playing with it right away: we tell `rails g` the names and types of attributes the model is going to have. So let's go ahead and create the `Story` model with its attributes (and their respective types), then examine each of the generated files in turn.

From the `readit` folder, enter the following:

```
$ rails g model Story name:string link:string
```

As you can see, the attributes we want our `Story` model to have are specified simply as space-separated arguments to the `rails g` command using the notation attribute `name:attribute` type. In this case, we specify that our `Story` model receives two attributes of type `string` (Rails defines the `string` type as up to 255 alphanumeric characters): one named `name`, which holds the title of our stories, and one named `link`, which holds, as you might have guessed, a link to the story on the Internet.

The output of this command will list exactly what has been done:

```
$ rails g model Story name:string link:string
Running via Spring preloader in process 42036
    invoke  active_record
    create    db/migrate/20160313140034_create_stories.rb
    create    app/models/story.rb
    invoke  test_unit
    create    test/models/story_test.rb
    create    test/fixtures/stories.yml
```

Let's take a closer look at what the **generate** command has done here.

Understanding the Output

generate has created some files (indicated by the word create, followed by the name of the file that was created) and a folder. Let's look at each of the files:

app/models/story.rb

This file contains the class definition for the Story model. Locate the file in the app/models folder and examine its contents in your text editor—the class definition is identical to the one that we typed out in Saving an Object in Chapter 4:

```
class Story < ApplicationRecord
end
```

What happened to the attributes we specified? They're nowhere to be found! Don't panic—Rails has used the information we provided to create the database table definition. It turns out Rails doesn't require you to declare each attribute of a model explicitly in the model's class definition. Rails determines a model's attribute by reading the columns of the database table to which the model is mapped. This technique is called introspection, which we'll meet again later on.

The ApplicationRecord class can be found in the app/models/ application_record.rb file. ApplicationRecord is an "abstract" class, which means, in this case, that ApplicationRecord is **not** to be mapped to a database table. The ApplicationRecord class allows us to write methods and include code that will be inherited by all of our models.

If the magic behind these attributes makes you uncomfortable, Rails 5 has added a new Attributes API that provides the ability to specify attributes and their types. In this case, if you wanted add an attribute called is_published to Story and ensure the value in that attribute is a boolean (true or false), then you could do:

```
class Story < ApplicationRecord
  attribute :is_published, :boolean
```

```
end
```

This will handle type conversion, making everything a string that is assigned to `name`:

```
s = Story.new(name: 1023, is_published: "yes")
s.is_published
=> true
```

Above, the string value of `yes` was converted to the boolean `true`. So, "truthy" values like `yes`, `1`, and `t` all are converted to `true`. If you like specifying types, this is good stuff.

Better yet, if you had custom types, like a Money type, you could create a class to handle the type conversion of that type. This, however, is beyond our scope today, which means:

EXTRA CREDIT: The Attributes API

Check out the documentation and code[1] behind the new Attributes API.

Okay, being able to generate these two lines of code is far from groundbreaking. But stay with me here!

```
test/models/story_test.rb
```

This file is much more exciting: it's an automatically generated unit test for our model. We'll look at it in detail in Chapter 6, but, briefly, building up the contents of this file allows us to ensure that all of the code in our model is covered by a unit test. As we mentioned back in Chapter 1, once we have all our unit tests in place, we can automate the process of checking that our code behaves as intended.

[1.] https://github.com/rails/rails/blob/master/activerecord/lib/active_record/attributes.rb `test/fixtures/stories.yml`

To help with our unit test, a file called `stories.yml` is created. This file is referred to as a **fixture**. Fixtures are files that contain sample data for unit testing purposes: when we run the test suite, Rails will wipe the database belonging to the testing environment and populate our tables using the fixtures. In this way, fixtures allow us to ensure that every unit test of a given application is run against a consistent baseline.

The `stories.yml` fixture file will come prepared with two sample story records for our `stories` table, prepopulated with values for each of the attributes we defined. You can see that it is another YAML file. I told you we'd see them again.

`db/migrate/xxxxx_create_stories.rb`

This file is what's known as a migration file; we'll be exploring migrations shortly. It's worth noting that the name of the migration file is based on the time the `rails g` command was run. As a result, your migration filename will be different. If it's the same, it means we're in the Twilight Zone.

Understanding YAML

YAML (a tongue-in-cheek recursive acronym that stands for YAML Ain't a Markup Language) is a lightweight format for representing data. YAML files have the extension `.yml`. As they employ none of the confusing tags that XML uses, YAML files are much easier for humans to read, and are just as efficiently read by computers.

Rails uses YAML files extensively to specify fixtures. We've seen a couple of examples of YAML files so far: the `database.yml` file that we used to configure our database connection was one; the `stories.yml` file that we just created with the `rails generate` command is another.

Let's dissect the `stories.yml` file. Open it up in a text editor (you'll find it in the `test/fixtures` directory), and you'll see the following code:

```
one:
  name: MyString
  link: MyString

two:
  name: MyString
  link: MyString
```

This YAML file represents two separate records (one and two). Each record contains values for the two attributes we defined. These values are obviously made up and not exactly descriptive.

Let's expand on each of these records by filling in meaningful values for the name and link fields. Edit the file so that it looks like this:

```
one:
  name: My old weblog
  link: http://ruprict.net/

two:
  name: SitePoint Forums
  link: http://community.sitepoint.com
```

As you can see, each record in a YAML file begins with a unique name that is *not* indented. This name is not the name of the record, nor any of the fields in the database; it's simply used to identify the record within the file. (It's also utilized in testing, as we'll see in Chapter 11.) In our expanded stories.yml file, one and two are these identifying names.

After the unique name, we see a series of key/value pairs, each of which is indented by one or more spaces (we'll be using two spaces, to keep consistent with our convention for Rails code). In each case, the key is separated from its value by a colon.

Now, let's take a look at the last file that was generated: the migration file. If your experience with modifying databases has been limited to writing SQL, this next section is sure to be an eye-opener, so buckle up! This is going to be an exciting ride.

Modifying the Schema Using Migrations

As we mentioned earlier, the last of the four files that our `generate` command created—20160313140034_create_stories.rb—is a migration file. A **migration file** is a special file that can be used to adjust the database schema in a variety of ways (each change that's defined in the file is referred to as a migration. Perhaps think of your database schema as flying south for production).

Migrations can be a handy way to make alterations to your database as your application evolves. Not only do they provide you with a means to change your database schema in an iterative manner, they let you do so using Ruby code rather than SQL. As you may have gathered by now, many folk are far from excited about writing lots of SQL, and migrations are a great way to avoid it.

Migration file names are based on the date they were created, as I've mentioned, so that they can be executed sequentially. In our case, the file for creating stories was created on March 13, 2016 at around 10.00 a.m. NAEST (North American Eastern Standard Time), so our migration file has the number 20160313140034 in its name.

Like SQL scripts, migrations can be built on top of each other, which reinforces the need for these files to be executed in order. Sequential execution removes the possibility of, for example, any attempt to add a new column to a table that is yet to exist.

Let's examine the migration file that was generated for us.

Creating a Skeleton Migration File

Open the file 20160313140034_create_stories.rb in your text editor (again, remember that the number in at the start of your filename will be different). It lives in db/migrate and should look like this:

```ruby
class CreateStories < ActiveRecord::Migration[5.0]
  def change
    create_table :stories do |t|
    t.string :name
    t.string :link

    t.timestamps null: false
        end
  end
end
```

As you can see, a migration file contains a class definition that inherits from the `ActiveRecord::Migration[5.0]` class. The class that's defined in the migration file is assigned a name by the `generate` command, based on the parameters that are passed to it. In this case, our migration has been given the name `CreateStories`, which is a fairly accurate description of the task that it will perform: we're generating a new model (a `Story`), so the code in the migration file creates a `stories` table in which to store our stories.

 Migrations, Compatibility, and 5.0

You may be wondering what the `[5.0]` signifies in `ActiveRecord::Migration[5.0]`. Rails 5.0 introduced versioning to the Migration API due to some breaking changes between versions 4 and 5 of the platform. The `[5.0]` tells Rails to use a compatibility layer with the migrations, allowing users of Rails 4 to upgrade more easily.

The class contains a single method: `change`. This method creates the table when the migration is run, and drops the table when the migration is, well, undone. That's right, a migration can be "run", which is called "migrate," and can be "undone", which is called "rollback". This is nifty, because if we want to add a column to a table, it's a simple matter of rolling back the migration, adding the column to the `change` method, and then running the migration again. Before migrations, changing existing database tables drove many a programmer to insanity and middle management.

What may come as a surprise is that the `change` method already does what we need it to do. Since we took the time to tell the `generate` command which columns the generated model should have, the generator auto-filled the migration with instructions to create a table including (but not limited to, as we'll see shortly) the two attributes to hold the name and the link of a story. But let's take a few minutes to walk through the generated code line by line.

Creating the `stories` Table

In the generated migration code in the `change` method, the first line includes a call to the `create_table` method, into which we pass the name of the table we'd like to create (`stories`) as a symbol (`:stories`). The method is also being passed a block (jump back to <u>Blocks, Procs, and Lambdas</u> in Chapter 3 if you need a refresher), used to define the individual columns in the table:

```
create_table :stories do |t|
  ⋮ block body…
end
```

Within the block, we have two lines to define the attributes we specified on the `generate` command line as columns in our SQL table. Like an SQL script, each column in our migration file should have a name and a type of data storage (such as a string, number, or date):

```
create_table :stories do |t|
  t.string :name
  t.string :link
  ⋮ block body…
end
```

Here, the first line defines the column `name` as type `string`, and the second line defines the column `link` also of type `string`. This could even be rewritten in shorthand syntax, as you see here:

```
create_table :stories do |t|
  t.string :name, :link
  ⋮ block body…
end
```

The third line in the block is a little special. Instead of creating a single `timestamps` column of questionable value, the `timestamps` method automatically creates two "magic" columns in the `stories` table named `created_at` and `updated_at`:

```
create_table :stories do |t|
  ⋮ block body…
  t.timestamps
end
```

We'll take an in-depth look at this magic functionality in Chapter 9.

In addition to creating completely new tables, migrations can be used to alter existing tables. If you were to decide tomorrow that your `stories` table needed to store a description for each story, it would be a painful having to recreate the whole table just to add the extra column. Once again, good old SQL can be used to perform this job efficiently, but to use it, you'd have to learn yet *another* awkward SQL command. The migrations option, on the other hand, allows you to add this column to an existing table without losing any of the data that the table contains.

We'll use migrations to alter the `stories` table when we get to Chapter 9. For now, let's just add one minor parameter to the `change` method:

```
def change
  create_table :stories, force: true do |t|
    t.string :name
    t.string :link

    t.timestamps
```

```
    end
  end
```

The `force: true` at the beginning of the block isn't usually required; we've included it in this case because we already created a table for this model back in Chapter 4 using raw SQL. Without it, our `create_table` call would fail, because the table already exists; however, leaving `force: true` in this migration will mean that `Story` records will be wiped with each future migration, so set it back to `false` after you've performed the migration to prevent this from happening.

In addition to the explicitly named columns we've talked about in this section, this code will also create a column named `id`, which will serve as the primary identifier for each row in the table.

This approach to schema definitions reflects the *pure* Rails method of creating and altering database tables that we talked about earlier in this section.

Now that we have a migration file complete with methods for setting up and tearing down our schema, we just need to make the migration happen. Yet again, we use the `rails` command to achieve this task.

Running the Migration

To apply the migrations in the migration file that we created earlier, we'd type the following:

```
$ rails db:migrate
```

When executed without any other arguments, this command achieves the following tasks:

1. checks the database for the unique number of the migration that was most recently applied

2. steps through the migrations that are yet to be applied, one by one

3. for each migration, executes the up method for that migration class to bring the database in line with the structure specified in the migration files

Go ahead and execute our database migration task from the readit folder. Here's the output you should receive:

```
$ rails db:migrate
 == 20160313140034 CreateStories: migrating
↳ ====================================
-- create_table(:stories, {:force=>true})
   -> 0.0025s
 == 20160313140034 CreateStories: migrated (0.0026s)
↳ ============================
```

As the output indicates, running this task has caused the CreateStories migration we created to be applied to our database. Assuming it was applied successfully, you should now (once again) have a stories table within your database.

With this table in place, we can create data about stories!

Rollbacks up Close

As our database schema evolves, so do the migration files that represent it. Rolling back to a previous version of the schema is easy with migrations. Simply type the following to revert to a previous version of the database (where n represents the version number that you want to restore):

```
$ rails db:migrate VERSION=n
```

The following command would undo the `stories` table that we just created, resulting in the blank database with which we began:

```
$ rails db:migrate VERSION=0
```

If you simply wish to roll back the most recent migration, it's even easier:

```
$ rails db:rollback
```

And the last migration is undone.

Managing Data Using the Rails Console

While we've developed a solid architecture for our application and created a table to store data, we're yet to have a nice front-end interface for managing that data. We'll start to build that interface in Chapter 6, but in the meantime we need to find a way to add stories to our table.

That's right—it's the Rails console to the rescue once again!

Creating Records

We can use two approaches to create records from the console. Let's look at the long-winded approach first. We create the object, then populate each of its attributes one by one, as follows:

```
$ rails c
Running via Spring preloader in process 63637
Loading development environment (Rails 5.0.0)
2.3.0 :001 > s = Story.new
 => #<Story id: nil, name: nil, link: nil, created_at:
↪ nil, updated_at: nil>
2.3.0 :002 > s.name = "SitePoint"
 => "SitePoint"
2.3.0 :003 > s.link = "https://sitepoint.com"
 => "https://sitepoint.com"
2.3.0 :004 > s.save
   (0.2ms)  begin transaction
 SQL (1.1ms)  INSERT INTO "stories" ("name", "link",
↪ "created_at", "updated_at") VALUES (?, ?, ?, ?)  [["name",
↪ "SitePoint"], ["link", "https://sitepoint.com"],
↪ ["created_at", "2016-03-13 14:43:29.351489"], ["updated_at",
↪ "2016-03-13 14:43:29.351489"]]
   (0.7ms)  commit transaction
 => true
2.3.0 :005 >
```

Let's step through what we've done here. After loading the Rails console, we created a new Story object. We assigned this object to a variable named s (the s is for Story—no awards for creativity, I know). We then assigned values to each of the columns that exist on a Story object. Finally, we called the save method, and our Story was stored in the database.

By default, Rails displays the SQL that was run in order to save the story. Aren't you glad you don't have to type *that* in every time? It's a constant reminder of how much time and typing Rails is saving you.

How can we be sure that the data was written successfully? We could look at the raw data using a trusty SQL database console, but we're trying to keep our distance from SQL. Instead, we can confirm that our story saved correctly by checking its id (the unique identifier that the database generates automatically when an object is saved). We can do this from within the Rails console:

```
>> s.id
=> 1
```

Our object's id is not nil, so we know that the save was successful. Of course, there's another way to ensure that the data was written successfully, and that is to use the new_record? method, which you may remember from the Saving an Object section in Chapter 4:

```
>> s.new_record?
=> false
```

Hooray! As this method returns false, we know for certain that the object was written to the database. Just in case you need even more reassurance, there's one more check that we can use: the count class method of the Story class. This method allows us to query the database for the number of stories it currently contains:

```
2.3.0 :007 > Story.count
   (0.1ms)  SELECT COUNT(*) FROM "stories"
 => 1
2.3.0 :008 >
```

Okay, that makes sense.

Let's create another Story now, this time using the second technique: this one's a shortcut! Oh, and from now on, I am not going to include the SQL in the text:

```
2.3.0 :008 > Story.create(
2.3.0 :009 >      name: 'SitePoint Forums',
2.3.0 :010 >      link: 'http://community.sitepoint.com')
 => #<Story id: 2, name: "SitePoint Forums", link:
↪ "http://community.sitepoint.com", created_at: "2016-03-13
↪ 14:47:48", updated_at: "2016-03-13 14:47:48">
```

The `create` class method achieves the same task as the long-winded approach we just saw, but it only uses one line (not counting word wrapping). This method also—very conveniently—saves the record to the database once the object has been created. And it allows us to assign values to the columns of the record (in this case, in the columns `name` and `link`) at the same time as the record is created.

Hang on—we forgot to assign the object to a variable! How can we query it for additional information?

Retrieving Records

It's all very well to be able to create and save new information, but what good is that information if we're unable to retrieve it? One approach to retrieving a story from our database would be to guess its id; the ids are auto-incremented, so we could anticipate the number of the record that we're after. We could then use the `find` class method to retrieve a row based on its id:

```
2.3.0 :012 > Story.find(2)
 => #<Story id: 2, name: "SitePoint Forums", link:
↳ "http://community.sitepoint.com", created_at: "2016-03-13
↳ 14:47:48", updated_at: "2016-03-13 14:47:48">
```

This approach might be fine for our testing setup, but once our application has deleted and created more than a handful of records, it will fail to work.

Another approach is to retrieve every row in the table. We can do this by using the `all` class method:

```
2.3.0 :014 > Story.all
 => #<ActiveRecord::Relation [#<Story id: 1, name:
↳ "SitePoint", link: "https://sitepoint.com", created_at:
↳ "2016-03-13 14:43:29", updated_at: "2016-03-13 14:43:29">,
↳ #<Story id: 2, name: "SitePoint Forums", link:
↳ "http://community.sitepoint.com", created_at: "2016-03-13
↳ 14:47:48", updated_at: "2016-03-13 14:47:48">]>
```

This process returns an object of class `ActiveRecord::Relation`. I bet you're wondering what this is, as you're probably expecting it to return a list (or `Array`) of all the stories. Well, back in the olden days it did just that, which was good when we had two records, but bad the rest of the time. Consider in the future when Readit is crazy popular, *the* site to share all things web. There are thousands, nay, millions of stories in our database. We then call `Story.all` and everything grinds to a halt while millions of records are copied into application memory. This is a bad situation, and an example of what inspired the creation of `ActiveRecord::Relation`.

`ActiveRecord::Relation` is an implementation of **lazy loading**, which is exactly what it sounds like. When records are lazily loaded, they are only placed into memory the moment they're needed. So, `Story.all` doesn't hit the database or load any records into memory. It waits until you tell it that you need the records first. You tell an `ActiveRecord::Relation` the records are needed, basically, by telling it to become that `Array` we were expecting before:

```
2.3.0 :014 > Story.all.to_a
 => [#<Story id: 1, name: "SitePoint", link:
↪ "https://sitepoint.com", created_at: "2016-03-13 14:43:29",
↪ updated_at: "2016-03-13 14:43:29">, #<Story id: 2,
↪ name: "SitePoint Forums", link:
↪ "http://community.sitepoint.com", created_at: "2016-03-13
↪ 14:47:48", updated_at: "2016-03-13 14:47:48">]
```

`to_a` tells `ActiveRecord::Relation` to become an `Array`. In the process of doing so it hits the database, selects the records, and loads them into memory. Perhaps the best way to show what's happening is to look at the SQL that's being executed again:

```
2.3.0 :019 > Story.all
Story Load (0.2ms)  SELECT "stories".* FROM "stories"
 => #<ActiveRecord::Relation [#<Story id: 1, name:
↪ "SitePoint", link: "https://sitepoint.com", created_at:
↪ "2016-03-13 14:43:29", updated_at: "2016-03-13 14:43:29">,
↪ #<Story id: 2, name: "SitePoint Forums", link:
```

```
↳ "http://community.sitepoint.com", created_at: "2016-03-13
↳ 14:47:48", updated_at: "2016-03-13 14:47:48">]>
2.3.0 :020 > Story.all.first
  Story Load (0.2ms)  SELECT  "stories".* FROM "stories"
↳ ORDER BY "stories"."id" ASC LIMIT 1
 => #<Story id: 1, name: "SitePoint", link:
↳ "https://sitepoint.com", created_at: "2016-03-13 14:43:29",
↳ updated_at: "2016-03-13 14:43:29">
```

In the first case, the SQL selects `stories.*`, or, all the stories. But when we chain the `first` method onto the call, it adds `ASC LIMIT 1` to the SQL, which tells the database to sort the records by id and load the first one. As you can imagine, reducing the amount of data that the database retrieves is good for performance as well as your application as a whole. Oh, and there is a corresponding `last` method we could use in place of the `first` call here. Can you guess what it does?

In short, `ActiveRecord::Relation` allows the record selection process to be handled by the database itself. There are many other methods that you can chain onto the `find` and `find_by` (which we'll see soon) methods that tell the database to do your bidding, such as `:order` and `:limit`.

The `:order` argument allows us to specify the sort order of the returned objects.

The `order` method should contain a tiny bit of SQL that tells the database how the records should be ordered. To retrieve the last element, for example, we would call `order` with a value of `id DESC`, which specifies that the records should be sorted by the `id` column in descending order:

```
>> Story.all.order('id DESC').first
=> #<Story id: 2, name: "SitePoint Forums", …>
```

The object that's returned is identical to the one we retrieved if we'd used `last`.

The `:limit` argument allows us to specify the number of objects to return.

The `:limit` method takes a number indicating how many records to return. To obtain the first two stories, for example, we would call `limit(2)`:

```
2.3.0 :029 > Story.all.limit(2)
 => #<ActiveRecord::Relation [#<Story id: 1, name:
↳ "SitePoint", link: "https://sitepoint.com", created_at:
↳ "2016-03-13 14:43:29", updated_at: "2016-03-13 14:43:29">,
↳ #<Story id: 2, name: "SitePoint Forums", link:
↳ "http://community.sitepoint.com", created_at: "2016-03-13
↳ 14:47:48", updated_at: "2016-03-13 14:47:48">]>
```

Now, while all of these retrieval techniques have worked for us so far, any approach that retrieves an object on the basis of its `id` is fundamentally flawed. It assumes that no one else is using the database, which certainly won't be a valid assumption when our social news application goes live!

What we need is a more reliable method of retrieving records—one that retrieves objects based on a column other than the `id`. What if we were to retrieve a `Story` by its name? Easy:

```
>> Story.find_by(name: 'SitePoint')
=> #<Story id: 1, name: "SitePoint", …>
```

We can even query the database using the `link` column, or any other column in our `stories` table! Cool, huh?

Updating Records

We know how to add stories to our database, but what happens when someone submits a story riddled with typos or (gasp!) factual errors to our Readit application? We have to be able to update existing stories, to ensure the integrity and quality of the information on Readit, and the continuation of our site's glowing reputation.

Before we can update an object, we must retrieve it. Any of the techniques outlined in the previous section would suffice, but for this example, we'll retrieve a `Story` from the database using its name:

```
>> s = Story.find_by(name: 'SitePoint')
=> #<Story id: 1, name: "SitePoint", …>
>> s.name
=> "SitePoint"
>> s.name = 'SitePoint.com'
=> "SitePoint.com"
```

As you can see, the task of changing the value of an attribute (`name`, in this case) is as straightforward as assigning a new value to it. Of course, this change is not yet permanent—we've simply changed the attribute of an object in memory. To save the change to the database, we call the `save` method, just as we did when we learned how to create new objects earlier in this chapter:

```
>> s.save
=> true
```

Once again, there's a shortcut—`update_attribute`—which allows us to update the attribute and save the object to the database in one fell swoop:

```
>> s.update_attribute(name: 'A weblog about Ruby on
↳ Rails')
=> true
```

This is straightforward stuff. Just one more command, then we'll leave the console for good. (Well, for this chapter, anyway!)

Deleting Records

To destroy a database record, simply call the `destroy` method of the `ActiveRecord` object:

```
>> s.destroy
=> #<Story id: 1, name: "SitePoint.com", …>
```

This will remove the record from the database *immediately*.

If you try to use the `find` method to locate an object that has been destroyed (or never existed in the first place), Rails will throw an error:

```
>> Story.find(1)
 => ActiveRecord::RecordNotFound: Couldn't find Story with
↪ 'id'=1
```

As you can see, deleting records is a cinch—at least, for Rails developers! In fact, SQL happens to be doing a good deal of work behind the scenes. Let's now exit the Rails console and pull back the curtain for a closer look at the SQL statements resulting from our commands.

Generating a Controller

Now that our model is in place, let's build a controller. In the same way that we generated a model, we generate a controller by running the `rails generate` command from our application's root folder.

Running the generate Command

Run the `rails g` command from the command line again, but this time pass `controller` as the first parameter:

```
$ rails g controller
```

The output of this command is depicted below

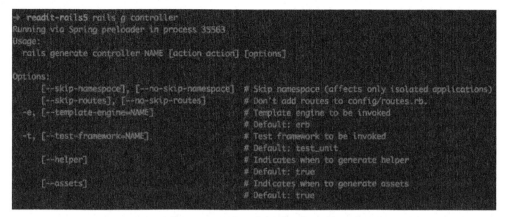

5-3. The output of the rails g controller command

As you may have deduced from the output, calling the `rails generate` command to create a controller requires us to pass the desired name of the controller as a parameter. Other parameters that we could pass include any actions that we'd like to generate.

Let's try it out. Type in the following:

```
$ rails g controller Stories index
Running via Spring preloader in process 93557
  create  app/controllers/stories_controller.rb
   route  get 'stories/index'
  invoke  erb
  create    app/views/stories
  create    app/views/stories/index.html.erb
  invoke  test_unit
  create    test/controllers/stories_controller_test.rb
  invoke  helper
  create    app/helpers/stories_helper.rb
  invoke    test_unit
  invoke  assets
  invoke    coffee
  create      app/assets/javascripts/stories.coffee
  invoke    scss
  create      app/assets/stylesheets/stories.scss
```

The output of the `generate` command tells us exactly what it's doing. Let's analyze each of these lines of output.

Understanding the Output

The meaning of the messages output by the controller generator should be quite familiar by now.

- The `generate` command created the file for our controller and a route. I'll cover routes in more details in Chapter 7.
- The `app/views/stories` folder was created. As mentioned when we first looked at `ActionView` in Chapter 4, the templates for our newly created `StoriesController` will be stored in this folder.
- Controllers have tests, as well, and the generator created a test file and folder for that purpose.
- Rails creates a helper file for each controller with the aim of reusing code in the controller and the views. We'll cover helpers in Chapter 6.
- Finally, each controller can have a set of assets. Here a CoffeeScript and Sass file are created. CoffeeScript and Sass are language abstractions of JavaScript and CSS respectively. We'll cover these later, so don't worry about those files right now.

Let's talk about the items created by generating our controller.

`app/controllers/stories_controller.rb`

This file houses the actual class definition for our `StoriesController`. It's mostly empty, though; all it comes with is a method definition for the index action, which is empty as well. We'll expand on it shortly!

```ruby
class StoriesController < ApplicationController
  def index
  end
end
```

Astute readers will notice that our `StoriesController` doesn't inherit from the `ActionController::Base` in the way we'd expect. The `ApplicationController` class that we see here is actually an empty class that inherits directly from `ActionController::Base`. The class is defined in the `application_controller.rb` file, which lives in the `app/controllers` folder, if you're curious. The resulting `StoriesController` has exactly the same attributes and methods as if it had inherited directly from `ActionController::Base`. Using an intermediary class such as this provides a location for storing variables and pieces of functionality that are common to all controllers, just as we saw with our models and `ApplicationRecord`.

`route  get 'stories/index'`

Remember, from our whirlwind tour of Rails, a controller handles the browser requests to your application. In other words, when a user goes to `http://readit.com/stories`, for example, Rails *routes* that request to the `index` method on `StoriesController`. When you generate a controller with methods, each method receives a route in `config/routes.rb` (known as the "routes" file.) If you open up `config/routes.rb`, you'll see:

5-4. config/routes.rb *(excerpt)*

```
Rails.application.routes.draw do
  get 'stories/index'
  ...lots of comments..
end
```

The `get 'stories/index'` line tells Rails to create an HTTP GET route for `/stories` to the `index` method on the `StoriesController`. This is another Rails convention. Like I said, routing is kind of a big deal, and I'll talk much more about it later.

`app/helpers/stories_helper.rb`

This is the empty helper class for the controller (**helpers** are chunks of code that can be reused throughout your application). We'll look at helpers in more detail in <u>Chapter 6</u>.

```
app/views/stories/index.html.erb
```

This file is the template that corresponds to the index action that we passed as a parameter to the `generate` command. For the moment, it's the only one in the `app/views/stories` directory, but as we create others, they'll be stored alongside `index.html.erb` and given names that match their actions; for example, the `show` action will eventually have a template named `show.html.erb`.

```
test/controller/stories_controller_test.rb
```

This file contains the tests for our controller. We'll skip over it for now, but expand the test cases that this file contains in <u>Chapter 6</u>.

With this knowledge, we're finally in a position to breathe life into our little Rails monster in the true spirit of Frankenstein.

Take Care When It Comes to Naming Parameters

You'll notice the controller class that was created by the `generate` command is called `StoriesController`, even though the first parameter we specified on the command line was simply `Stories`. If our parameter had been `StoriesController`, we'd have ended up with a class name of `StoriesControllerController`!

Starting Our Application ... Again

It's time to fire up our application again. While our previous experience with Puma was somewhat uneventful, our application should do a little more this time.

Start up the web server with the following command:

```
$ rails s
```

Once the server has completed its startup sequence, type the following address into your web browser: `http://localhost:3000/stories/index`. If everything goes to plan, you should be looking at a page similar to the one in Figure 5-5.

5-5. Accessing our `StoriesController` from a browser

What does this display tell us? Well, this simple (and not especially pretty) page confirms that:

- The routing between controllers and views is working correctly—Rails has found and instantiated our `StoriesController` based on the URL that we asked it to retrieve.
- Our controller is able to locate its views—the HTML for the page we see rendered in the browser is contained in the file that's mentioned onscreen (`app/views/stories/index.html.erb`).

If you think about it, this is actually quite an accomplishment, given that we've really only executed two commands for generating code from the command line.

So that we can complete the picture, let's pull some data from our model into our `index` action.

Creating a View

We can use two approaches to build views for our Rails application. One approach is to make use of scaffolding; the other is to "go it alone."

We'll only look at scaffolding briefly as we won't be using it much in the development of our Readit application. It'll be just enough to give you a taste of the topic–then it's up to you to decide whether or not you use it in your own projects.

After that, we'll roll up our sleeves and build some views from scratch.

Generating Views with Scaffolding

In the early days of Rails, scaffolding was one of the features that the Rails community used as a selling point when promoting the framework. This feature also received a considerable amount of criticism, though this was largely due to critics failing to fully understand its intended uses.

So what is scaffolding, anyway?

Scaffolding is a tool that quickly creates a web interface for interacting with your model data. The interface lists the existing data in a table, providing an easy way to add new records, as well as manipulate or delete existing ones.

While there used to be a way to use scaffolding in a temporary fashion (as a one-line addition to one of your controllers, which would then perform all sorts of behind-the-scenes magic), these days scaffolding is Yet Another Generator invoked through the `rails generate` command.

When a scaffold is generated, you end up with a model, a controller with several actions, and numerous view templates for these actions. The generated code can then be built upon and extended over time as you progress with your application. Features provided by the template code can be tweaked or implemented in a different manner, and code that's unsuited to your project can be removed.

We won't be generating any permanent scaffolding in this project, but I do encourage you to experiment with this approach in your own projects, as there may be cases in which you'll find it useful. The syntax to generate a model with scaffolding code is as follows:

```
$ rails g scaffold Story name:string link:string
```

The inline help is available as shown below.

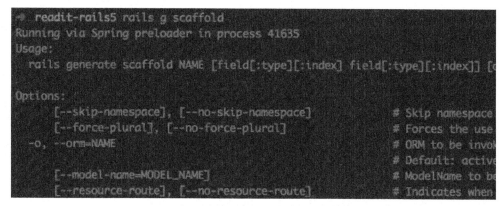

5-6. The inline help for script/generate scaffold

 When You Go Off the Rails ...

If you ever mess up a call to `rails generate`, you may find its alter ego `rails destroy` (alias `rails d`) very helpful. This takes exactly the same arguments as `rails generate` but attempts to reverse what it did, removing newly generated files and modifications to existing files. To undo the scaffold we created above, you would use `rails d scaffold Story`. Pretty cool, eh?

An example screen from a generated scaffold for our `Story` model is shown in Figure 5-7.

Listing stories

Name	Link	
My shiny weblog	http://poocs.net/	Show Edit Destroy
SitePoint Forums	http://sitepoint.com/forums/	Show Edit Destroy

New story

5-7. Example screen from a generated scaffold

A Great Tool–but with Limitations

Scaffolding is a tool designed for quick interaction with models, and should only be used as such. It is by no means intended to be a fully automated tool for generating web applications (or even administration interfaces).

Scaffolding also has its limits in providing automated access. For example, it's unable to cope with `ActiveRecord` associations such as "a `Story` belongs to a `User`," which we'll see later. Additionally, since most applications do require a fully fledged administrative interface, you're advised to just create the real thing rather than fiddle around with a dummy interface.

Scaffolding is certainly a powerful feature of Rails, and it's rewarding to gain instant visual feedback with the views created for us; however, it's now time to create some views of our own, which will give us a much better insight into what each part of the MVC stack does.

Creating Static Pages

Back in Chapter 4, we looked briefly at the `ActionView` module, but only in theory. Let's create some custom views that we can use a web browser to view.

As a quick refresher, `ActionView` represents the view part of the model-view-controller architecture. Files that are used to render views are called templates, and they usually consist of HTML code interspersed with Ruby code. These files are referred to as ERb templates.

One of these templates (albeit, a not so interesting one) has already been created for us—it's the `index.html.erb` file that's located in `app/views/stories`:

```
<h1>Stories#index</h1>
 <p>Find me in
↳ app/views/stories/index.html.erb</p>
```

Does it look familiar? This is the HTML code that we viewed in our web browser earlier in the chapter. As you can see, it's a static page (so it's without any Ruby code). Dynamic pages (which pull in data from a database or an alternative source) are much more interesting! We'll have a closer look at dynamic pages now.

Creating Dynamic Pages

Let's begin our adventure in building dynamic pages. We'll add a value—the current date and time—to the HTML output of our view. Although simple, this value is considered to be dynamic.

Open the template file in your text editor and delete everything that's there. In its place, add the following line:

```
<%= Time.now %>
```

Here we call the class method that lives on the `Time` class, which is part of the Ruby Standard Library. This method call is wrapped in ERb tags (beginning with `<%=` and ending with `%>`).

You may remember from Chapter 4 that the equal sign attached to the opening ERb tag will cause the return value of `Time.now` to be output to the web page, instead of executing silently.

If you refresh your browser now, the page should display the current time, as shown in Figure 5-8. To confirm that this value is dynamic, reload your page a few times—you'll notice that the value does indeed change.

2016-03-14 08:37:55 -0400

5-8. Our first dynamic page: displaying the current time

Passing Data Back and Forth

There's one fundamental problem with what we've done here. Can you spot it?

In order to adhere to the model-view-controller architecture, we should avoid performing any hefty calculations from within any of our views—that's the job of the controller. Strictly speaking, our call to `Time.now` is one such calculation, so it should really occur within the controller. But what good is the result of a calculation if we can't display it?

We introduced the concept of passing variables between controllers and views briefly in Chapter 4, but at that point, we had no views that we could use to demonstrate it in action. Now's our chance to do just that!

We learned that any instance variable that's declared in the controller automatically becomes available to the view as an instance variable. Let's take advantage of that now. Edit /app/controllers/stories_controller.rb so that it contains the following code:

```ruby
class StoriesController < ApplicationController
  def index
    @current_time = Time.now
```

```
    end
end
```

Next, replace the contents of `app/views/stories/index.html.erb` with the following:

```
<%= @current_time %>
```

I'm sure you can see what's happened here:

1. We've moved the "calculation" of the current time from the view to the controller.

2. The result of the calculation is stored in the instance variable `@current_time`.

3. The contents of this instance variable are then automatically made available to the view.

The result is that the job of the view has been reduced to simply displaying the contents of this instance variable, rather than executing the calculation itself.

Voilà! Our application logic and our presentation logic are kept neatly separate.

Pulling in a Model

All we do now is pull some data into our view, and we'll have the entire MVC stack covered.

In case you deleted all of your model records when we experimented with scaffolding earlier, make sure you create at least one story. Type the following into a Rails console:

```
>> Story.create(name:  'SitePoint Forums', link:
↪ 'http://community.sitepoint.com')
```

To display this model data within a view, we retrieve it from within the controller, like so:

```
class StoriesController < ApplicationController
  def index
    @story = Story.find_by(name: 'SitePoint Forums')
  end
end
```

We'll also change our view accordingly:

```
A random link:
  <a href="<%= @story.link %>"><%= @story.name
↪ %></a>
```

Reload the page to see the result. It should look like Figure 5-9.

5-9. MVC in action: a view displaying model data via the controller

Of course, Rails would be failing in its job of saving you effort if it required you to manually create links the way we just did. Instead of typing out the HTML for a link, you can use the link_to function, which is much easier to remember and achieves the same result. Try it for yourself:

```
A random link:
<%= link_to @story.name, @story.link %>
```

One other point: I'll be the first to admit that the text on the page is a little misleading. Our link is hardly random—it simply retrieves the same link from the database over and over again.

It's actually quite easy to make our application retrieve random stories, though. Simply modify the part of the controller that fetches the story to this:

```
@story = Story.order('RANDOM()').first
```

This modification selects a single story, just like before (using the `:first` parameter). This time, however, the database is being instructed to shuffle its records before picking one. When you reload your page, random stories should now appear—assuming you have more than one story in your database, that is! You might like to save a few more stories (using `Story.create` in a Rails console) and see the random link feature of our Readit application in action.

There we have it: the beginnings of our story-sharing application. Admittedly, displaying a random story from our database is only a small achievement, but hey—it's a start!

Summary

This chapter saw us create some real code for each component of an MVC application. We generated a model with a corresponding migration to handle the storage of our stories; we generated a controller to handle communication between the models and the views; and we created a view that dynamically renders content supplied by our controller.

With the functionality provided by `ActiveRecord`, we've been creating, updating, and deleting data from our SQL database without resorting to any SQL.

I also introduced you to the `rails` commands that can be used to run migrations and other tasks. And we learned about the YAML data representation language that's used to store test fixture data for our application.

In the next chapter, we'll add a layout to our application using HTML and CSS; talk about associations between models; and extend the functionality of our application.

Let's get into it!

Chapter

Helpers, Forms, and Layouts

In the last chapter, we put in place some basic architecture for our application—a model, a view, and a controller—and were able to display a link to a random story in the database. The foundation of our application is sound, but users are unable to really interact with it yet.

In this chapter, we'll use helpers to implement the basic functionality for our application: the capability that allows users to submit stories to the site.

We'll also start to build our test suite, and create some functional tests to confirm that the submission form is working as intended. We'll expand on this suite of tests in the coming chapters.

Calling upon Our Trusty Helpers

And I'm not talking about Santa's little helpers. Let me explain.

In Chapter 5, we discussed the importance of keeping application logic in a controller, so that our views contain only presentational code. Although not apparent in the basic examples we've used, extracting code from a view and moving it into a controller often causes clumsy code to be added to an application's controllers.

To address this problem, another structural component exists: the helper. A **helper** is a module–a Ruby module–that can be reused throughout an application, and is stored in a helper file. A helper usually includes methods that contain relatively complicated or reusable presentation logic. Since any views that include the helper are spared this complexity, the code in the view is kept simple and easy to read, reflecting our adherence to DRY principles. Dozens of helpers are built into Rails, but you can create your own to use throughout your application.

Code that renders a screen element on a page, for example, is a good candidate for a helper. Repeating this type of code from one view to another violates the DRY principle, but sticking it all into a controller makes no sense either.

As we saw in Generating a Controller in Chapter 5, when we generate a controller (using the `generate` command that we've come to know and love), one of the files that's created is a new helper file called `controllername_helper.rb`. In the case of our `StoriesController`, the helper file associated with this controller is `stories_helper.rb`, and lives in `app/helpers`.

We'll be relying on a few of Rails' built-in helpers for much of the story submission interface we'll be building in this chapter.

Enabling Story Submission

In our brief foray into the world of scaffolding in Chapter 5, we saw that it's possible in Rails to create a quick (and dirty) front end for our data; however, this approach doesn't necessarily constitute best practice.

In this section, we'll build a web interface for submitting stories to our Readit website without relying on scaffolding. First, we'll create a view template that contains the actual submission form; then we'll add a new method to our `StoriesController` to handle the task of saving submitted stories to the database. We'll also implement a global layout for our application, and create feedback to present to our users, both when they're filling out the form and after they've submitted a story.

Creating a Form

HTML forms is an area that even seasoned front-end developers have traditionally found intimidating. While it's possible to create form elements manually, it's unnecessary: Rails offers plenty of helpers and shortcuts that make creating forms a breeze. One of those is the `form_for` helper.

Introducing the `form_for` Helper

Rails offers a few helper functions for writing forms. `form_for` is the most common among these and is recommended when generating a form that's bound to one type of object. "Bound" here means that each field in the form maps to the corresponding attribute of a single object, rather than to corresponding attributes of multiple objects. In other words, it creates a *form for* an object. Clever naming, eh? At its most basic, using the `form_for` helper to bind a simple form to a `Story` object looks like this:

```erb
<%= form_for @story do |f| %>
  <%= f.text_field :name %>
  <%= f.text_field :link %>
<% end %>
```

This `form_for` helper syntax boasts a few points that are worth highlighting:

- The last line uses the ERb tags for silent output (`<% … %>`), while the other lines of the helper use ERb tags that display output to the browser (`<%= … %>`).

- The parameter that immediately follows `form_for` is the object to which the form will be bound (`@story`). Can you guess where this will come from?

- The fields that make up the form live inside a block. As you'll no doubt remember, a Ruby block is a statement of Ruby code that appears between the keywords `do` and `end`, or between curly braces. This is the first time we've encountered a block within an ERb file, but the principle is the same.

- A new object—which I've named `f` as shorthand for "form" in this case—must be passed as a parameter to the block. This object is of type `FormBuilder`, which is a class that contains instance methods designed to work with forms. Using these methods, we can easily create the HTML form input elements such as `text_field`, `password_field`, `check_box`, and `text_area`.

We receive a number of benefits in exchange for following this syntax:

- The HTML form tags that signify the start and end of our HTML form will be generated for us.

- We gain access to a number of instance methods via the `FormBuilder` object that we can use to create fields in our form. In the example, we've used the `text_field` method to create two text fields; these fields will be mapped to our `@story` object automatically.

- Appropriate `name` and `id` attributes will be applied to each of these fields; these attributes can then be used as hooks for CSS and JavaScript, as we'll see later in the chapter.

- Rails automatically figures out to which URI this form should be posted when submitted by the web browser if our model has been defined as a resource (a term that you will recall from REST-ful Style in Chapter 4). More on this in a moment.

As you can see, using `form_for` and the `FormBuilder` object that comes with it is a powerful way to create comprehensive forms with minimal effort.

Help on Helpers

As I mentioned, helpers are modules, so the `form_for` method (as well as the rest of the form helper methods) are all defined in the `ActionView::Helpers::FormHelper` module, which you can read all about on the Ruby on Rails documentation[1].

Creating the Template

Now that we have a handle on `form_for`, let's use it to create the form that site visitors will use to submit stories to Readit.

A form is a presentational concept, which means it should be stored as a view. Our form will allow users to submit *new* stories to Readit, so we'll give this view the name new. Let's make a template for it: create a new file called `new.html.erb` in the `app/views/stories` folder. It should contain the following:

```erb
<%= form_for @story do |f| %>
  <div>
    <p><%= f.label :name  %></p>
    <%= f.text_field :name %>
  </div>
  <div>
    <p><%= f.label :link  %></p>
    <%= f.text_field :link %>
  </div>
  <%= submit_tag %>
<% end %>
```

Let's break down the ERb code here:

```erb
<%= form_for @story do |f| %>
```

---

[1]. http://api.rubyonrails.org/classes/ActionView/Helpers/FormHelper.html

As we discussed, the `form_for` helper creates a form that's bound to a specific object—in this case, it's bound to the `@story` instance variable.

```
<%= f.label :name %>
<%= f.text_field :name %>
```

These lines create a label and text field called "name," which is mapped to the `name` attribute on our `@story` object. It will display a text field in which the user can enter the name of the story being submitted.

```
<%= f.label :link %>
<%= f.text_field :link %>
```

Here we have another label and text field combination, this time named `link`, which is also mapped to our `@story` object. It will display a text field in which the user can enter the URL of the story being submitted.

```
<%= submit_tag %>
```

This helper generates the HTML code to display a submit button in our form. This is a stand-alone helper and not part of the `form_for` helper, which means we don't need the FormBuilder (`f`) to call it.

Next, make sure that your web server is running (refer to Chapter 2 if you need a refresher on starting the server). Open your web browser and type the following URL into the address bar: `http://localhost:3000/stories/new`. You should see—yikes!—an error similar to the below.

6-1. Error resulting from having no route

The Console Is Key

If you see a different error message when you try to open this URL, I recommend that you monitor the console window from which you launched your web server. This process is the heart of our application; if it's not beating, you'll be unable to access any of the functionality added in this chapter. Errors that appear in the console should give you an idea of what went wrong.

Now, what happened here? Well, there's no route for /stories/new, so Rails cannot know which controller and method to invoke. I'll talk a bit more about routing in a minute. For now, let's add the route to config/routes.rb:

```
Rails.application.routes.draw do
  get 'stories/index'
  get 'stories/new'
  ....
```

Now refresh the page ... and as seen in Figure 6-2 we have *another* error!

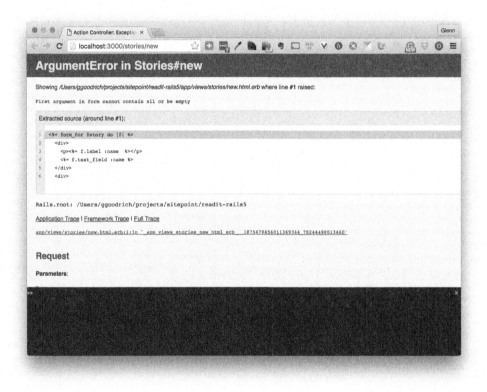

6-2. For argument's sake! Another error

So, what's up? Well, we handed the `form_for` helper the instance variable called `@story`, but we never actually assigned an object to that variable, so it ended up being `nil`. Adhering to the MVC principles, we must turn to the controller as being responsible for putting a value into `@story`, which we'll do in the next section.

Modifying the Controller

To create an action that will populate the @story instance variable, edit the file
app/controllers/stories_controller.rb so that it looks as follows (the
method to be added is in bold):

6-3. app/controllers/stories_controller.rb *(excerpt)*

```ruby
class StoriesController < ApplicationController
  def index
    @story = Story.order("RANDOM()").first
  end


  def new
    @story = Story.new
  end
end
```

It doesn't matter whether you place this new method above or below the existing
index method. Some people prefer to sort their methods alphabetically, while
others group their methods by purpose; the decision is entirely up to you and has
no impact on your application's functionality.

The code that we've added to our new method simply instantiates a new Story
object and places it in the @story instance variable. As it's an instance variable,
@story will now be available to our view and thus to the form_for helper.

Reloading the page in your browser should now yield ... yet another error!

6-4. Even after implementing the "new" action, we still receive an error on our submission form

As I mentioned earlier in the chapter, a benefit of using the `form_for` helper to set up our form is that it automatically figures out where to submit the form. Now it's showing that something's missing from our equation: we're yet to declare `Story` as a resource anywhere. Let's do that now.

RESTful Resources in Rails

As covered in Chapter 4, Rails encourages a RESTful architectural approach to development, especially for sites that create, retrieve, update, and delete *resources*. In our case, a Story is a perfect candidate for a RESTful resource. Although the Rails creators would prefer that every model generated is automatically declared a RESTful resource, we're yet to reach that stage—and, admittedly, it makes no sense to make it so in every case.

Resources in Rails are declared in the file responsible for the routing configuration: `config/routes.rb`. In Rails, the routing module is responsible for mapping URLs to controllers and actions. Take the following URL, for example:

```
/stories/new
```

The routing module maps this URL to the `new` action of `StoriesController`. But you already knew that. Here are the contents of the `routes.rb` file with its comments removed:

```
Rails.application.routes.draw do
  get 'stories/index'
  get 'stories/new'
end
```

As outlined previously, the first part of the URL is mapped to the controller and the second part is mapped to the action.

This being the default configuration, mapping RESTful resources is a little different. Resources always consume the second spot in the URL—we're talking about resource-centric development, after all. So for any given resource, the paths along with their respective HTTP verbs outlined in Table 6.1 are recognized.

6.1. The Mapping of RESTful URLs to Controller Actions

URL	Action
GET /stories	index
GET /stories/new	new
POST /stories	create
GET /stories/1	show
GET /stories/1/edit	edit
PUT /stories/1	update
PATCH /stories/1	update
DELETE /stories/1	destroy

When you're looking at the table, the actions can be divided into two groups: actions that operate on a single, existing story (show, edit, update, and destroy) and those that don't (index, new, and create). The actions that do operate on a single story use the second part of the URL to identify the resource they're operating on with its numeric *id*.

That leaves us with seven distinct ways to interact with stories. But are we supposed to define all those by hand for every resource our application is going to have? Rails wouldn't be Rails if we had to jump through all those hoops. So let's take a look at the magic that's behind `resources`, Rails' method for automatically mapping RESTful routes.

Mapping a New Resource

We can discuss the theory of resources in Rails until we're blue in the face, but nothing stimulates the brain like actually doing it for yourself. In the `config/routes.rb` file, add the following line:

6-5. config/routes.rb (excerpt)

```
Rails.application.routes.draw do
  resources :stories
end
```

This one line of code will give us all sorts of exciting features. Among them is a working—albeit unstyled—story submission form we can see upon reloading the page in the browser. The result is shown in Figure 6-6. We'll explore the remainder of those features in the upcoming chapters.

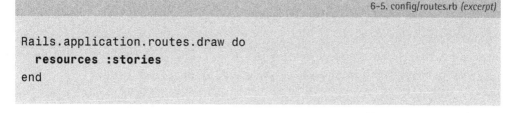

Name

Link

Save changes

6-6. Our unstyled story submission form

Analyzing the HTML

The time has come to find out what kind of HTML the Rails helpers have generated. Using your browser's **View Source** option, check the HTML in forms for this page and you should see the following:

```
<form class="new_story" id="new_story" action="/stories"
↪ accept-charset="UTF-8" method="post">
<input name="utf8" type="hidden" value="✓">
 <input type="hidden" name="authenticity_token"
↪ value="J7MBWtcQCU9UJMPb2AiDiOelUt7sTNDS91SeyMj4TaGlvIyesHI4kh
↪QBF4ExmwmKI5x6Q6iuzwVS7+jWASgCIw==">
```

```
  <div>
 <p><label
↪ for="story_name">Name</label></p>
    <input type="text" name="story[name]" id="story_name">
  </div>
  <div>
 <p><label
↪ for="story_link">Link</label></p>
    <input type="text" name="story[link]" id="story_link">
    <p></p>
  </div>
 <input type="submit" name="commit" value="Save changes"
↪ data-disable-with="Save changes">
</form>
```

This markup is basically what we would expect: two text fields, a couple of labels, and a submit button have been created for us, and everything has been wrapped up in a form element. Rails has also figured out the correct target URL (the `action` attribute of the form element) to create a new `Story` object according to the RESTful URL mapping outlined in the last section. Submission of the form will lead us to the `create` action of `StoriesController`, which we've yet to implement.

Of note is that strange hidden `<input>` element named `authenticity_token` inside it. This is one aspect of Rails' attempt to counteract so-called **Cross-Site-Request-Forgery (CSRF)** attacks, ensuring that submitted forms originate at the current web application as opposed to a third party. The content of `authenticity_token` is based on the user's session and is verified against a token set for the application (in `config/secrets.yml`, if you're curious). If there is a mismatch, an error is raised and the form submission is discarded.

So our markup looks fine. But if you were to submit the form in its current state, you would be less than thrilled with the results: we'd receive another error, because the `create` method in `StoriesController` is yet to exist. Let's add some code to save the story data to the database.

Saving Data to the Database

Remembering when we made `Story` a resource, submitting the form will `POST` the form data to the `create` action of the `StoriesController`. We'll create (heh) that now by adding a method to the `app/controllers/stories_controller.rb` file:

```
def create
  @story = Story.new(params[:story])
  @story.save
end
```

The `params` object in the first line of our method is a Hash that contains all of the content that the user submitted; you can revisit Hashes in Chapter 3 if you'd like a refresher.

All of the form data passed to Rails will be added to the `params` Hash. If you look again at the HTML source of the submission form, you'll notice that the `input` element name attributes all have a `story[]` prefix. This prefix groups all the submitted form fields for the story we're creating in `params[:story]`.

We can then reference individual elements within the Hash by passing the name of the attribute (as a symbol) to the Hash. For example, the value of the `name` attribute could be accessed as `params[:story][:name]`. You get the idea.

The point of all this is that user data submitted via the form can be assigned to an object very easily. We just pass the `params[:story]` Hash to the `Story.new` method, and we have ourselves a populated `@story` object.

Not coincidentally, this is exactly what we've done in the first line of our method:

```
@story = Story.new(params[:story])
```

The newly created `@story` object is then sent the `save` method to store it permanently into our database.

Now, before you go ahead and enter some data into your form and click **Save**, let's pause for a second and think about what Rails would do if you submitted the form. Can you hazard a guess? We'd end up with *yet another* error screen stating that Rails was unable to locate the `create.html.erb` template.

After Rails has finished processing the code in the controller action, (unless instructed otherwise) it will try to render a template named after the controller and action. In this case, it would be `app/views/stories/create.html.erb`.

But we don't actually want to do any rendering. We have saved the object to the database and can return to the random story selector that we created in <u>Chapter 5</u>, located within the `index` action.

Redirecting with URL helpers

If we don't want to render a template after an action has finished, preferring to go elsewhere instead, we need to use the `redirect_to` method. This method takes a single argument, namely, the destination of the redirection. What *is* the destination of the redirection? Well, we know we've accessed the story randomizer at `http://localhost:3000/stories`, so could we simply redirect there with the following command?

```
redirect_to 'http://localhost:3000/stories'
```

We certainly could. But since it's likely that we'll be using these kinds of URLs in many places, it seems a little tedious to go down that path. And, after all, `form_for` was able to figure out paths on its own, why wouldn't `redirect_to`, too?

Albeit a lot of magic and mind-reading on the part of Rails, it turns out in this case that we *do* need to tell Rails what we want it to do. But to ease our pain, there are quite a few methods provided by the `resources` call in the `config/routes.rb` file that we use to define our stories as resources. These are known as **URL helpers**.

Table 6.2 shows a list of URL helpers that are being defined for every `Story` resource.

6.2. URL Helpers for the `Story` Resource

Helper	URL
stories_path	/stories
new_story_path	/stories/new
story_path(@story)	/stories/1
edit_story_path(@story)	/stories/1/edit

URL helpers use singular or plural naming conventions depending on whether they're dealing with a specific story (singular) or no specific story (plural).

You may wonder why there's no such thing as a `destroy_story_path(@story)` or `create_stories_path`. It's because the actual URL generated from these wouldn't differ from `story_path(@story)` and `stories_path` respectively. Remember that the only difference is the actual HTTP verb used to access the resource. We'll learn in the forthcoming chapters how to specify a different HTTP verb. This HTTP verb/URL combination is the very heart of Mr. Fielding's RESTful vision.

Now that we know about the URL helpers available to us, it's easy to spot the helper to use for our `redirect_to` call to redirect the browser back to the story index: `stories_path`. The new `create` method should now look as follows:

```
def create
  @story = Story.new(params[:story])
  @story.save
  redirect_to stories_path
end
```

As we can see in Figure 6-7, submitting the form now—after filling in a proper name and story link, of course!—should ... *result in yet another error*. Wait, what?

6-7. Error prone!

What the what? Forbidden attributes? But, we only submitted the `name` and `link`. What's going on?

Well, we've hit another example of a Rails convention that's put in to protect our site from basic security problems. The security issue here is called **Mass Assignment Protection**. If we simply let all the keys of the `params[:story]` Hash be passed to `Story.new`, an inscrutable person could pass all kinds of attributes. For example, if the model has an attribute that, say, affects administrative privileges, a user could manual set that attribute to `true` and compromise our site.

To save us from having to handle this every time we want to create (or update) a model, the superheroes that make Rails created automatic Mass Assignment protection, which is affectionately known as "strong parameters" in the community. To make this error go away, we **whitelist** (or `permit`) the attributes that are on the safe list. The conventional way this is done is by creating the following private method on `StoriesController`:

```
def story_params
  params.require(:story).permit(:name, :link)
end
```

Then, change the `create` action to this:

```
def create
  @story = Story.new(story_params)
  @story.save
  redirect_to stories_path
end
```

 EXTRA CREDIT: Going Private

How would you make `story_params` private? If you did your extra credit in Chapter 3, you would know ...

Simply add the keyword `private` above the method and all methods defined after that keyword will be private.

Now, we have whitelisted our parameters, so submitting the new Story form will create the story and redirect you back to the random story selector. This is a good thing; however, our application does look a little sparse. Let's make it pretty.

Creating a Layout

In Rails, a **layout** is a specialized form of a view template. Layouts allow page elements that are repeated globally across a site to be applied to every view. Examples of such elements are HTML headers and footers, CSS files, and Javascript includes.

Layouts can also be applied at the controller level. This ability can be useful if, for example, you want to apply different layouts to a page depending on whether it's being viewed by an administrator or a regular user.

We'll begin our foray into layouts by creating a global layout for the entire application.

Establishing Structure

Layouts should be stored in the `app/views/layouts` folder. A layout template can have any name, as long as the file ends in `.html.erb`. Rails, by convention, creates a "global" application layout called—wait for it—`application.html.erb`.

Let's take advantage of that convention. Open the file named `application.html.erb` in the `app/views/layouts` folder and add the content where indicated:

```erb
<!DOCTYPE html>
<html>
  <head>
    <title>Readit</title>
    <%= csrf_meta_tags %>

  <%= stylesheet_link_tag    'application', media: 'all',
↪ 'data-turbolinks-track': 'reload' %>
  <%= javascript_include_tag 'application',
↪ 'data-turbolinks-track': 'reload' %>
  </head>
  <body>
    <div id="content">
      <h1>Readit</h1>
      <%= yield %>
    </div>
  </body>
</html>
```

There's nothing too radical going on here—it's a regular HTML5 document with a proper DOCTYPE declaration; however, a couple of ERb calls here warrant an explanation.

The following code generates the HTML that includes the default external CSS stylesheet called `application.css` in the `app/assets/stylesheets` folder:

```
<%= stylesheet_link_tag    'application', media: 'all',
↪ 'data-turbolinks-track': 'reload' %>
```

Rails (and the asset pipeline, which we'll talk about soon) will create a URL for this stylesheet that looks like `/assets/application.css`.

```
<%= javascript_include_tag 'application',
↪ 'data-turbolinks-track': 'reload' %>
```

I bet you can guess what this does. Just as we have `stylesheet_link_tag` for CSS, `javascript_include_tag` generates the `<script>` element for the default application JavaScript file. This file is, as you've no doubt guessed, located at `app/assets/javascripts/application.js`.

The `data-turbolinks-track` attribute on each of those tags tells Rails to reload the files only when they change, otherwise they will be cached. Rails is so smart!

 Built-in Abettors

> Rails ships with a number of helpers similar to `stylesheet_link_tag` and `javascript_include_tag`, in that they make generating HTML pages easy. They mostly save tedious typing and thus potential errors.

I mentioned Cross-Site-Request-Forgery earlier, and how Rails takes measures to protect our site from basic attacks. `csrf_meta_tags` is one of those measures, as it creates a couple of `meta` tags that hold the parameter name and value for the authenticity token in our forms:

```
<%= csrf_meta_tags %>
```

This line is the point at which the content for our specific view is displayed:

```
<%= yield %>
```

Telling our layout to "yield" might not seem intuitive here, but it does actually make sense. Let me explain.

Remember that our layout will be used by many different view templates, each of which is responsible for displaying the output of a specific action. When the layout receives the command `yield`, control is handed to the *actual* view template being rendered—that is, the layout *yields* to the view template. Once that template has been rendered, control returns to the layout, and rendering is resumed for the rest of the page.

Since we've linked a stylesheet, we'd better make use of it.

Adding Some Style

Let's use CSS to pretty up our page.

 CSS Mastery Not Required

Fear not if CSS isn't your forte. All that's required for this project is to type out the CSS rules exactly as you see them—or, even better, copy and paste them from the code archive. If you're interested in improving your CSS skills, a good place to start is with Louis Lazaris' book, *Jump Start CSS* https://www.sitepoint.com/premium/books/jump-start-css.

To apply a stylesheet to your application, open the file called `application.css` in the `app/assets/stylesheets` folder and drop in the following code after the comments in the file:

```
body {
  background-color: #666;
  margin: 15px 25px;
  font-family: Helvetica, Arial, sans-serif;
}
p { margin: 0 }
input {
  margin-bottom: 1em;
}
#content {
  background-color: #fff;
  border: 10px solid #ccc;
  padding: 10px 10px 20px 10px;
}
```

Reload the page in your browser. You should see a slightly prettier version of the form, as shown below.

6-9. Fully functioning form styled with CSS

Excellent! We now have a form that functions correctly, is well structured under the hood, *and* looks good on the outside; however, our app is yet to deliver any feedback to the user to confirm whether a story submission was successful. Enter: the flash!

Enabling User Feedback with the Flash

Yes, you read that correctly: flash.

And no, we're not going to be switching to Adobe's Flash technology to provide submission feedback. **The flash** also happens to be the name for the internal storage container (actually a kind of hash) that Rails uses for temporary data. In this section, we'll use the flash to pass temporary objects between actions. We'll then apply some validation to the data that's entered.

Adding to the Flash

When I say that the flash is used to store *temporary* items, I'm not referring to items that exist in memory only without being saved to the database. Items stored in the flash exist for the duration of one sole request, and then they're gone.

What good is that? Well, using the flash allows us the convenience of communicating information between successive actions without having to save information in the user's browser or database. The flash is well positioned to store short status messages, such as notifications that inform the user whether a form submission or login attempt was successful.

Flash content is usually populated from within a controller action. Using the flash is very easy; to place a message in the flash, simply pass it an identifying symbol and a corresponding message. Here's an example:

```
flash[:error] = 'Login unsuccessful.'
```

In our story-sharing application, we want to place a message into the flash immediately after the story is saved to confirm to the user that the submission was successful. Add the following line to the **create** action of your **StoriesController**:

```
def create
  @story = Story.new(story_params)
  @story.save
  flash[:notice] = 'Story submission
↪ succeeded'
  redirect_to stories_path
end
```

> **Flash Naming Conventions**
>
> In general, Rails applications use conventions named after common UNIX logging levels to indicate a message's level of severity. The common area names are `:notice`, `:warning`, and `:error`.
>
> As the message is not critical in this case, we'll use `:notice`; however, the name of the flash area is entirely up to you.

Retrieving Data from the Flash

To retrieve contents from the flash (usually done in the successive action), access the flash from a view in the same way that you would access any other hash in Rails. There's no need to explicitly populate it in the controller, nor purge the Flash once the view has been rendered—Rails takes care of this for you.

Since flash content is universally applicable, we'll change our layout file (located at `app/views/layouts/application.html.erb`) so that it renders a notification box as long as there's content to render. Modify your layout file as follows:

6-10. app/views/layouts/application.html.erb *(excerpt)*

```
<div id="content">
  <h1>Readit</h1>
  <% unless flash[:notice].blank? %>
  <div id="notification"><%= flash[:notice]
↪ %></div>
  <% end %>
  <%= yield %>
</div>
```

The condition that we've added here checks whether the `flash[:notice]` variable is blank; if not, the code renders a simple HTML div element to which an id is attached. Rails considers an object to be blank if it's either `nil` or an empty string.

Before we switch to the browser to test this addition, let's add a few rules to our stylesheet to display our notification:

6-11. app/assets/stylesheets/application.css *(excerpt)*

```
#notification {
  border: 5px solid #9c9;
  background-color: #cfc;
  padding: 5px;
  margin: 10px 0;
}
```

If you submit another story now, you should see a nice green box on the subsequent page informing you that the submission succeeded as shown here.

6-12. Green signals success with flash

If you're curious, reload the landing page to make sure the contents of the flash disappear.

Our form submission process, however, is still flawed; it's possible for a user to submit stories without entering a name, or a link, or both!

Applying Validations

To ensure that all the stories submitted to Readit contain both a name and a link before they're saved, we'll make use of the `ActiveRecord` functionality called **validations**.

Validations come in a variety of flavors: the simplest flavor says "Check that this attribute (or form input) is not empty." A more complex validation, for example, might be "Make sure this attribute (or form input) matches the following regular expression."[2] There are varying degrees of complexity in between. A more involved validation might be used, for example, to validate an email address.

Validations are defined in the model. This ensures that the validation is always applied, and that an object is always valid before its data is saved to the database.

Let's look at a simple validation. To add validations to our `Story` model, edit the model class in `app/models/story.rb` so that it looks like this:

6-13. app/models/story.rb

```ruby
class Story < ApplicationRecord
  validates :name, :link, presence: true
end
```

You'll note that the line we've added here is fairly verbose, so it's quite readable by humans. This line ensures that the name and link attributes have a value before the model is saved.

---

2. A regular expression is a string of characters that can be used to match another string of characters. The syntax of regular expressions can be confusing, with particularly long expressions looking much like random characters to a newcomer to the syntax. One of the most common uses of regular expressions is validating whether or not an email address is in the correct format.

Tweaking the Redirection Logic

We want to ensure that the user will only be redirected to the story list if the model passes its validation checks. To do so, we must modify the `create` action in our controller as follows:

```
6-14. app/controllers/votes_controller.rb (excerpt)

def create
  @story = Story.new(story_params)
  if @story.save
    flash[:notice] = "Story submission succeeded"
    redirect_to stories_path
  else
    render action:'new'
  end
end
```

As you can see, we've added an `if` clause so that it checks to see whether `@story.save` returns true.

The validations we defined will be called before the `save` method writes the object to the database. If the validations fail, this method will return `false`—the object will not be saved, and the user will not be redirected.

It's quite common to use Ruby statements directly within conditions, as we've done with the `save` method here. In general, many of the methods provided by the Rails core classes return `true` or `false`, making them an excellent choice for use in conditions.

In the `else` part we instruct the controller to re-render the template associated with the `new` action, which is our story submission form. This enables the user to correct his or her submission and resubmit without reentering the form values. Please note that the render call does *not* execute any of the controller code associated with the new action.

Fantastic! Our logic for processing the form is sound. If you were to try to submit a blank name or link now, our app would not allow the object to be saved nor the redirect to occur, and the form would be re-rendered; however, the user still requires some guidance for correcting any errors that result from a failed validation.

Improving the User Experience

The generated HTML of the re-rendered form provides a hint as to how we might implement additional feedback for the user when a validation error occurs:

```
<div class="field_with_errors">
  <label for="story_link">Link</label>
</div>
<div class="field_with_errors">
 <input type="text" value="" name="story[link]"
↳ id="story_link">
</div>
```

As you can see, using the Rails `form_for` helper has paid off. It has wrapped our label and text field in `div` elements, and assigned them a class called `field_with_errors`. It has also given them a custom style, making the background red to indicate an error. We could override this if we wanted to, so let's do that. Add the following rule to the `application.css` file:

```
                                    6-15. app.assets/stylesheets/application.css (excerpt)

.field_with_errors {
  color: red;
  background: transparent;
}
.field_with_errors input {
  border: thin solid red;
}
```

The helper's other neat trick is that it populates each field with values that the user entered in the previous submission, as shown below.

6-16. Showing errors to the user

It's also good practice to tell our users what *exactly* is wrong with a particular field. Further along, we may want to add a validation to our model to ensure that each URL is submitted only once.

Add the following line to the top of the `new.html.erb` template (above the `form_for` call):

6-17. apps/views/stories/new.html.erb *(excerpt)*

```erb
<% if @story.errors.any? %>
  <div class="form_errors">
    <h3>Errors</h3>
    <ul>
      <% @story.errors.full_messages.each do |message| %>
        <li><%= message %></li>
      <% end %>
    </ul>
  </div>
<% end %>
```

Then add a CSS rule for our `form_errors` into `app/assets/stylesheets/application.css`:

```css
.form_errors { color: red }
```

Now if a user submits the form without entering content into every field, the browser will display:

- a useful error message that indicates how many fields are blank
- some textual hints as to the nature of the error for each field
- a red border that clearly highlights which fields need attention

See Figure 6-18 for an example.

6-18. Story submission form with validation

A fairly functional form submission process, no? And it doesn't look too shabby, either.

Before we begin loading our application with additional features, we should add some unit and functional test coverage. This will ensure that future modifications don't break any of our existing functionality.

Testing the Form

Making a habit of writing tests for newly added code is more than just a good idea—it may save your hide in the future!

As I've mentioned before, by writing tests for *all* of your code, you can evolve a suite of automated testing facilities as your application evolves. This suite can then be run periodically or on demand to reveal any errors in your application.

A Rails test suite can be split into three fundamental parts:

- *Unit tests*-also called model tests-cover model-level functionality, which for simple apps can encompass an application's core business logic. Unit tests can test validations, associations (which we'll cover in Chapter 7), and generic methods that are attached to models.
- *Functional tests*-also called controller tests-cover controller-level functionality and the accompanying views. A functional test can be quite specific; ensuring, for example, that a certain HTML element is present in a view, that a variable is populated properly, or that the proper redirection takes place after a form has been submitted. Functional testing of controllers has fallen out of favor and given way to integration testing.
- *Integration tests* go beyond the relatively isolated approaches of functional and unit testing. An integration test allows you to test complete stages of user interaction with your application. The registration of a new user, and the story submission process as a whole, are good candidates for integration testing.

We'll look at functional and unit testing in this chapter and cover integration testing in Chapter 11.

Generally speaking, test cases in Rails exist as classes that descend from `ActiveSupport::TestCase`; however, when we generated our models and controllers in Chapter 5, the `generate` command created some skeleton files for us. These are located in the `test` folder, which is where all the files that make up our testing suite reside.

> ### EXTRA CREDIT: Minitest versus RSpec
>
> While our test cases do inherit from `ActiveSupport::TestCase`, they are really subclasses of `Minitest::Test`. Minitest is the default testing framework for Rails, but many people use other frameworks, such as RSpec. Your extra credit? Do a bit of searching around the web on Minitest and RSpec.

Testing the Model

While our `Story` model is still yet to have a great deal of functionality, it does have some validations, and we should definitely make sure that they operate as expected. We'll add them to the skeleton test file, then run the test to confirm that our validations are behaving themselves!

Analyzing the Skeleton File

The skeleton test file for our `Story` model is located at `test/models/story_test.rb`. Upon opening it, you should see the following code:

```
require 'test_helper'

class StoryTest < ActiveSupport::TestCase
  # test "the truth" do
  #   assert true
  # end
end
```

That first line aside, what we have here is a basic class definition by the name of `StoryTest`. The name of this class, which was created when the file was generated, suggests that its purpose is for testing our `Story` model—and so it is.

The `require` command at the top of the file is a simple example of one file gaining access to the functionality of another file; the external file in such arrangements is known as an **include file**. By including this file, we gain access to a large amount of testing-related functionality.

Of course, Rails includes other files all the time, but we don't see dozens of `require` commands littered throughout our code. Why not? The Rails conventions allow it to autoload many files by deducing what is needed, when it's needed, and where it can be found. This is another reason why following Rails conventions is so important.

Using Assertions

Code is tested in Rails using assertions. **Assertions** are tiny functions that confirm that an item is in a certain state. A simple assertion may just compare two values to check that they're identical. A more complex assertion may match a value against a regular expression, or scan an HTML template for the presence of a certain HTML element. We'll look at various types of assertions in this section.

Once written, assertions are grouped into tests (of assertions). A test is an instance method that is prefixed with `test_`. An example of a test is the `test_truth` method in the previous code listing. These tests are executed one by one via the `rails test` command. If one of the assertions in a test fails, the test is immediately aborted and the test suite moves on to the next test.

Now that we know what assertions are and how they work, let's write one!

Writing a Unit Test

The `test "the truth"` test in our unit test file is just a stub that was created by the `generate` command. Let's replace it with a real test:

6-19. test/models/story_test.rb *(excerpt)*

```ruby
test "is not valid without a name" do
  s = Story.create(
    name: nil,
    link: 'http://www.testsubmission.com/'
  )
  assert s.errors[:name].any?
  refute s.valid?
end
```

💡 A Choice of Syntaxes for Testing

It's worth noting that you can write Minitest tests using a couple of different syntaxes. The first one uses the **test** method and a block that runs your tests and assertions. This is the syntax I prefer and am using. The other syntax involves using a method with a **test_** prefixed name, such as **test_is_not_valid_without_a_name**. So, the second syntax for the aforementioned test is:

```
def test_is_not_valid_without_a_name
  s = Story.create(
    name: nil,
    link: 'http://www.testsubmission.com/'
  )
  assert s.errors[:name].any?
  refute s.valid?
end
```

Pick whichever you like, or use both. The test world is your oyster.

The **test** method allows us to use a descriptive string to specify what we are testing here. As you may have guessed, this method will test the validation of the name. Let's examine each line within the method:

```
s = Story.create(
  name: nil,
  link: 'http://www.testsubmission.com/'
)
```

This line creates a new **Story** object—a task that we might perform in a regular controller action. Note, however, that this time we've purposely left the required **name** attribute blank (**nil**). As the **create** method will attempt to save the new object immediately, the validations that we defined in the model will be checked at the same time. At this point, we can check the result of the validation by reading the **errors** attribute of our newly created object.

```
assert s.errors[:name].any?
```

Every model object in Rails has an `errors` attribute, which acts like a Hash. This attribute contains the results of any validations that have been applied to it. If the validation failed, the `errors` attribute will have a key for that attribute. In this case, we deliberately left the `name` attribute empty; passing the symbol `:name` to `errors[]` to test for `any?` error entries on the `name` attribute should therefore return `true`, and our assert statement confirms it.

```
refute s.valid?
```

Simply put, `refute` is the opposite of `assert`. Calling `valid?` on a model will run the validations and return `true` if they all pass or `false` if they don't.

Errors and ActiveModel Errors

I said that the `errors` attribute *acts like a hash*, which implies that it's **not** a hash. That's because it isn't. It's an `ActiveModel::Errors`. Feel free to do some more research on what that is.

The `name` attribute is not the only required attribute for our `Story` model, though—the `link` attribute must be assigned a value before a story can be saved. We've already added one test, so adding a second should be straightforward. Let's add a test that covers the validation of the `link` attribute:

6-20. test/models/story_test.rb *(excerpt)*

```
test "is not valid without a link" do
  s = Story.create(name: 'My test submission', link: nil)
  assert s.errors[:link].any?
  refute s.valid?
end
```

Easy, huh?

Lastly, to complete our first batch of tests, we'll add a test that checks whether a new `Story` object can be successfully created and saved when being instantiated with all the required attributes, thereby passing all of our validations:

6-21. test/models/story_test.rb *(excerpt)*

```
test "is valid with required attributes" do
  s = Story.create(
    name: 'My test submission',
    link: 'http://www.testsubmission.com/')
  assert s.valid?
end
```

In this test, a new `Story` object is created, and all mandatory attributes are assigned a value. The assertion then confirms that the created object has indeed passed all validations by calling its `valid?` method.

Running Model Tests

With the testing code in place, let's run our small unit test suite. From the applications root folder, execute the following command:

```
$ rails test:models
```

Ensure the Test Database is Set Up

If you get an error that says "Migrations are pending", be sure to set up your test database by running

```
rails db:migrate RAILS_ENV=test
```

before running the tests.

This command will execute all the test cases located in the `test/models` folder one by one, and alert us to any assertions that fail. The output of a successful test execution should look a little like:

```
$ rails test:models
Run options: --seed 5658

# Running:

...

 Finished in 0.026414s, 113.5773 runs/s, 189.2955
↳ assertions/s.

3 runs, 5 assertions, 0 failures, 0 errors, 0 skips
```

As you can see, `rails` gives us a nice summary of our test execution. The results suggest that a total of three test cases and five assertions were executed, which is exactly what our test suite contains at the moment.

You'll notice some dots between the "Running" and the "Finished" lines of the test suite output: one dot for each test passed. Whenever an assertion fails, an uppercase F will be displayed, and if one of your tests contains an error, an uppercase E will be displayed, followed by details of the error that occurred.

Instead of boldly assuming that our tests work correctly, let's change one so that we *know* it's going to fail. In our `test "is required with valid attributes"` test, modify the last line so that its output is reversed:

```
assert !s.valid?
```

Save the file and run the unit testing suite again:

```
$ rails test:models
Run options: --seed 53603

# Running:

F..
```

```
Finished in 0.022360s, 134.1698 runs/s, 223.6163
↳ assertions/s.

  1) Failure:
StoryTest#test_is_valid_with_required_attributes
↳ [/Users/ggoodrich/projects/sitepoint/readit/test/models/
story_test.rb:23]:
Failed assertion, no message given.

3 runs, 5 assertions, 1 failures, 0 errors, 0 skips
```

The output now displays an F, indicating a test failure, along with a description of the assertions that may have caused the test to fail.

Armed with this information, locating and fixing an error unit test is easy. We're provided with the name of the test that failed (test_is_valid_with_required_attributes), the test case to which it belongs (StoryTest), and the line on which it failed (line 23). Thus, the (admittedly forged) culprit is easily located and fixed.

For now, undo the change you made to the last line of test "is required with valid attributes", so that the test will again pass:

```
assert s.valid?
```

That's it—we've tested the model. We'll add more tests in later chapters as we add more functionality to the model.

Testing the Controller

The testing of controllers is, at first glance, fairly similar to testing models—it's just a different part of the MVC stack; however, there *is* some extra housekeeping involved in setting up the environment properly.

Analyzing the Skeleton File

Once again, a skeleton integration test was created as a result of our generating the `StoriesController`. This skeleton file resides in `test/controllers/stories_controller_test.rb`:

```
require 'test_helper'

class StoriesControllerTest <
↳ ActionDispatch::IntegrationTest
  test "should get index" do
    get stories_index_url
    assert_response :success
  end
end
```

On first inspection, this *looks* similar to the `StoryTest` class from the previous section. Here, however, the example test is being useful: it's actually running the action and ensuring that it returns a `:success`.

Writing a Controller Test

Let's modify that first test for our `StoriesController` by adding the following code:

```
test "should get index" do
  get stories_url
  assert_response :success
end
```

We'll now look at each line in this test:

```
test "should get index" do
```

As you may have deduced from the name of the test, we're checking that the `index` action is correctly displayed in the user's browser when the `/index` path is requested.

The next line simulates a user requesting the index action of the `StoriesController` class:

```
get stories_url
```

It uses the HTTP request method `GET`; similarly, the methods `post`, `put`, `patch`, and `delete` exist for testing actions requiring that respective HTTP verb. Also, we use Rails route helpers (`stories_url`) to grab the correct URL when running the test.

The `assert_response` assertion checks that the HTTP response code we receive is the code we expect:[3]

```
assert_response :success
```

 HTTP Code Aliases

As HTTP codes are numeric, they're sometimes hard to remember. As a result, Rails has implemented a few aliases for the more common codes. In this example we've used the `:success` symbol, which maps internally to the **200 OK** response code that's returned when a page request is successful. Other mappings that can be used with the `assert_response` function include `:redirect` for HTTP redirect headers and `:missing` for the all-too-common **404 Not Found** error when there's a request for a file that doesn't exist. Oh, and a site where they are correlated to cats[4].

We also need fixtures for this test. Fixtures in controller tests are dummy model objects that provide a consistent data set against which our tests can run. Fixtures

---

[3.] A complete list of HTTP response codes can be found at http://en.wikipedia.org/wiki/List_of_HTTP_status_codes
[4.] https://http.cat/

are model based, so there's a fixture file for every model class in our application. By default, Rails makes all YAML files stored in `test/fixtures/` available to our tests, so there's no requirement to specify explicitly which fixtures we want to load for each test.

Running a Controller Test

Now that we've created our test case, we can invoke the controller test suite. Once again, we turn to the trusty `rails` tool to execute controller tests:

```
$ rails test:controllers
```

Here's the output that results from the successful execution of our test suite:

```
$ rails test:controllers
Run options: --seed 30514

# Running:

.

Finished in 0.254726s, 3.9258 runs/s, 11.7774 assertions/s.
1 runs, 3 assertions, 0 failures, 0 errors, 0 skips
```

Writing More Controller Tests

There are two actions for which we are yet to write a test: the `new` and `create` actions. We should create a few different tests for these actions. Let's do that now.

For the purpose of testing the inner workings of our new action in GET mode, we'll use a test case that we'll name `test "should get new"`. Add the following method below the index test that we created previously:

```
test "should get new" do
  get :new
  assert_response :success
```

```
  assert_template 'new'
  assert_not_nil assigns(:story)
end
```

Apart from a few textual differences, this test is almost identical to what we did for test "should get index"; however, our work isn't done yet!

There's a form element in the new template, so we should certainly test that it appears correctly. Here's another test to do just that:

6-22. test/controllers/stories_controler_test.rb *(excerpt)*

```
test "new shows new form" do
  get new_story_path
  assert_select 'form div', count: 2
end
```

This test starts with another get request, but this time to the new_story_path. This merits a brief sidenote on the Rails route helpers.

The route helpers come in two flavors: _url and _path. The former (_url) is an *absolute path*, meaning it includes the protocol (like http://) and the domain (like example.com). The _path helpers are *relative*, meaning, it includes just the *path*, which is the bit **after** the domain, like /stories/new. I prefer the _path helpers for these tests, but it's only a preference.

The assert_select helper assertion used here is a very flexible and powerful tool for verifying that a certain HTML element is present in a document returned from a request. assert_select can even verify the hierarchy of the HTML element, regardless of how deeply it's nested. It can also test the element's attributes: for example, the value of its class or id. In fact, it's so flexible that we could potentially devote an entire chapter to its features alone.

But now we're getting sidetracked. Back to this line! assert_select checks for the existence of one form element in which two div elements are nested; the count is supplied using the :count argument. These three paragraphs contain the fields that comprise our story submission form.

How do we specify an element in this hierarchy? Easy: by following the simple rules of CSS selectors.

In this example, we want to reference a div element that resides within a form element. Now, if we were writing a CSS rule to style these elements in bold, it would look like this:

```css
form div {
  font-weight: bold;
}
```

In the same way that we reference paragraphs in CSS, the parameter that we use with `assert_select` assertion is simply `'form div'`. We'll look at a few more of the CSS selector features of `assert_select` in the tests we write in later chapters.

Lastly, to test the posting of a new story, we'll write a few more short tests for the `create` action:

6-23. test/controllers/stories_controler_test.rb *(excerpt)*

```ruby
test "adds a story" do
  assert_difference "Story.count" do
    post stories_path, params: {
      story: {
        name: 'test story',
        link: 'http://www.test.com/'
      }
    }
  end
  assert_redirected_to stories_path
  assert_not_nil flash[:notice]
end
```

Let's break this test down line by line.

The test uses the `assert_difference` before-and-after check to confirm that this action, which is supposed to modify data, is indeed doing its job. The first line sets up the count we want to check for the test block:

```
assert_difference "Story.count" do
```

assert_difference will confirm that the story we submitted was created successfully, by counting the number of stories before and after the code in the block is run, and subtracting the difference. It defaults to checking for a difference of 1.

As I mentioned earlier in the chapter, post is another way to invoke an HTTP request programmatically from a test:

```
post stories_path, params: {
  story: {
    name: 'test story',
    link: 'http://www.test.com/'
  }
}
```

post takes a few parameters—in this case, we're simulating the submission of a story. To do this, we pass a hash of params that contains values for the required attributes of a story: symbols representing the name and link attributes.

When a story submission has been successful, our application issues a redirection. We can test that this redirection occurs using assert_redirected_to:

```
assert_redirected_to stories_path
```

Lastly, we assert that the contents of the notice flash area is not nil:

```
assert_not_nil flash[:notice]
```

Whew! Our rapidly expanding test suite is evolving to the point where we can be confident the story submission process is functioning correctly.

The final test case we'll add covers the scenario in which posting a new story fails. We'll cause the submission to fail by omitting one of the required fields:

6-24. test/controllers/stories_controler_test.rb (excerpt)

```ruby
test "rejects when missing story attribute" do
  assert_no_difference "Story.count" do
    post stories_path, params: {
      story: { name: 'story without a link' }
        }
  end
end
```

In the first line of this code, we attempt to post a story without a link:

```ruby
post stories_path, params: {
  story: { name: 'story without a link' }
}
```

That's it! We've written all the tests we need for the time being. Now, let's run the suite.

Running the Complete Test Suite

Now that we have these additional tests in place, we have to run all our tests again. This time, we'll use a slightly different approach: instead of invoking our model and controller tests separately, we'll use a `rails` task to run these test suites in succession:

```
$ rails test
```

The output of a successful test run should look like:

```
$ rails test
Run options: --seed 26531
```

```
# Running:

........

Finished in 0.310305s, 25.7811 runs/s, 54.7848 assertions/s.

7 runs, 13 assertions, 0 failures, 0 errors, 0 skips
```

Congratulations! Not only have you created a full test suite, but you've found upon running it that your application is error-free—a discovery that should earn even the most seasoned developer a self-pat on the back. To finish up, let's turn our thoughts to the application's performance as we inspect the log files generated by `ActionPack`.

Visiting the Logs

We talked briefly about logs when we looked at the structure of a Rails application. You'll be glad to learn that `ActionPack` is a prolific logger, with a full record of user activities within the application, complete with SQL statements, page redirections, page requests, templates rendered, time taken, and more.

The level of detail in Rails' log files is of real benefit when you're hunting down a problem with your code—the logs provide insight into what's actually happening as a page is requested. The same level of detail is captured for unit and controller tests in the test log file, which is located in `log/test.log`.

The timing values that are written to the log file are particularly interesting. Consider the following snippet:

```
(0.2ms)  begin transaction
 SQL (0.6ms)  INSERT INTO "stories" ("name", "link",
↪ "created_at", "updated_at") VALUES (?, ?, ?, ?)  [["name",
↪ "Goodrichs.NET"], ["link", "http://goodrichs.net"],
↪ ["created_at", "2016-03-20 16:54:50.285226"], ["updated_at",
↪ "2016-03-20 16:54:50.285226"]]
```

```
 (0.6ms)  commit transaction
Redirected to http://example.com/stories
```

From this log entry, we can conclude that:

- 0.6ms (milliseconds) were burned by Rails talking to the database
- the whole exercise took 1ms

While this information might seem useless (after all, it only took *1 millisecond*), there will definitely come a time when performance is hurting and you need help in figuring out why. Starting with the logs is recommended.

We'll skip digging any deeper into the logs here, but be aware that it's worth keeping an eye on your log files. Incidentally, this is the same information that has been flying past in the terminal window you launched your web server from, too. This is another way that you can check your application's log entries in real time, although you'll probably find using a text editor more practical.

We'll revisit the log files once more when we reach <u>Chapter 11</u>.

Summary

We certainly increased the functionality of our application in this chapter; we even made it look a little prettier. We used the Rails form helpers to create a fully functional web interface for submitting stories in a RESTful way, and we added a global layout to our application, complete with stylesheets.

Along the way, we looked briefly at the flash, Rails's short-term memory container that can be used to pass messages between successive actions. Some of the many ways that Rails' conventions protect our site were explored, including strong parameters and CSRF protection. We also added some validations to our Story model, to ensure that our story submissions adhere to our own high standards—or that, at the very least, each story has a title and a URL!

Finally, we wrote our first unit and controller test cases, which we used to automate the testing of our models, controllers, and views. We also took a scroll through the Rails log files to see what kind of logging the `ActionPack` module performs, and how those log entries are useful when we debug our application.

In the next chapter, we'll add the much anticipated voting feature to our story-sharing application—and we'll do it using cutting-edge XHR (XMLHttpRequest) technology, spiced up with some visual effects. Yes, it's going to be one good-looking chapter! On with the show!

Chapter

Ajax and Turbolinks

The success of a social bookmarking or content-sharing application doesn't rest solely on the submission of users' stories; there must also be a way for site visitors to know the *value* of each content item.

Now, in the world of social bookmarking, popular opinion rules. That's why the value of each story on our Readit site will be gauged by its popularity–indicated by votes the story receives from Readit users.

In this chapter, we'll expand the feature set of our story-sharing application to include this crucial voting functionality. And, as you might expect, Rails comes with some client-side technology to make this a good user experience. We'll also cover what's known as "Turbolinks," as well as the JavaScript library that comes with Rails–jQuery–in the coming pages.

Generating a Vote Model

At the core of our app's voting functionality lies a data model—a Vote—which we'll now create. Once that's in place, we'll make the necessary changes to our database schema. We learned how to do this using migrations in Chapter 6, so there's no reason to return to the old ways now!

Creating the Model

Using the `rails generate` command (you should be reasonably at home with this by now), let's add a new model to our application:

```
$ rails generate model Vote story_id:integer
Running via Spring preloader in process 65396
   invoke  active_record
   create    db/migrate/20160403175119_create_votes.rb
   create    app/models/vote.rb
   invoke    test_unit
   create      test/models/vote_test.rb
   create      test/fixtures/votes.yml
```

Just like the last time we generated a new model, we gave the `generate` command some insight into the attributes the new model will have, which we'll explore in a moment. As you might expect, this command generates, among others, a new migration file: `db/migrate/20160403175119_create_votes.rb` (remember, your file will have a slightly different name). Let's look at it right now.

Examining the Vote Migration

The migration file that was generated for us contains the basic code to create a `votes` table in our database. Currently, the `change` method should look like this:

```
                                            7-1. db/vote/migrate/xxx_create_votes.rb

class CreateVotes < ActiveRecord::Migration[5.0]
  def change
    create_table :votes do |t|
      t.integer :story_id

      t.timestamps
    end
  end
end
```

As you can see, we're following the format we used in Chapter 5 to create the schema, but this time the column types are different. Let's look at them briefly:

```
    t.integer :story_id
```

This line creates a `story_id` column of type `integer`. It will be used to store the numerical ID of a story that has received a vote from a user. The column will be populated using associations, which we'll talk about in the next section.

Rails has a handful of *magical* column names; two of the most handy are `created_at` and `updated_at`, each of type `datetime`. Since they're so useful, Rails has a shortcut for creating those two columns in a migration. It even includes that shortcut by default every time we create a new migration:

```
    t.timestamps
```

Whenever a new model is saved to the database using the `save` method, Rails will automatically populate the column called `created_at` with the current date and time.

Its companion, `updated_at`, operates in a similar manner. It automatically populates the column with the current date and time of any successive call to the save method, although we won't be using this column for the Vote model. (A vote, once cast, is a vote, right?)

As with the last migration we created, the change method is also able to reverse this migration by simply getting rid of the whole table.

Applying the Migration

Our migration is in place, so let's apply it using the rails tool once more:

```
$ rails db:migrate
Running via Spring preloader in process 67380
  == 20160403175119 CreateVotes: migrating
↳ ======================================
-- create_table(:votes)
-> 0.0013s
  == 20160403175119 CreateVotes: migrated (0.0015s)
↳ ==============================
```

Excellent! Now, I suggest you sit down before we begin the next topic, because matters could get a little heavy. It's time for you and me to have an in-depth talk about relationships.

Introducing Relationships

Contrary to received wisdom, relationships don't have to be hard work.

I'm not talking about human relationships—I'm referring to the relationships (also commonly referred to as associations) between objects in our model. We touched on some of this back in Chapter 4 when we discussed the features of ActiveRecord. Now we have a practical use for all that theory.

The Vote model that we created needs to be associated with our Story model. After all, what good is a vote if it's unclear which story it's for?

As we saw in Chapter 4, Rails can cater to a variety of associations between models. One of the more popular associations is the one-to-many relationship, which we'll add to our model now.

Introducing the has_many Clause

A **one-to-many relationship** exists when a single record of type A is associated with many records of type B.

In our application, a single story is likely to be associated with many votes. This relationship is shown in Figure 7-2.

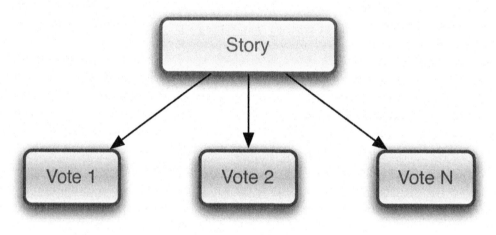

7-2. Illustrating a one-to-many relationship

Relationships are usually declared *bidirectionally*, so that the relationship can be utilized from both sides. Let's begin by examining the Story model's relationship to a Vote; we'll look at the reverse relationship later in the chapter.

To define the first aspect of the relationship, edit the Story class (located in app/models/story.rb) by adding the line in bold:

7-3. app/models/story.rb *(excerpt)*

```ruby
class Story < ApplicationRecord
  validates :name, :link, presence: true
  has_many :votes
end
```

The addition of this one line has ignited a flurry of activity behind the scenes—fire up a Rails console, and I'll show you what I mean. First, retrieve an existing Story record from the database:

```
$ rails console
>> s = Story.first
=> #<Story id: 2, name: "SitePoint Forums", …>
```

Next, invoke this object's newly acquired votes method:

```
>> s.votes
  => #<ActiveRecord::Associations::CollectionProxy
↪ []>
```

The name of this method is derived directly from the has_many :votes relationship that we defined in our class definition (we'll discuss declaring associations in Chapter 9). Invoking the method grabs all votes for the Story and returns them in a CollectionProxy.

> **Collection Proxy Helps Efficiency**
>
> If you remember from Chapter 5, ActiveRecord does all it can to not execute SQL before it's needed. The `CollectionProxy` exists for much of the same reason. Rather than querying the database to see if our story has any votes, ActiveRecord returns a proxy object. A **proxy** is like a middleman between the story and its votes, waiting to see what we want to do with the votes. Do we want an array of all the votes? Then call `s.votes.to_a`. Do we want to know how many votes have been cast? Call `s.votes.count`. These two options require sending different SQL to the database, and the proxy ensures that the most efficient SQL query is used.

So, how do we go about adding votes to this story? The easiest way is to call the `create` method of the object returned by `story.votes`, like so:

```
>> s.votes.create
=> #<Vote id: 1, story_id: 2, …>
```

This approach instantiates a new `Vote` object, and saves the object to the database immediately. It works because we have yet to specify any validations for the `Vote` model, so there's nothing to prevent empty fields from being saved; however, if you assume that the record we just saved to the database is completely empty, you'd be completely off the mark.

Let's look at the number of votes that have been created. Call the `size` method for our `Story`'s associated votes:

```
>> s.votes.size
=> 1
```

This is another method to which we gained access by defining the `has_many` relationship and our good friend, the `CollectionProxy`. It instructs Rails to calculate the number of records associated with the current model object. A result of 1 indicates that the `Vote` object we just created does indeed contain some information, since one `Vote` is associated with the `Story` we retrieved.

To find out more, let's retrieve the same `Vote` object independently from the `Story` with which it's been associated and inspect its attributes:

```
>> v = Vote.first
=> #<Vote id: 1, story_id: 2, …>
>> v.attributes
 => {"id"=>1, "story_id"=>2, "created_at"=>Sun,
↪ 03 Apr 2016 18:33:08 UTC +00:00, "updated_at"=>Sun, 03 Apr
↪ 2016 18:33:08 UTC +00:00}
```

As you can see, not only has our `Vote` object automatically been populated with a creation and update date (the two start out being the same value), but a value has been assigned in its `story_id` field. This value was obtained from the `id` attribute of the `Story` object that was used to create the vote. (In this case, the value is equal to 2, as that's the id of the first `Story` in the database.) Figure 7-4 shows this relationship.

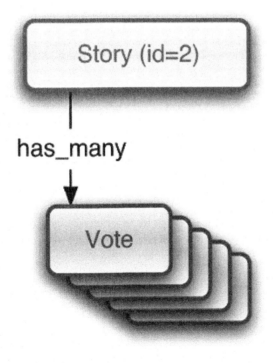

7-4. A one-to-many relationship

To complete our relationship definition, we'll add its counterpart—the `belongs_to` clause—to the Vote model.

Introducing the `belongs_to` Clause

As in life, there are usually two sides to the story when it comes to relationships. We'll now add the second part of our one-to-many relationship. First, edit the Vote model class (in `app/models/vote.rb`) as follows:

```ruby
class Vote < ApplicationRecord
  belongs_to :story
end
```

Now that we've defined the relationship within both models that are affected by it, not only can we access the `votes` of a `Story`, we can also access the `story` of a Vote. And I'm sure you can guess how we accomplish the latter—back to the Rails console!

```
>> v = Vote.first
=> #<Vote id: 1, story_id: 2, …>
>> v.story
=> #<Story id: 2, name: "SitePoint Forums", …>
```

Revise, Reload, Revise, Reload

If you make a change to your models or controllers while you have a running Rails console, you'll be unable to call any of your new code; your console has to reload your models and controllers. Doing this is as simple as issuing the `reload!` console command, where you'll then see the following:

```
>> reload!
Reloading...
=> true
```

You'll also have to recreate any existing instances of your models, because they'll still be using the old class.

By adding just one line to our `Vote` class definition, we've gained access to the associated `Story` object. As the code listing shows, access to this object is possible via a new instance method (`story`) on the model. This method is available as a direct result of the relationship clause that we put in place, and obtains its name from the first parameter of the association call: `belongs_to :story`.

Figure 7-5 shows how this relationship works.

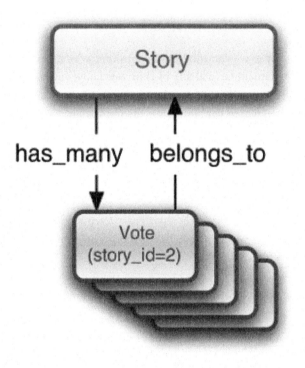

7-5. Depiction of a has many, belongs to relationship

How's our schema looking?

Now that we've established both sides of our one-to-many relationship, let's look at how the information representing this relationship is stored in the database.

If you recall each of the migrations that we've created and applied so far, you'll notice that although the `Vote` model contains a `story_id` column, the `Story` model has no corresponding `vote_id` column.

In fact, this column is unnecessary. There's no need to store association information in both models when defining a one-to-many relationship; the information is always stored on the "many" side of the relationship. With this information in place, Rails is intelligent enough to query the correct table when we instruct it to find objects with an association.

Notice also how the terminology used to define the relationship accurately reflects what's going on: the `Votes` *belong to* the `Story`, hence the `belongs_to` call. And the Vote model represents the "many" side of the relationship, so each Vote stores its own reference to its associated Story.

Now that we understand the data structures that underlie our voting functionality, let's jump into building some user interactivity.

Making a Home for Each Story

In terms of viewing stories that have been submitted to Readit, our users currently only have access to a page displaying a random story. To address this issue, we'll add a new action that displays a single story, along with all of its details, before we implement the voting actions themselves. The story page will serve as a reference point for any given story on the Readit site, as it will contain a range of information—voting actions, voting history, and so on—about the story.

Determining Where a Story Lives

The first step in displaying our stories is to find out what the URLs to access a single Story should look like, and then which action we need to teach StoriesController to handle these requests.

If you flip back to the section about resources in Rails, which we talked about in Chapter 6, and take another look at the table with the mappings of URLs to controller actions, you'll find the promising mention of a show action to handle URLs such as /stories/2. This is the action we'll implement over the next few pages.

Before we implement said show method in StoriesController, let's think for a moment about what it will do. Our controller action has to retrieve a story with a specific ID from the database. This ID is contained in the URL; Rails routing extracts it from there and makes it available to us as params[:id]. The controller then needs to hand the object it finds to the view, which is in turn responsible for displaying it.

We'll start by adding the following method to our StoriesController class. Once again, the order of the method definitions within the class definition is of no importance:

```
                                    7-6. app/controllers/stories_controller.rb (excerpt)
def show
  @story = Story.find(params[:id])
end
```

The single line of code in our show method executes a find by passing the value of params[:id] to it. We're instructing ActiveRecord to retrieve from the database all rows with an ID that's equal to the value in the URL requested by the user; there should only ever be a single row returned.

The result of the find operation is then assigned to the instance variable @story, which is automatically made available by Rails to the corresponding view internally. Speaking of which, let's create that view now.

Displaying Our Stories

We need a template with which to display a story. Create a new template file at app/views/stories/show.html.erb, and fill it with the following simple HTML and ERb code:

```
<h2><%= @story.name %></h2>
  <p><%= link_to @story.link, @story.link
↳ %></p>
```

This displays the name of the Story, wrapped in h2 tags, and adds a link to the URL that's stored as part of the story.

Let's check that this functionality works as expected. Open the following URL in your browser (if you've deleted some of your stories, substitute a higher number at the end to see a story): http://localhost:3000/stories/2.

As you can see below, our story now has its own page that displays its name and a link to the story content.

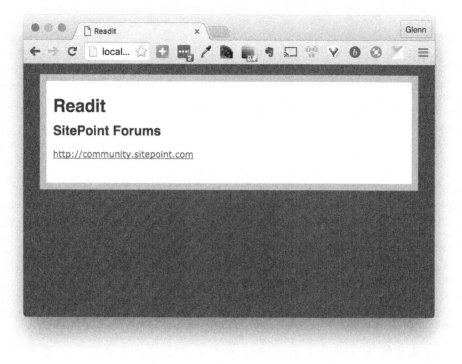

7-7. The Readit story page

 Recap on Making Sure the Server Is Up

As with all of our examples, connecting to your application requires the Rails web server to be running. If you need a refresher on how to launch it, flip back to Starting Our Application in Chapter 2.

Improving the Story Randomizer

While we're at it, let's change our front page so that the random link displayed no longer uses the story's external URL. Instead, we'll direct users to the story's internal page, to which we'll soon add some voting functionality.

Open up the template responsible for the index action of `StoriesController` (located at `app/views/stories/index.html.erb`) and change the `link_to` call so that it reads as follows:

```
<%= link_to @story.name, story_path(@story) %>
```

That a `story_path` function exists for our use is a direct result of the `resources`
`:stories` call in the route configuration—this is another benefit of using Rails
resources and following their conventions, which include using the action `show`
to display a single resource. The `story_path` function accepts a `Story` object
that's used dynamically to generate the URL we're looking for.

Reload the `index` page at `http://localhost:3000/stories`. It should now link to
the internal story page, as demonstrated below.

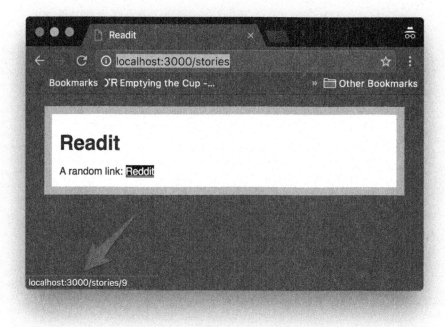

7-8. The index page is now linking to the story page

If you thought that was a simple and straightforward way to generate a link to a
story, it gets even better! The aforementioned `link_to` call can be shortened to
just the following:

7-9. app/views/stories/index.html.erb *(excerpt)*

```erb
<%= link_to @story.name, @story %>
```

Rails's `link_to` helper will automatically invoke the `story_path` helper behind the scenes, all because of that simple one-line declaration that made `Story` into a resource in the first place.

Well, this is already functional, but I think we can still improve in terms of readability within the URLs we're exposing to our users. Let's look at the concept of a clean URL.

Implementing Clean URLs

The URLs we put to use in the last section are simple enough– and definitely simpler than some we're plagued by on our daily travels through some niches of the Internet. But we can do better!

To recap, we've employed the following URL to refer to a single story:

```
/stories/1
```

This is all well and good, but an ID of 1 is hardly meaningful to our users; they're more likely to remember the title of a story. Even if the title was slightly modified–with special characters removed, escaped, or replaced–it would still make for a more usable URL, and be much friendlier to our search engine friends as well!

So, to refer to a story titled "My Shiny Weblog," the following URL would be perfect:

```
/stories/my-shiny-weblog
```

The implementation we're about to commence comes close to this ideal. Soon enough, we'll have our stories found at URLs such as this one:

```
/stories/1-my-shiny-weblog
```

As you can see, the URL *still* has the ID of the `Story`, but in addition it contains a simplified version of the story name. To implement this URL, we'll pull a little Ruby trick that's worth exploring in the console first.

Converting from Strings

We've talked about different object classes that are available in Ruby, and more or less any other programming language on the planet. There are ways to convert between them, and there are some conversions that make sense and others that don't. We'll now look at the conversion of a `String` object into an `Integer` object, and a neat side effect of that.

First off, why would you want to convert an object to a different class? Well, everything our web application receives from a user's browser is treated as a string, because the HTTP protocol doesn't specify values with a class. It's better to be safe than sorry, given that `String` is the most universal choice and able to represent *almost* everything.

With that established, it's fairly clear that the value 1 we receive in `params[:id]` from a URL such as `/stories/1` is actually not a number, but a string. The difference is illustrated by the following Rails console output:

```
>> 1.class
=> Fixnum
>> "1".class
=> String
```

But how do we make a number out of a string representation of a number? To convert a string into an integer (that is, whole numbers without a decimal component, such as the number 1), every `String` object ships with a `to_i` method:

```
>> "1".to_i
=> 1
```

The flipside of this is the to_s method provided by the Fixnum class:

```
>> 1.to_s
=> "1"
```

Armed with that knowledge, here's the little trick that will make our permalinks work with minimal effort:

```
>> "1-my-shiny-weblog".to_i
=> 1
```

So how does this work? Strings to_i method simply discards anything after the first numeric content it encounters, leaving us just with the ID of the story nicely extracted. Now we just have to put that simplified title into our story URLs, the topic of the next section.

Investigating Link Generation

When Rails' URL generation helpers need to create URLs that point to specific objects such as Story, they ask the model being passed in how it wants to be represented.

The view template we created for the show action originally included a call to the story_path helper. This is like a shortcut that Rails gives us for declaring Story a resource. I know you've come across this point a number of times now, but it's really important and well worth repeating.

If we weren't to use resources and had to do without story_path, we'd use the following code to achieve the same result:

```
url_for controller: 'stories', action: 'show', id: @story
```

But even that snippet of code carries a bit of Rails magic. If you pass an
ActiveRecord model to url_for, it will automatically call the to_param method
of the model (@story in the previous example). This method, by default, returns
the value of the id attribute.

So the url_for call is actually equivalent to:

```
 url_for controller: 'stories', action: 'show', id:
↪ @story.to_param
```

And it's this to_param method that we can use to our advantage in getting our
simplified title into the URL.

I know you're champing at the bit to make a start with the nifty Ajax stuff, so
quickly throw this method into the Story class definition (stored in app/models/
story.rb):

7-10. app/models/story.rb (excerpt)

```
class Story < ApplicationRecord
  ...
  def to_param
    "#{id}-#{name.gsub(/\W/, '-').downcase}"
  end
end
```

This rather cryptic snippet of code overrides the to_param method defined by the
ActiveRecord::Base class. Now it no longer returns just the ID, but includes a
simplified version of the story's name. It's this new return value that we'll use in
URLs that point to stories.

In the new to_param method, I'm using *regular expressions* to turn non-
alphanumeric characters (anything that's not a number or alphabetical character)

in the story name into a dash, and everything else to lowercase. This string is then appended to the original ID of the story to generate the new, more representative URL. Of course, like a lot of methods in Rails, you're free to play with it in the console as well:

```
>> s = Story.first
=> #<Story id: 2, name: "SitePoint Forums", …>
>> s.name
=> "SitePoint Forums"
>> s.to_param
=> "2-sitepoint-forums"
```

At this point we can let Rails go and do its magic. There's no other tasks required to make our clean URLs work. Give it a try—reload the story index in your browser (`http://localhost:3000/stories`) and marvel at your sparkling clean URLs!

Now we're ready to start implementing the app's voting functionality; however, as we're going to be using Ajax techniques, we'll take another slight detour to learn a bit about Ajax and see how it's implemented in Rails.

Ajax, Pjax, and Turbolinks

We mentioned back in Chapter 1 that Rails is a full-stack framework, encompassing code on the client, the server, and everything in between. Ajax is a technique for communicating between client and server, so the Rails implementation of Ajax is therefore one of the key parts making up this full stack.

Introducing Ajax

Ajax stands for Asynchronous JavaScript and XML, but represents a technique that encompasses more than just these specific technologies. You may have heard of the term, or perhaps you've heard of **Single-page Applications** where there is a single HTML file and all interactions between the browser client and the server are done using asynchronous technology, such as Ajax. Strictly speaking, Ajax is not a new invention—it's actually existed for quite some time.

Ajax enables a web browser to continue to communicate with a web server without having to completely reload the page it's showing—a technique also known as **remote scripting**. This communication may include the exchange of form data, or the request of incorporating additional data into a page that has already been displayed. The end result is that a web application using Ajax has the potential to compete with more traditional desktop applications by providing the user with a more dynamic and responsive experience.

At the heart of Ajax is the `XmlHttpRequest` **object**. `XmlHttpRequest` was originally invented by Microsoft in the late 1990s for Internet Explorer 5 to improve and enhance the user experience of Microsoft's web-based email interface. It has since been implemented in all modern browsers. In 2005, a user-experience designer named Jesse James Garrett invented the term Ajax to describe the approach of using the `XmlHttpRequest` object–along with HTML, CSS, and the Document Object Model (DOM)–to create interactive websites that *feel* like desktop applications. While compatibility with certain web browsers was lacking when the first applications using Ajax hit the Web, this is no longer an issue; all popular web browsers support the `XmlHttpRequest` object, including Internet Explorer, Firefox, Safari, and Chrome.

The term Ajax itself is a bit dated, and there's been other similarly named approaches, such as Pjax. **Pjax** is, in some folk's opinion, an evolution of Ajax: when the user clicks on a navigational link, the browser performs the request in the background and replaces all or part of the HTML content. This avoids reloading other assets, such as JavaScript, CSS, and images files. Additionally, Pjax handles well-known user experience items, such as the browser history, ensuring that going back and forth with browser buttons still works. Before Pjax, the developer handled the history manually: adding URLs to the browser history included some rather clunky solutions involving iframes and third-party libraries. The development of some new APIs in HTML5 (namely, the History API), led to Pjax and easier development. Again, behind the scenes, Pjax is just doing what Ajax already did: asynchronously requesting content from the server and replacing it in the browser, avoiding a full page load. What's different is that Pjax uses some APIs and conventions to help programmers avoid writing boilerplate code to do the same task over and over.

As you know by now, Rails is all about reducing boilerplate code with convention. As such, Rails ships with **Turbolinks**, which (some may say) is an evolution of Pjax. Turbolinks automatically takes all requests to the same domain and asynchronously performs the request, just like Pjax. The browser history is maintained and updated as needed, and any JavaScript or CSS assets are merged. And guess what you, as the Rails developer, have to do in order to use Turbolinks?

Nothing. It just works.

As you define links to parts of the app, such as the link to the current story on the stories page, Turbolinks takes care of A/Pjaxing them up. If you go to `http://localhost:3000/stories` for a random story, then click on the link to that story, Turbolinks will request the page for that story and load it in the background. If you look at the browser, you'll notice the loading/reload icon never changes, meaning a full page load was avoided! Superb!

In fact, the excellent Rails team has enabled a cool little progress bar that loads along the top of the page so that the user knows things are going down, as seen below.

7-11. The progress bar in action

Pretty cool, eh? Now your users won't be left wondering if anything is happening. It's great to have all these built-in tools in our Rails toolbox.

An additional benefit of using Rails' built-in helpers to enable Ajax functionality in your application (compared with writing all the code from scratch) is that they make it easy to provide a fallback option for browsers not supporting Ajax—a concept known as **graceful degradation**. The browsers that fall into this category include older versions of web browsers not supporting Ajax, some browsers on newer platforms such as mobile phones, and browsers for which the user has deliberately disabled JavaScript. Visitors using these browsers will still be able to use your web application. It won't be as dynamic as it is for other users, but at least they won't be faced with an application that fails to work at all—a scenario that's almost guaranteed to drive them away from your site.

Armed with this knowledge, we'll make use of the Rails Ajax helpers to implement functionality that allows users to vote on stories in our Readit application without waiting for page reloads. We'll also provide those users with a nice visual effect to highlight the altered element after their vote actions are successful.

Making Stories

Okay, we've walked through the ins and outs of Ajax/Pjax/Turbolinks. We've discussed some of the capabilities of Turbolinks and explored one of the tools it provides. We're now in a good position to add voting functionality to our application while indicating to users that their votes have been recorded. We'll also provide a fallback option for users whose browsers are without Ajax support.

Controlling Where the Votes Go

Before we can tackle the design details of the vote button, we need to lay down the foundation of where the votes go as soon as they're cast. We need another controller!

Here's the `rails generate` call for generating a new controller (`VotesController`) with a single action (`create`):

```
$ rails g controller Votes create
```

The output of that command is shown:

```
$ rails g controller Votes create
Running via Spring preloader in process 59403
  create  app/controllers/votes_controller.rb
  route   get 'votes/create'
  invoke  erb
  create    app/views/votes
  create    app/views/votes/create.html.erb
  invoke  test_unit
  create    test/controllers/votes_controller_test.rb
  invoke  helper
  create    app/helpers/votes_helper.rb
  invoke    test_unit
  invoke  assets
  invoke    coffee
  create      app/assets/javascripts/votes.coffee
  invoke    scss
  create      app/assets/stylesheets/votes.scss
```

Additionally, being RESTful citizens, we're going to declare a new set of resources in `config/routes.rb`. You might be tempted to declare `Vote` as a stand-alone resource. But what good is a vote without a story? It turns out that Rails has something in store to adapt our use of a one-to-many relationship between a story and its votes to the resource declarations. Change the routing configuration as follows:

7-12. config/routes.rb

```
Rails.application.routes.draw do
  resources :stories do
    resources :votes do
  end
  ⋮ routes…
end
```

Now, what do we have here? At this point, it makes sense to introduce a task that provides a list of all the RESTful routes and their helper names that Rails generates for you, based on the configuration in `config/routes.rb`:

```
$ rails routes
```

Go ahead and run the command for yourself. See if you can spot what the declaration of `has_many: :votes` in the routing configuration achieved in terms of URL helpers. The result of the command run locally on my machine is as follows:

```
→  readit-rails5 git:(chapter7) rake routes
Running via Spring preloader in process 12434
          Prefix Verb   URI Pattern                                 Controller#Action
     story_votes GET    /stories/:story_id/votes(.:format)          votes#index
                 POST   /stories/:story_id/votes(.:format)          votes#create
  new_story_vote GET    /stories/:story_id/votes/new(.:format)      votes#new
 edit_story_vote GET    /stories/:story_id/votes/:id/edit(.:format) votes#edit
      story_vote GET    /stories/:story_id/votes/:id(.:format)      votes#show
                 PATCH  /stories/:story_id/votes/:id(.:format)      votes#update
                 PUT    /stories/:story_id/votes/:id(.:format)      votes#update
                 DELETE /stories/:story_id/votes/:id(.:format)      votes#destroy
         stories GET    /stories(.:format)                          stories#index
                 POST   /stories(.:format)                          stories#create
       new_story GET    /stories/new(.:format)                      stories#new
      edit_story GET    /stories/:id/edit(.:format)                 stories#edit
           story GET    /stories/:id(.:format)                      stories#show
                 PATCH  /stories/:id(.:format)                      stories#update
                 PUT    /stories/:id(.:format)                      stories#update
                 DELETE /stories/:id(.:format)                      stories#destroy
```

7-13. Checking out the routes

You've guessed right if you've pointed at all the routes with a declaration of `votes#<method>` in them. What's interesting to see here is that the URLs look like this:

```
/stories/:story_id/votes
```

What we've created is a so-called **nested route**. A vote object is nested below the story object and cannot be accessed by simply going to a URL like `/votes` or

/votes/1, but must be accessed with a prefix naming the associated story first, such as /stories/1/votes.

Of note is the naming of the URL helpers. Instead of employing the standard votes_path method to refer to the votes index, our nested route has provided us with the story_votes_path method. Similarly, the helper to access a single vote would not be vote_path but story_vote_path. We'd receive an error if we tried to use incorrectly named helpers. In addition, we must specify the parent story of the vote when generating vote URLs. Confused yet? Let's see it in practice!

The Asset Pipeline

First, however, we have to perform a quick side step to discuss how JavaScript and CSS assets are included in our pages.

In a standard HTML page, JavaScript and CSS assets are included via tags and elements in the head of the HTML page. This is Web Development 101 and it's no different for pages in a Rails application. By default, the generated application layout (app/views/layouts/application.html.erb) has helpers for including CSS and JavaScript files. If you open up that layout and look in the head section, you'll see:

7-14. app/views/layouts/application.html.erb *(excerpt)*

```
<%= stylesheet_link_tag    'application', media: 'all',
↳ 'data-turbolinks-track': 'reload' %>
<%= javascript_include_tag 'application',
↳ 'data-turbolinks-track': 'reload' %>
```

These are the two helpers I was talking about. Let's break down the attributes of each helper.

stylesheet_link_tag:

- application tells it to look for an application.css file. By default, Rails will look for CSS files in app/assets/stylesheets and vendor/assets/stylesheets.

- ▨ media: 'all' adds an attribute to the link tag to include this file for all media. This is a CSS setting.
- ▨ 'data-turbolinks-track': 'reload' means that Turbolinks will track this asset and reload it if it changes.

javascript_include_tag:

- ▨ application tells it to look for an application.js file. By default, Rails will look for JavaScript files in app/assets/javascripts and vendor/assets/javascripts.
- ▨ 'data-turbolinks-track': 'reload' indicates that Turbolinks will track this asset and reload it if it changes, just as with the previous tag.

To confirm that the helpers are indeed doing their jobs, take a look at the source of any of the pages that exist in our application. Remember, since we added these files to the application's layout template, this change will be visible on *every* page. In the header of the page source, you should find script tags that closely resemble the following:

```
<link rel="stylesheet" media="all"
↪ href="/assets/scaffolds.self-d2f648f...786.css?body=1"
↪ data-turbolinks-track="reload" />
<link rel="stylesheet" media="all"
↪ href="/assets/stories.self-e3b0c...855.css?body=1"
↪ data-turbolinks-track="reload" />
<link rel="stylesheet" media="all"
↪ href="/assets/votes.self-e3b0c...855.css?body=1"
↪ data-turbolinks-track="reload" />
<link rel="stylesheet" media="all"
↪ href="/assets/application.self-1165b...b34.css?body=1"
↪ data-turbolinks-track="reload" />
<script src="/assets/jquery.self-c64a7...da4.js?body=1"
↪ data-turbolinks-track="reload"></script>
<script
↪ src="/assets/jquery_ujs.self-d602b...b09.js?body=1"
↪ data-turbolinks-track="reload"></script>
<script
↪ src="/assets/turbolinks.self-c377...fff.js?body=1"
↪ data-turbolinks-track="reload"></script>
```

```
<script src="/assets/stories.self-877ae...c05.js?body=1"
↪ data-turbolinks-track="reload"></script>
<script src="/assets/votes.self-877ae...c05.js?body=1"
↪ data-turbolinks-track="reload"></script>
<script
↪ src="/assets/application.self-0c76c...75e.js?body=1"
↪ data-turbolinks-track="reload"></script>
```

Whoa! What the what? So, each helper put out multiple tags with multiple scripts and stylesheets. What's going on? And why does each file look like it was named to win a Scrabble game?

Relax. Take a deep breath. You're just seeing the output of one of Rails' tools: the asset pipeline[1].

Geek Etymology

The asset pipeline comes from a Ruby gem called "sprockets", which is why you'll often hear "asset pipeline" and "sprockets" used interchangeably.

Why do we need an asset pipeline?

The asset pipeline was created to solve a few problems that websites can have with external static assets, such as JavaScript, CSS, and image files. These issues comprise:

- most sites using more than one JavaScript or CSS file, where each one involves a call to the server from the browser
- there being many languages that make CSS and JavaScript more developer-friendly, but requiring a preprocessor, which can be tedious to use
- most JavaScript and CSS files containing comments or whitespace that are unnecessary for the production site
- browsers wanting to cache static assets to save on bandwidth and improve performance, so there needs to be an easy indicator that a static asset is different, or changes will never make it to the browser

---

[1] http://guides.rubyonrails.org/asset_pipeline.htm

These are fairly difficult issues to solve, or used to be. The Rails core team set out to solve them with the asset pipeline, and they have done well. Let's talk about each issue and how it's solved.

Multiple Source Files

Going back to the previously generated HTML, there are six JavaScript files: two from jQuery, one for Turbolinks, and three from our application. How'd they get there?

The asset pipeline uses a file called a **manifest** to let the developer list the files to be included in the application. There is a manifest file for both JavaScript and CSS. The JavaScript manifest file is located in `app/assets/javascripts/application.js` and looks like this:

```
// This is a manifest file that'll be compiled into
↪ application.js, which will include all the files
// listed below.
//
// Any JavaScript/Coffee file within this directory,
↪ lib/assets/javascripts, vendor/assets/javascripts,
// or any plugin's vendor/assets/javascripts directory can
↪ be referenced here using a relative path.
//
// It's not advisable to add code directly here, but if you
↪ do, it'll appear at the bottom of the
// compiled file.
//
// Read Sprockets README
↪ (https://github.com/rails/sprockets#sprockets-directives) for
↪ details
// about supported directives.
//
//= require jquery
//= require jquery_ujs
//= require turbolinks
//= require_tree .
```

The manifest file lists all the JavaScript files we want to use in our application, like so:

```
//= require jquery
```

This requires the jQuery source. **jQuery** is a popular JavaScript framework that ships, by default, with Rails. You can see the jquery_ujs and turbolinks lines, as well. That last line, //= require_tree . tells the asset pipeline to look in the default directories (app/assets/javascripts and vendor/assets/javascripts) and include all the JavaScript (and CoffeeScript) files it finds. The Rails generators we used to create our controllers also automatically create a

CoffeeScript. Finally, the `app/assets/javascripts/application.js` file is created as a part of every Rails application. That accounts for the six files.

I know what you're thinking: what in the wide wide world of programming is CoffeeScript? Don't worry, we'll address that soon. First, though, let's quickly cover the CSS manifest.

The CSS manifest is located in `app/assets/stylesheets/application.css` and looks like:

```
/*
 * This is a manifest file that'll be compiled into
↪ application.css, which will include all the files
 * listed below.
 *
 * Any CSS and SCSS file within this directory,
↪ lib/assets/stylesheets, vendor/assets/stylesheets,
 * or any plugin's vendor/assets/stylesheets directory can be
↪ referenced here using a relative path.
 *
 * You're free to add application-wide styles to this file
↪ and they'll appear at the bottom of the
 * compiled file so the styles you add here take precedence
↪ over styles defined in any styles
 * defined in the other CSS/SCSS files in this directory. It
↪ is generally better to create a new
 * file per style scope.
 *
 *= require_tree .
 *= require_self
 */

body {
  background-color: #666;
  margin: 15px 25px;
  font-family: Helvetica, Arial, sans-serif;
}

p { margin: 0 }
input {
  margin-bottom: 1em;
}

#content {
  background-color: #fff;
  border: 10px solid #ccc;
  padding: 10px 10px 20px 10px;
}
```

```css
#notification {
  border: 5px solid #9c9;
  background-color: #cfc;
  padding: 5px;
  margin: 10px 0;
}

.field_with_errors {
  color: red;
  background: transparent;
}
.field_with_errors input {
  border: thin solid red;
}

.form_errors {
  color: red;
}
```

This file plays the same role for CSS that `application.js` does for JavaScript. The major difference is the comment syntax between JavaScript (`//`) and CSS (`/*...*/`). Going back to the `link` tags created by the `stylesheet_link_tag` helper, there are four files: `scaffolds.css`, `stories.scss`, `votes.scss`, and `application.css`. `scaffolds` and `application` are Rails defaults, whereas the `stories` and `votes` files are SCSS files created by the controller generator. The CSS styles in the manifest are added by Rails.

Now I know what you're asking: what in the wide wide world of programming is SCSS? Let's find out.

Asset Preprocessors

Not everyone knows or likes JavaScript and CSS. Both of these languages can have a steep learning curve and their syntax, to some, leaves much to be desired. As such, pragmatic programmers have created language abstractions for both JavaScript and CSS. The Rails core team has included a couple of these language abstractions in the framework, which we'll discuss now.

CoffeeScript

CoffeeScript[2] is a "little language that compiles into JavaScript." It attempts to make JavaScript easier to write by removing some syntax and adding other language features. Figure 7-17 shows a side-by-side comparison of CoffeeScript (left) to JavaScript (right) from the CoffeeScript website.

```
# Assignment:                          var cubes, list, math, num, number, opposite, race, square,
number   = 42                            slice = [].slice;
opposite = true
                                        number = 42;
# Conditions:
number = -42 if opposite                opposite = true;

# Functions:                            if (opposite) {
square = (x) -> x * x                     number = -42;
                                        }
# Arrays:
list = [1, 2, 3, 4, 5]                  square = function(x) {
                                          return x * x;
# Objects:                              };
math =
  root:   Math.sqrt                     list = [1, 2, 3, 4, 5];
  square: square
  cube:   (x) -> x * square x           math = {
                                          root: Math.sqrt,
# Splats:                                 square: square,
race = (winner, runners...) ->          cube: function(x) {
  print winner, runners                    return x * square(x);
                                          }
# Existence:                            };
alert "I knew it!" if elvis?
                                        race = function() {
# Array comprehensions:                   var runners, winner;
cubes = (math.cube num for num in list)   winner = arguments[0], runners = 2 <= arguments.length ?
                                        slice.call(arguments, 1) : [];
                                          return print(winner, runners);
                                        };

                                        if (typeof elvis !== "undefined" && elvis !== null) {
                                          alert("I knew it!");
                                        }

                                        cubes = (function() {
                                          var i, len, results;
                                          results = [];
                                          for (i = 0, len = list.length; i < len; i++) {
                                            num = list[i];
                                            results.push(math.cube(num));
                                          }
                                          return results;
                                        })();                          run, cubes
```

7-17. CoffeeScript and JavaScript

As you can see, CoffeeScript removes semicolons and the need for keywords such as `var` to declare a variable. It has shortcut syntax for creating a function (`square = (x) -> x * x`) and uses whitespace to delineate blocks. It's less code for the same functionality. We'll be using CoffeeScript in this book, as needed, so you might want to spend some time looking at its syntax.

---

2. http://coffeescript.org

> **CoffeeScript or JavaScript?**
>
> While Rails encourages the use of CoffeeScript, it does not mandate it; you're free to write plain JavaScript for your site as well. The asset pipeline will run any file with the `.coffee` extension through the CoffeeScript preprocessor, and leave `.js` files alone. If you want to know more about CoffeeScript, check out *Jump Start CoffeeScript*[3] by Earle Castledine.

Sass

Sass[4] stands for "Syntactically Awesome Style Sheets" and is an extension to CSS. It allows you to nest CSS selectors, create variables, and create functions in your CSS. For example, if you use a color such as #333 throughout your CSS files, you can define a variable called `$main_color` and use that where you'd use the value. This allows you to change the value of that color in one spot. Here's an example of Sass:

```
$main_color: #333
nav {
  ul {
margin: 0;
padding: 0;
list-style: none;
  }

  li { display: inline-block; }

  a {
display: block;
padding: 6px 12px;
text-decoration: none;
        color: $main_color;
  }
}
```

---

3. https://www.sitepoint.com/premium/books/jump-start-coffeescript
4. http://sass-lang.com/

You can see the nested CSS selectors: instead of `nav ul`, the `ul` tag is nested inside the `nav` brackets. Sass has some excellent time-saving techniques, so it's worth becoming familiar with it. (Did someone say "EXTRA CREDIT"?)

Syntactically Awesome, or Simply Cascading?

As with JavaScript, you can write `.scss` files or `.css` files, of which the former will be run through the Sass preprocessor by the asset pipeline. Sass has a couple of flavors, so be sure to use the `.scss` extension. A great book on Sass I'd recommend is *Jump Start Sass*[5] by Hugo Giraudel and Miriam Suzanne.

Asset Compression and Minification

On the Internet, every ounce of bandwidth is sacred. The performance of your site can be improved greatly by reducing the size of the assets that the browser retrieves. As a result, best practice for any website is to compress and minify the static assets–the JavaScript and CSS. The asset pipeline does that for you in the right environment.

Just so that we understand each other, **minifying** and **compressing** an asset means removing all of its whitespace and combining it with other assets of the same type. All JavaScript files are given a *whitespace-ectomy* and combined into a single file so that the browser receives all the JavaScript for the site with a single request. It's the same for the CSS.

The JavaScript files undergo more complex minification where the code is changed to be as small as possible. For example, the development version of a JavaScript file may have the following line:

```
var orderAmount = 0;
```

When minified, this looks like:

---

[5] https://www.sitepoint.com/premium/books/jump-start-sass

```
var o=0;
```

The asset pipeline will replace all references to orderAmount with o when it compresses the file, so you end up with the smallest file possible. I mentioned that this compression happens in the "right environment," meaning the "production environment." Remember back in Chapter 1 that Rails has a development, test, and production environment? The assets are not compressed in the development environment. A task has to be run for the compression to happen, which we'll discuss when we deploy our app in Chapter 12.

Asset Digests

The last aspect we'll cover on the asset pipeline is asset digests. As I've mentioned, browsers love to cache static assets; this is great, because caching assets that seldom change is a good thing. But, how does the browser know when a cached asset has changed? This can be especially dire if you are using a Content Delivery Network (CDN) for your asset, which expects it to be a long-lasting asset.

Let's look at one of the tags from the generated HTML:

```
<script
 ↪ src="/assets/application.self-0c76c...75e.js?body=1"
 ↪ data-turbolinks-track="reload"></script>
```

In this filename, the .self-0c76c1... is the digest of the asset. A **digest** is a hashed value that is created based on the *contents of the file*. That means that the value of the digest will change when the contents of the file changes. So, the easiest way to invalidate a cached file is to stop using it. By making the name of the file dependent on its content, we always know when the file has changed.

The asset pipeline is an incredibly useful tool that does a lot for the Rails developer. Arguably, an entire book could be written on just the asset pipeline and what it provides. Alas, we have votes to count and must move on ...

Get Out the Vote

The next step is to change our existing show view (located at app/views/stories/show.html.erb) to display the current number of votes that the story has received. Then we'll add a link that allows users to vote on stories. Modify your view so that it looks like this:

```
<h2>
  <span id="vote_score">
    Score: <%= @story.votes.size %>
  </span>
  <%= @story.name %>
</h2>
<p>
  <%= link_to @story.link, @story.link %>
</p>
<div id="vote_form">
 <%= form_tag story_votes_path(@story), remote: true do
 %>
    <%= submit_tag 'Vote for it' %>
  <% end %>
</div>
```

Let's take a look at what's new here:

```
<h2>
  <span id="vote_score">
    Score: <%= @story.votes.size %>
  </span>
  <%= @story.name %>
</h2>
```

The heading that previously displayed just the name of the story now also contains a span tag that holds its vote score. To calculate this number, we use the size method on the votes association that we looked at earlier to add up the number of votes submitted for that story. We've also given the span element a unique ID, which we'll use later as a hook to update the score when a user casts a vote. We'll add some CSS to float this span to the right of the page, too.

We've also added the following:

```
<div id="vote_form">
  <%= form_tag story_votes_path(@story), remote: true do
↳ %>
    <%= submit_tag 'Vote for it' %>
  <% end %>
</div>
```

This is where the magic happens! The extra `div` houses a form created by the `form_tag` helper, complete with a `remote: true` option. This generates the bits of HTML and Javascript that are necessary to invoke the form submission using Ajax, rather than as a regular page-loading form.

What we handed to `form_remote_tag` is a call to one of the nested resource helpers we talked about earlier (the ones that might have made you feel a little dizzy, remember?), specifically to the `story_votes_path` helper. This helper takes `@story` as its argument to specify that we're dealing with votes associated with that given story.

In particular, we'd like to create a new vote for this story, which means we need to send a `POST` request to `/stories/1/votes`. Rails then routes to the create action of `VotesController`.

Styling the Scoreboard

Next, let's expand our CSS (it lives in the file located at `app/assets/stylesheets/stories.scss`) to style and position our new elements:

7-18. app/assets/stylesheets/stories.scss *(excerpt)*

```scss
$vote_color: #393;

#vote_score {
  float: right;
  color: #9c9;
}

#vote_form {
  margin: 10px 0;
}

#vote_form input {
  padding: 3px 5px;
  border: 3px solid $vote_color;
  background-color: #cfc;
  text-decoration: none;
  color: $vote_color;
}

#vote_form input:hover {
  background-color: #aea;
}
```

There's nothing too mysterious happening here—it's all cosmetic. But who said cosmetics weren't important?

If you access one of your stories through your browser (using the link to a random story on `http://localhost:3000/stories`, for example), you should see a page similar to the one in Figure 7-19; however, clicking the *Vote for it* link will do very little right now (except that your application may spit out some weird warnings and error messages).

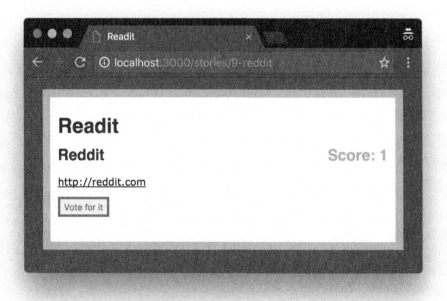

7-19. The story page

To store the votes that have been submitted, we'll implement the `create` method of our `VotesController` that we generated earlier in the chapter. Here it is:

7-20. app/controllers/votes_controller.rb *(excerpt, incomplete)*

```ruby
class VotesController < ApplicationController
  def create
    @story = Story.find(params[:story_id])
    @story.votes.create
  end
end
```

This new method contains nothing we haven't seen before. In the first line, we find the appropriate story record using the unique ID of `Story` for which a vote has been cast. This ID is given to us by Rails in the form of `params[:story_id]`, since `params[:id]` is in this case reserved for a potential ID of a `Vote` object. You can also see this pattern displayed in the routes list we looked at earlier (the route syntax looked like: `/stories/:story_id/votes`).

The second line creates and saves a new `Vote`. It only contains auto-generated values, such as the creation date and the IDs that receive a value because of the `Votes` association with a `Story`.

If you were to try clicking the **Vote for it** link on your story page now, it would store your vote. But nothing on the page would change yet—we can only perform so much magic at once, even in Rails land.

To update the voting score that's displayed on the page and highlight it with a visual effect, we'll use a different (prepare yourself for another new term) **response format**.

Response Formats

One of the tenets of REST is the ability to request a resource in multiple formats. By default, requests that are made for dynamic content (and are not static assets) are expected to be in HTML format. When you visit `http://localhost:3000/stories`, the format is presumed to be HTML. This is driven by the `Accept` header on a request, which has the value of `text/html` for that request; however, when we involve technologies such as Ajax, we want a different format. In this case, when we cast a vote using the `form_tag, remote: true`, we are using Ajax to submit the form via JavaScript, so it'd be great if we could get a JavaScript response. For the vote request, the `Accept` header has a value of `application/javascript` or `text/javascript`, which tells Rails to respond using JavaScript. But what does that mean?

Since the `VotesController` is receiving the request and needs to formulate a response from the `create` method, we can use a method on `ActionController::Base` (`VotesController`'s grandparent) called `respond_to` and tell it to handle HTML *and* JavaScript. Modify the `VotesController#create` method to look like:

```
                                      7-21. app/controllers/votes_controller.rb

class VotesController < ApplicationController
  def create
    @story = Story.find(params[:story_id])
    @story.votes.create
    respond_to do |format|
 format.html { redirect_to @story, notice: 'Vote was
↳ successfully created.' }
      format.js {}
    end
  end
end
```

You can see that I've added a `respond_to` method call and passed in a block with a `format` argument. We can tell `format` which formats we are interested in by calling the appropriate method and passing in a block to handle it:

- `html` is handled by redirecting to the Story (`story_path(vote.story)`) and putting a message in the flash. The `redirect_to` function will be familiar to you from <u>Chapter 6</u>. It also uses the same shorthand syntax we've used for `link_to` earlier in this chapter.
- `js` is handled by ... doing nothing. Just render the view for this format which, by convention, is `app/views/votes/create.js.erb`.

Just like an `html.erb` file has HTML to render, a `js.erb` file has JavaScript to execute. Let's look at `create.js.erb`:

```
                                      7-22. app/views/stories/create.js.erb

$("#vote_score").html("Score: " + <%= @story.votes.size
↳ %>)
$("#vote_score").css({backgroundColor: "#ffffcc"});

setTimeout(function(){
  $("#vote_score").css({backgroundColor: "#ffffff"});
}, 2000);
```

As I've said, this view is all JavaScript, specifically jQuery. The view grabs the `#vote_score` element, changes its content, then highlights it for two seconds. We won't win any awards for it, but this shows how easy it is to call JavaScript and manipulate the page based on the results of an action.

Furthermore, our `respond_to` block will handle HTML, so this approach degrades gracefully—so if their browser isn't using JavaScript, they can still vote! Isn't it amazing how much you can do with as little code as this?

 Shorthand Awesomeness

Speaking of shorthand syntax, I have an even shorter version of our gracefully degraded form. This is just in case you were wondering why you suddenly needed to type in all these characters to have such a, well, simple thing as a form that simultaneously caters to both traditional and Ajax-enabled browsers, submits to a nested route, and looks pretty. Turns out you *don't*!

```
<div id="vote_form">
  <%= form_for [ @story, Vote.new ], remote: true do |f|
  ↳ %>
     <%= f.submit 'Vote for it' %>
  <% end %>
</div>
```

Now we're using `form_for`, a slightly more specialized cousin of `form_tag`. If we hand that helper an array containing the parent story and a new `Vote` object, we get exactly the same result as before, only with a little less typing. You've got to love that!

Introducing Partials

I've mentioned before that templates ending in `.html.erb` can be used to display certain pieces of the page independent from the rest of the page. When used in this way, these files are called **partials**. Partials can be helpful for dealing with parts of a page that are constantly being reused (such as a navigation menu), or for retrieving and formatting the items in a collection (such as a list).

In this section, we'll use partials to implement a voting history box for our story page. The history box will show the dates and times at which each vote for a story was submitted.

Adding Voting History

We'll implement the voting history as a list, using the HTML elements for an unordered list (ul). Each vote will be represented as a list item (li) that shows the voting timestamp. The list items themselves will be rendered as partials, so a single template that contains a single list item will be rendered as often as there are votes for a given story.

To begin with, we'll modify the show template located at app/views/stories/show.html.erb to render an unordered list of the votes a story has received. To accomplish this, we'll add to the template code right above the paragraph container that houses the story link, like so:

7-23. app/views/stories/show.html.erb

```erb
<ul id="vote_history">
  <% if @story.votes.empty? %>
    <em>No votes yet!</em>
  <% else %>
    <%= render partial:'votes/vote',
        collection: @story.votes %>
  <% end %>
</ul>
<p>
  <%= link_to @story.link, @story.link %>
</p>
```

In this code, we've started out with a straightforward ul element that has a unique ID, and we've added a condition using an if … else … end construct. This causes the message "No votes yet!" to be displayed whenever a story without any votes is rendered:

```
<% if @story.votes.empty? %>
  : template code…
<% else %>
  : template code…
<% end %>
```

While the `if` construct is familiar to us from Chapter 3, the `votes.empty?` part is new. The `empty?` method brought to us by declaring the association between votes and stories will return `false` if a story has associated votes, and `true` if not.

It's in this call to render that we add the partial to our page:

```
<%= render partial: 'votes/vote',
  collection: @story.votes %>
```

We instruct Rails to render a template for every `Vote` added to a story. The `render partial` syntax can be used to render a partial once or many times (as in this case). It's the addition of the `collection` argument that indicates we'll be rendering the partial multiple times.

The value `votes/vote` of the `:partial` option actually asks Rails to look for a `vote` partial in the `votes/` subdirectory of `app/views/`, since this is the place where we'll store the new partial.

Creating the Partial

Partials, like regular full-page templates, have a `.html.erb` extension and are stored right alongside their full-page cousins in an application's directory structure. A partial is identified by an underscore (_) prefix in its filename. Let's create the new partial at `app/views/votes/_vote.html.erb`, and populate it with the following line of code:

7-24. app/views/votes/_vote.html.erb

```
><li><%= vote.created_at.to_formatted_s(:short)
↳ %></li>
```

That's all there is to it! This line simply wraps the date on which a vote was made—the value of which is stored in the `created_at` attribute—in a pair of `li` tags.

Note that we have access to an object named `vote`. Rails has created this object for us—it does so for every partial—and the object takes the name of the partial (`vote`, in this case). This object is automatically set to the current element of the collection that's being rendered.

The upshot of all this is that a partial doesn't concern itself with determining which `Vote` it's currently processing, or where that `Vote` sits within the larger collection of votes. The partial simply operates on a single `vote` object and lets Rails take care of the rest.

Styling the Voting History

If we printed the date and time exactly as they appear in the database, we'd produce this regimental-looking style:

```
2016-02-01 11:47:55
```

To address this issue, we've made use of Rails' date-formatting helper. This helper, appropriately named `to_formatted_s`, is available as an instance method for objects of the classes `Date` and `Time`. The helper takes a single argument, one of several pre-defined symbols representing the format that should be applied to the output. Some of the formats include `:short` and `:long`; for a `Time` object, these render as `01 Feb 11:47` and `February 01, 2016 11:47` respectively.

Again, to make this a little more pleasing to the eye, we'll add a few CSS rules to our stylesheet to define how our voting history box should look. These rules arrange our voting history nicely, but they also introduce some minor CSS quirks

that relate to floated elements. Thankfully, we can rectify these problems easily
by adding a few more lines to our stylesheet. The additions are marked in bold:[6]

7-25. app/assets/stylesheets/application.css

```
#content {
  background-color: #fff;
  border: 10px solid #ccc;
  padding: 10px;
  overflow: hidden; /* added */
}
* html #content { /* added */
  height: 1%; /* added */
} /* added */
```

7-26. app/assets/stylesheets/stories.scss

```
#vote_history {
  padding: 5px;
  margin: 0;
  list-style: none;
  border: 3px solid #ccc;
  background-color: #eee;
  float: right;
  color: #999;
  font-size: smaller;
}
```

With all this code in place, go ahead and reload a story page in your browser—the
result should look similar to Figure 7-27 (depending on how much fun you had
clicking the vote link earlier).

[6.] The explanation of what's happening here—and why these cryptic CSS rules are
necessary—is well beyond the scope of this book. If you're interested in learning more, this
topic (amongst myriad others) is explained in Rachel Andrew's *The CSS3 Anthology*
(https://www.sitepoint.com/premium/books/the-css3-anthology-4th-edition).

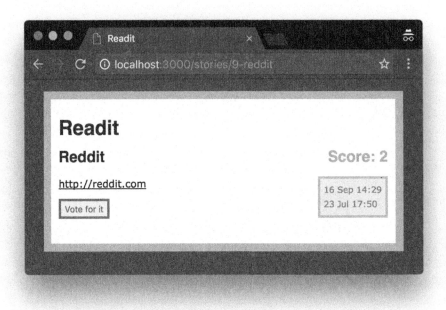

7-27. A history of voting

While the page is looking good, there are a few more details to add: update the list of votes with a new vote, sort the votes by descending ID (so that the newest is displayed at the top), and limit the number of votes that are displayed.

We can achieve the first task easily by adding a single line of code to our JavaScript template, located at `app/views/votes/create.js.ejb`. These additions will deal with the voting actions:

```
7-28. app/views/votes/create.js.ejb

$("#vote_history").html('<%= j(render partial:
↳ "votes/vote",
collection: @story.votes) %>')
```

This is the same approach: use jQuery to grab the `vote_history` list, then replace its content with the output of our partial that includes the new vote. That's right, we reuse the same partial inside our JavaScript. Because our ERb partial emits HTML, we have to escape it so that the JavaScript file can handle it. That's what the j function does. j is an alias for `escape_javascript`, which allows us to handle the output of the partial and append it to the list.

Tweaking the Voting History

Lastly, we'll add an instance method to the association between the `Vote` and the `Story` model to return a limited number of votes sorted by descending ID. Why would we write this as a separate method, and not just retrieve the data from within the view? Well, for a couple of reasons. For one, MVC principles state that we shouldn't be retrieving any data from our view. But as we'll be calling this method from a couple of separate places, moving it to the model makes more sense.

Let's create the method first, then add the references to it. Edit the `Story` class so that it looks like this:

7-29. app/models/story.rb (excerpt)

```
class Story < ApplicationRecord
  validates :name, :link, presence: true
  has_many :votes do
    def latest
      order('id DESC').limit(3)
    end
  end
```

This `latest` method will take advantage of the story's association with the `Vote` model, and will use a scope of the records we want, up to a total of three records (as specified by the `limit(3)` method). The `order('id DESC')` method will ensure that they're ordered so that the newest vote is located at the top.

A Methods of Sorts

In case you're curious, the argument passed to the `order` method is actually a tiny piece of SQL. DESC, quite obviously, stands for descending; there's also ASC for ascending, which is often left off as it's the default for ordering records in Rails.

The rest of the argument constitutes a column name by which the records will be ordered (or multiple column names separated by commas—if you want to order by multiple columns—like so: `order('id, created_at')`).

Having added this new method to the `Story` class, you can go ahead and replace the two occurrences of `@story.votes` that are present in our views with `@story.votes.latest`. The first occurrence is the `render` call in show.html.erb:

```
<%= render partial: 'votes/vote',
  collection: @story.votes.latest %>
```

The second occurrence is the last line of the JavaScript template create.js.erb:

```
$("#vote_history").html('<%= j( render partial:
↪ "votes/vote",
  collection: @story.votes.latest )  %>')
```

Excellent. Reloading the story page should produce the expected results, with the number of votes being limited to three, and the votes ordered by descending ID. Hitting the vote button will update the voting history and place the new vote at the top of the list. Have a look at Figure 7-30 to see how the updated page looks.

7-30. An evolved history of voting

Testing the Voting Functionality

In Chapter 6, we mentioned that our plan is to provide test coverage for all of the functionality in our application. Let's expand our growing test suite by adding some unit and functional tests.

Testing the Model

While most of the work in this chapter has been on the controller side, we still made some changes to the model: modifying our Story model, adding a Vote model, and defining an association between the two. We also added an instance method called latest to retrieve the most recent votes of a given Story. All of these features can be tested programmatically, so let's write some unit tests to cover them.

Before we begin, can you think of something we need to do? Maybe to prepare the test environment? No? We added migrations in this chapter, so we have to be sure to run them against the test database:

```
rails db:migrate RAILS_ENV=test
```

Preparing the Fixtures

Before we write any tests, we'll add some test data to the fixtures for our `Vote` model, which resides in `test/fixtures/votes.yml`. Actually, Rails has already done this for you:

7-31. test/fixtures/votes.yml

```
one:
  story: one

two:
  story: one
```

Check One Two

Make sure that your `votes.yml` fixture file looks like this one. I've seen Rails generate faulty fixture files that break the tests.

We generated the original contents of this file using the `rails generate` command earlier in this chapter, but I've made some small changes. Both `story` attributes point to the first `Story`, named `one`, in the `stories.yml` fixture file, illustrating the point that one `Story` can have multiple `Votes`.

Testing a `Story`'s Relationship to a `Vote`

At this stage, we're ready to add a test that covers the `Story`'s relationship to the `Vote` model. To do this, open the file `test/models/vote_test.rb` and change the `VoteTest` class to read as follows:

```
class VoteTest < ActiveSupport::TestCase
  test "votes have a story" do
    assert_equal stories(:one), votes(:one).story
```

```
    end
end
```

The new `votes have a story` test undertakes the testing of the relationship between the `Story` and the `Vote` model. While the underlying Rails association has very good internal test coverage, it's good practice to test all associations that you create as you test your application's behavior.

The `assert_equal` assertion, as the name implies, confirms that two expressions are absolutely equal. In this case, we're simply comparing the return values of two methods:

```
assert_equal stories(:one), votes(:one).story
```

What's new on this line is the `stories(:one)` and `votes(:one)` syntax, which references our fixture data by name. Making use of a fixture file in a test does more than just load the contents of the file into the database, it also gives us a convenient way to access each record in the fixture file without having to resort to manual retrieval methods (for example, using `Vote.find(1)` to retrieve the first vote). The records we defined in the `votes.yml` fixture file are named `one` and `two`. Simply passing these identifiers as symbols to the votes method returns the corresponding record.

To give an example, take a look at these two calls. They are equal, given the `votes.yml` fixture we created earlier:

```
Vote.find(1)
votes(:one)
```

Incidentally, a method with a name identical to the name of the fixture file (minus the `.yml` extension) is made available for every fixture we include in a test case. As we've created two fixtures so far, we have access to both the `votes` and `stories` methods.

In our assertion line, we compare the Story named one with the Story object that's associated with the Vote named one. We know that this assertion should be true, because we associated both votes in the fixture file with the first story.

Testing the Voting History Order

To test the functionality provided by the latest method we added, we'll add two more tests to the story_test.rb file below the others:

7-32. test/models/story_test.rb (excerpt)

```
test "returns highest vote first" do
  highest_id = stories(:one).votes.map(&:id).max
  assert_equal highest_id, stories(:one).votes.latest.first.id
end

test "return 3 latest votes" do
  10.times { stories(:one).votes.create }
  assert_equal 3, stories(:one).votes.latest.size
end
```

Let's look at these tests line by line.

The returns highest vote first test confirms that the :order part of the latest method is indeed operating correctly. We have to grab the highest vote ID for our story votes first, because we have no control over when or in what order the fixtures are created:

```
  highest_id = stories(:one).votes.map(&:id).max
  assert_equal highest_id, stories(:one).votes.latest.first.id
```

The assertion compares the first element of the array returned by the latest method with the highest vote ID, to which we expect it to be equal.

To test whether the limit part of our latest method does indeed do its job, we need to add a few more votes to the database, as our fixture file currently contains only two votes. Because it's unlikely that we'll be using a large number of votes in any other test, we'll create the additional votes right there in the test, using a simple block of Ruby code:

```
10.times { stories(:one).votes.create }
```

This line programmatically creates ten votes on the fly by calling the `create` method on the `votes` association of the first `Story`.

These dynamically created votes will be wiped from the database automatically before the next test starts, so they won't affect any other tests.

The assertion then goes ahead and compares the size of the array returned by `latest` method with the expected number of 3, which is the maximum number of votes that latest` should return.

Running the Unit Tests

At this point, we're ready to run our model tests with all the newly added coverage. You remember how to do that, right?

The output should look similar to this:

```
$ rails test:models
Running via Spring preloader in process 52828
Run options: --seed 16833

# Running:

......

Finished in 0.083235s, 72.0847 runs/s, 96.1130 assertions/s.

6 runs, 8 assertions, 0 failures, 0 errors, 0 skips
```

Testing the Controller

Now that we've created tests that cover all the extra functionality we added to our model in this chapter, we'll do the same for the new controller actions: show in StoriesController and create in VotesController, as well as their accompanying views.

Testing Page Rendering

We'll add two tests for the show action to test/controllers/ stories_controller_test.rb; the first will be a test that deals with the basics of displaying a story. The code for the first test is as follows:

7-33. test/controllers/stories_controller_test.rb *(excerpt)*

```
test "show story" do
  get story_path(stories(:one))
  assert_response :success
  assert response.body.include?(stories(:one).name)
end
```

This code does nothing we haven't seen before. We request a page (the "show story" page) using HTTP GET, and make sure that the page returns a code indicating that it displayed successfully. We then check that the story name is included in the response, indicating we've rendered it correctly.

The next test we'll create will cover the new HTML elements that we added to the story page, specifically those relating to the voting functionality. Here's the test:

```
                                    7-34. test/controllers/stories_controller_test.rb (excerpt)

test "show story vote elements" do
  get story_path(stories(:one))
  assert_select 'h2 span#vote_score'
  assert_select 'ul#vote_history li', count: 2
  assert_select 'div#vote_form form'
end
```

This is quite a comprehensive test. It checks for the presence of correctly nested HTML tags on the rendered page, as well as proper element attributes. Let's examine it one line at a time:

```
assert_select 'h2 span#vote_score'
```

This assertion introduces more of the CSS selector syntax that can be used with `assert_select`, which we first encountered in Chapter 6. Just as you would regularly style an element on a page by referring to its ID, `assert_select` allows us to test for the presence of an element with a given ID using the same syntax we'd apply to style an element on the page.

Here, we're checking for a span tag with an ID of `vote_score` nested within an `h2` element. This test confirms that we have a proper story header in place, and that the current voting score appears beneath it.

The next assertion also uses `assert_select`:

```
assert_select 'ul#vote_history li', count: 2
```

Here, we check for the presence of a `ul` element that has a unique ID of `vote_history` and a specific number of `li` elements nested within it (reflecting the entries of the voting history for this particular story).

Our final check confirms the presence of a `div` element with a unique ID of `vote_form` with a nested `form` inside it:

```
assert_select 'div#vote_form form'
```

We now have a high level of confidence that our pages are displaying everything expected of them! Now, let's add some tests for our voting functionality.

Testing Vote Storage

To test the basics of the vote-casting functionality, add the following test to test/controllers/votes_controller_test.rb (and while you're in there, delete the test that Rails generated.) It simply confirms that new votes are stored correctly:

7-35. test/controllers/votes_controller_test.rb *(excerpt)*

```
class VotesControllerTest < ActionController::TestCase
  test "creates vote" do
    assert_difference 'stories(:two).votes.count' do
      post story_votes_path(stories(:two))
    end
  end
end
```

The test uses the assert_difference before-and-after check to confirm that this action, which is supposed to modify data, is indeed doing its job. Let's look at each line in turn.

The first line sets up the count we want to check for the test block:

```
assert_difference 'stories(:two).votes.count' do
```

We then submit the vote using HTTP POST:

```
post story_votes_path(stories(:two))
```

`assert_difference` will confirm that the vote we submitted was stored successfully, and is associated with our story.

Okay, we now have a test in place for the application's basic voting functionality. But our voting pages are far from being basic—they use that fancy Ajax stuff, remember? Can we test that, too? You bet we can!

Testing Ajax Voting

Let's test an Ajax voting action. Add the following test to your rapidly expanding collection of functional tests:

7-36. test/controllers/votes_controller_test.rb (excerpt)

```
test "create vote with ajax" do
  post story_votes_path(stories(:two)), xhr: true
  assert_response :success
end
```

>

Again, let's walk through each line of this test.

The first line is our test's way of pretending to perform an actual Ajax request:

```
post story_votes_path(stories(:two)), xhr: true
```

Obviously, this isn't really an Ajax request. It makes no use of a browser, and there's no `XmlHttpRequest` object in sight. But, by adding the `xhr: true` parameter to the `POST` call, our request receives a header that fools the application into thinking that this is a real Ajax request.

The next block of statements check for a proper response, and confirms that the correct template was rendered:

```
assert_response :success
```

There's nothing here that we haven't seen before, so let's move on to our last test.

EXTRA CREDIT: Make a Difference

Change the Ajax test to use `assert_difference`.

Testing Regular HTTP Voting

We still must test the process of vote submission using regular HTTP POST (that is, without Ajax). To do so, we'll add one more test to the `votes_controller_test.rb` file:

7-37. test/controllers/votes_controller_test.rb *(excerpt)*

```
test "redirect after vote with http post" do
  post story_votes_path(stories(:two))
  assert_redirected_to story_path(stories(:two))
end
```

Let's examine each line in this test. The first line casts the vote with a simple HTTP POST:

```
post story_votes_path(stories(:two))
```

After the vote has been submitted, we check whether the user is properly redirected to the story page. This is accomplished with an `assert_redirected_to` assertion:

```
assert_redirected_to story_path(stories(:two))
```

Excellent! All of our new functionality is covered. Time to run the tests.

Running the Full Test Suite

Invoking the full test suite (using the `rails test` command) will run through a total of 26 assertions contained in ten tests. The results of a successful test suite execution should look like this:

```
$ rails test
Running via Spring preloader in process 56718
Run options: --seed 3298

# Running:

................

Finished in 0.385701s, 41.4829 runs/s, 82.9658 assertions/s.

15 runs, 25 assertions, 0 failures, 0 errors, 0 skips
```

Summary

In this chapter, we've equipped Readit with some fully fledged voting functionality, and we've done it using cool technologies such as Ajax combined with some good-looking user-interface effects.

Along the way, we covered the principles of Rails routing helpers, and added to our application a page that shows the details of a story that has already been submitted.

We took a long look at the asset pipeline and how it compresses and minifies our assets, generates asset digests, and handles preprocessors such as CoffeeScript and Sass.

Turbolinks supplied us with some great tools out of the box, such as asynchronous page requests and a progress bar.

We also looked at using JavaScript templates to modify the contents of pages that have already been rendered, and discussed how we can use visual effects to enhance the usability of our application. We even covered partials: mini page templates that help reduce the amount of template code required to get the job done.

Finally, we established test coverage for all the functionality we added to our Readit application in this chapter, so that we'll know immediately if any future change to the application code breaks our existing functionality.

Whew! We covered a ton in this chapter. Take a break and get some coffee. You deserve it.

In the next chapter, we'll implement some protective measures in Readit with user authentication—with some additional benefits!

Chapter

8

Protective Measures

Over the last few chapters, we've spent a good deal of time implementing new features for our link-sharing application; however, we've yet to put any effort into preventing those features from being misused.

In this chapter, we'll implement some user authentication techniques that will allow us to protect certain actions from being used by individuals failing to register with or log into the site.

Introducing Sessions and Cookies

Before we write any code, let's learn a bit more about the technology behind user logins, including sessions and cookies.

If you already have some experience with sessions and cookies, you may prefer to skim through this section.

Identifying Individual Users

Generally speaking, **HTTP**—the protocol that a web browser uses to talk to an application—is **stateless**. This means it makes no assumptions about, nor relies upon, previous requests between the client and the server.

This is the crucial difference between stateless protocols and other protocols, including instant messaging systems such as Skype or Internet Relay Chat (IRC). When you start up an instant messenger client, it logs in to the instant messaging server and remains connected for the time that you use the service. Stateless protocols, such as HTTP, request only a single item—a web page, an image, or a stylesheet, for example—during each connection. Once the item has been requested, the connection is closed. If the requested item is a web page, it's impossible for the application to tell what the users are doing; they may be still reading the page, following a link to another site, or shutting down the machine altogether.

In the world of HTTP, it's also impossible to tell whether two pages requested in succession were actually done so by the same user. We cannot rely on the IP address of the user's computer,[1] as that computer might sit behind a proxy server or firewall, in which case it's entirely possible that thousands of other users share the IP address displayed by that machine.

Obviously, we need another technique to identify individual visitors. Without it, we'd have to force every user to log in to each and every page of our Readit application, and that's just not cool. This is where sessions and cookies come into play.

What's a cookie?

A **cookie** is a tiny snippet of information that a website places on a user's computer. The cookie is bound to the website that placed it there; no other site is

---

[1.] An IP address is a number that uniquely identifies a computer connected to the Internet. You've no doubt encountered them before—here's an example: 123.45.67.123.

able to access the cookie. You've probably encountered cookies when using the Web in the past, possibly without even knowing it.

A cookie consists of a name/value pair. For example, a cookie with the name `color` might have the value `green`. Additionally, the cookie's name must be unique. If a cookie is set with the same name as one that already exists, the older cookie will be overwritten.

All web browsers give users control over the cookies that websites set on their machines, although some make cookie management easier than others. Firefox, for example, provides a handy tool for inspecting—and removing—the cookies that have been set on a machine. To display the Firefox Storage Inspector shown in Figure 8-1, select *Tools > Web Developer*, click *Storage Inspector*. The top item in the list is called "Cookies." Select the address of the current site under "Cookies" (`www.google.com` in the figure) to show you the cookies for that site. Go take a look—chances are that many of the sites you've visited have left a cookie without even telling you about it.

8-1. The Storage Inspector

Cookies usually have an expiration date, with the browser deleting a cookie automatically once this has passed. It makes sense for sites to set expiration dates on cookies, as they occupy space on the user's computer. Additionally, once a cookie is set, it cannot be modified by the application that set it, so a cookie without an expiration date could wind up sitting on the user's hard disk forever.

A site can set the expiration date of a cookie in two ways:

- using an explicit date (for example, December 31, 2016)

- making the cookie expire when the user closes the browser

The latter is the default behavior for Rails' session cookies ... which brings us to the next topic.

What's a session?

Sessions are what's needed to identify returning visitors. A **session** is like a small container that's stored on the server for each user; it can be used as a temporary storage location for everything that needs to be remembered between successive page views made by the user. Though a session is a less permanent storage solution, the data stored in the session shouldn't be treated any differently from data in the application's database.

As an added bonus, the processes of creating sessions and retrieving information from them occurs without us having to write any code or provide specific instructions.

For our Readit application, we'll use a session to store information about where users are from; we'll use that information when users attempt to access pages or functionality to determine whether we should allow them access, or redirect them to the login form. Sessions can also be used to store shopping cart content, custom user preferences, and other information that allows us to enhance and customize users' experiences of a site.

Rails uses a session cookie to identify the session of a returning visitor. A session cookie, by default, will contain the actual session content in a safely encrypted fashion, although it's possible to store the session content on the server or in the database if you so desire later on.

In fact, if you've been following the code in this book, you may notice that a session cookie has been set by our application already: check your browser's cookie manager for a cookie set by `localhost` or `localhost.local`, with the name `_readit_session`. This is a cookie that Rails sets for us automatically, providing us with a session to use within our application.

Sessions in Rails

As I've previously noted, a session in Rails is automatically created for each of your application's users, and can be used to store and retrieve data without requiring any special code.

The session container for a user is accessed just like any other hash. To add a new value to the session, simply assign the value that you wish to store to a hash key that's yet to exist in the session, like so:

```
session[:page] = 'Index page'
```

The result of this assignment is that a cookie will be written to the user's machine. The cookie contains an encrypted representation of what was stored in the session previously. With the cookie in place, any data stored in the session becomes available for all successive pages that this user visits.

The retrieval of session values is equally simple. To access the value we stored in the previous code snippet and display it in a view, we'd use the following syntax:

```
<%= session[:page] %>
```

It's possible to store data other than strings in a session container—you can actually use a session to store any type of data you like. The only prerequisite for such storage is that your application has access to the class definition of the stored object; however, in practice, sessions should only be used to store simple objects, such as `String` and `Fixnum`. And since anything you store in the session will be stored in the user's browser, the objects you store had better be small.

> ### Session Storage Solutions
>
> As mentioned, we can store the contents of a session on the server or in different types of databases, as well as the default location of the session cookie itself.
>
> While the default option is fine for local development, it may not work so well in a production environment. It lacks some control, not least by its inability to purge data from the user's session and thus prevent data from becoming stale (that is, out of sync with data in our database).
>
> An in-depth discussion on the different session storage options is beyond the scope of this book, but we'll briefly explore some of the alternatives in Chapter 12.

Modeling the User

Now that we've stepped through the theory, let's return to the topic at hand: protective measures. In this section, we'll lay an architectural foundation for providing user authentication in Readit.

The first step is to generate a new model named User. Since we've covered model generation, I'll avoid dwelling on this step for long. Let's do it.

Generating a User Model

From the readit folder, run the rails generate command to generate the base class of the User model, along with its migration files, unit tests, and fixtures:

```
$ rails generate model User password_digest:string
↳ name:string email:string
Running via Spring preloader in process 61211
      invoke  active_record
      create    db/migrate/20160412173358_create_users.rb
      create    app/models/user.rb
      invoke    test_unit
      create      test/models/user_test.rb
```

To create the database table for this model, modify the generated migration file located at db/migrate/xxx_create_users.rb to this:

8-2. db/migrate/xxx_create_users.rb

```ruby
class CreateUsers < ActiveRecord::Migration[5.0]
  def change
      create_table :users do |t|
        t.string :password_digest
        t.string :name
        t.string :email

        t.timestamps
      end

      add_column :stories, :user_id, :integer
      add_column :votes, :user_id, :integer
  end
end
```

We'll use this migration to create a brand new users table. The three columns we've just defined will hold users' personal information: password digests (I'll get to this), names, and email addresses. Actually, the table has six columns if you include the automatically created id column as well as the created_at and updated_at columns that are a result from the t.timestamps call.

As you've probably figured out, we're going to store our users and their credentials in this table. The credentials consist of the email and password attributes. But, you must be shouting, there is no password attribute in the table. That's correct, and it's another example of Rails doing right by you. It is bad, bad, BAD practice to store a password in clear text (that is, not encrypted.) So, Rails has a shortcut that allows a developer to configure a model (the User model, in our case) to accept email and passwords in a secure, best practices kind of way. It's called has_secure_password and I'll walk you through it once we finish with this migration.

In addition to creating this table, we'll insert a new column into each of the existing stories and votes tables, which will store the ID of the user who created a particular story or vote respectively.

While we would normally split migrations into the components that handle small isolated changes, in this case it makes sense to group the creation of the `users` table with the modification of the two other tables. We'll keep our schema changes together as one migration, as they're so closely related. We use the good old `rails` tool to apply the migration we've just written:

```
$ rails db:migrate
Running via Spring preloader in process 63227
 == 20160412173358 CreateUsers: migrating
↳ =======================================
-- create_table(:users)
       -> 0.0028s
-- add_column(:stories, :user_id, :integer)
         -> 0.0003s
-- add_column(:votes, :user_id, :integer)
         -> 0.0004s
 == 20160412173358 CreateUsers: migrated (0.0037s)
↳ =============================
```

This snippet shows the result of a successful migration. We now have in place the database structure necessary to begin writing code for our `User` model.

Has Secure Password

As we've covered, Rails comes with a method called `has_secure_password` that can be applied to our `User` model to give us a solid, practical authentication solution. To configure it, open up the `User` model (`app/models/user.rb`) and change it to:

```
class User < ApplicationRecord
  has_secure_password
end
```

That one line does quite a bit. First, it adds two methods on the `User` model: password and password_confirmation. has_secure_password also adds validations to ensure that the `password` and `password_confirmation` attributes match when creating a user. Additionally, the password value is encrypted and stored in the `password_digest` field in the `users` table that we discussed earlier. Finally, `has_secure_password` adds an `authenticate` instance method to the `User`, model which we'll use to authenticate our users.

There is one small chore to perform to get all this working. `has_secure_password` encrypts the `password` value using a RubyGem called `bcrypt`. In order to use `has_secure_password`, we add the `bcrypt` gem to our `Gemfile` and update our bundle via `bundle install`.

Open up the `Gemfile` and search for `bcrypt` (a gem I'll explain in a bit). It should be in there, but commented out:

```
# Use ActiveModel has_secure_password
# gem 'bcrypt', '~> 3.1.7'
```

Change it to:

```
# Use ActiveModel has_secure_password
gem 'bcrypt', '~> 3.1.7'
```

Then go to your command line in the root directory of `readit` and run `bundle install`:

```
$ bundle install
Fetching gem metadata from https://rubygems.org/...........
Fetching version metadata from https://rubygems.org/...
Fetching dependency metadata from https://rubygems.org/..
Resolving dependencies...
Using rake 10.5.0
Using i18n 0.7.0
Using json 1.8.3
Using minitest 5.8.4
Using thread_safe 0.3.5
Using builder 3.2.2
Using erubis 2.7.0
```

```
Using mini_portile2 2.0.0
Using rack 1.6.4
Using mime-types 2.99
Using arel 6.0.3
Installing bcrypt 3.1.11 with native extensions
...
 Bundle complete! 13 Gemfile dependencies, 55 gems now
↪ installed.
 Use `bundle show [gemname]` to see where a bundled gem is
↪ installed.
```

Now, we can encrypt passwords and feel good about how they are stored.

Server Reboot Required

If your web server running, you'll need to kill it (CTRL+C) after a `bundle install` and restart it to see the changes.

Adding Relationships for the User Class

Our users will create votes and stories, so we need a way to track which user created or voted for what stories. As you've probably gathered from our past endeavors with `ActiveRecord`, a model requires little code in order to track relationships.

Open the `User` class definition and modify it as follows:

8-3. app/model/user.rb

```ruby
class User < ActiveRecord::Base
  has_secure_password
  has_many :stories
  has_many :votes
end
```

This code sets up a one-to-many relationship between the `User` class and each of the `Story` and `Vote` classes.

As you already know, relationships can (and should) be defined for both participating models. Our next step is to add complementary relationship definitions to the `Story` and `Vote` classes (located at `app/models/story.rb` and `app/models/vote.rb` respectively):

```
class Story < ActiveRecord::Base
  belongs_to :user
  : class definition…
end
```

```
class Vote < ActiveRecord::Base
  belongs_to :user
  : class definition…
end
```

These bidirectional relationship definitions allow us to retrieve not only the `Vote` and `Story` objects associated with a particular `User`, but also the `User` object associated with a particular `Story` or `Vote`.

All right, enough of the architectural building blocks—let's create a user. Then we can start to protect some of our actions from users not logged in.

Creating a User

Creating a `User` object is no different from creating any other `ActiveRecord` object. It's easily accomplished from the Rails console—feel free to create an account for yourself, rather than using my name.

```
>> u = User.new
=> #<User id:nil, …>
>> u.name = 'Glenn Goodrich'
=> "Glenn Goodrich"
 >> u.password = 'sekrit' # You should choose a better
↳ password
=> "sekrit"
```

```
>> u.password_confirmation = 'sekrit'
=> "sekrit"
>> u.email = 'glenn.goodrich@sitepoint.com'
=> "glenn.goodrich@sitepoint.com"
>> u.save
=> true
```

Excellent. The first user of millions (I am sure) has been added to Readit.

Developing Login Functionality

In order to handle login and logout actions (and cater for new user registrations down the track), we'll need another controller to complement our existing controllers StoriesController and VotesController. Once that's in place, we can create some functionality to let users log in and out. It's exciting stuff.

Creating the Controller

We'll name this new controller SessionsController (since it's dealing with the creation and deletion of sessions, rather than users), and generate it using the rails generate command:

```
$ rails generate controller Sessions new create destroy
Running via Spring preloader in process 78423
    create  app/controllers/sessions_controller.rb
     route  get 'sessions/destroy'
     route  get 'sessions/create'
     route  get 'sessions/new'
    invoke  erb
    create    app/views/sessions
    create    app/views/sessions/new.html.erb
    create    app/views/sessions/create.html.erb
    create    app/views/sessions/destroy.html.erb
    invoke  test_unit
    create    test/controllers/sessions_controller_test.rb
    invoke  helper
```

```
create      app/helpers/sessions_helper.rb
invoke      test_unit
invoke   assets
invoke      coffee
create         app/assets/javascripts/sessions.coffee
invoke      scss
create         app/assets/stylesheets/sessions.scss
```

Passing the additional `new`, `create`, and `destroy` parameters as arguments to the `generate` command will automatically produce blank `new`, `create`, and `destroy` actions in our new `SessionsController`, which saves us a few lines of typing. It will also form empty `ActionView` templates in the `app/views/sessions/` folder, with the names `new.html.erb`, `create.html.erb`, and `destroy.html.erb`. Since no template is required for the `create` action (this action is destined to redirect elsewhere after it performs its job), you're free to remove `create.html.erb`.

Before closing off this section, we'll revisit our routing configuration (stored in `config/routes.rb`), since we want to build our `SessionsController` in a RESTful way. Add the following line to make sure Rails knows our intentions and provides the appropriate helpers to generate RESTful URLs for the session that's about to begin:

8-4. config/routes.rb

```
Rails.application.routes.draw do
  ⋮ more routes…
  resource :session
end
```

Now delete all the `get` lines that the `generate` command added for sessions in that file.

Please note that we've used the *singular* form of `resource` instead of the plural form (`resources`), as well as the singular form of `session`, unlike what we did for `stories`. When using the singular form, Rails knows we're talking about a singleton resource, which means only one of it ever exists at a time. This is true here in the context of a `User` object, which will only ever have a single session at a time. As such, all the RESTful URLs for sessions will take the singular rather than plural form of the model name we've seen so far. For example, the URL that creates a new session will be: `session/new`.

All right, let's go ahead and create some forms.

Creating the View

To better understand what happens when we use extra parameters to generate `ActionView` templates, type `http://localhost:3000/session/new` into your web browser.

The result you see should be similar to Figure 8-5. It's basically a friendly message to inform us where we can find the template that's displayed in the browser.

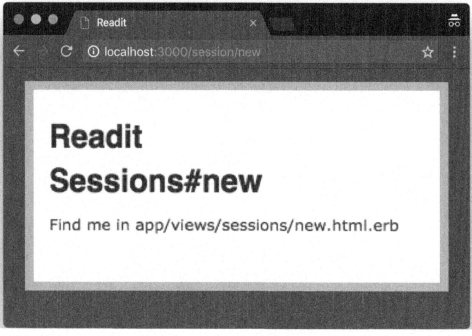

8-5. The generated login template

Start Your Engines...

As always, to use our Readit application, you must have the web server running. Flip back to <u>Starting Our Application</u> in Chapter 2 if you need a refresher on this.

Let's modify this template and turn it into an actual login form. As Rails indicates in the browser, the template is located at `app/views/sessions/new.html.erb`:

8-6. app/views/sessions/new.html.erb

```erb
<%= form_tag session_path do %>
  <p>Please log in.</p>
  <p>
    <label>Email:</label>
    <%= email_field_tag 'email' %>
  </p>
  <p>
    <label>Password:</label>
    <%= password_field_tag 'password' %>
  </p>
  <p><%= submit_tag 'login' %></p>
<% end %>
```

Once again, we've created a form using simple HTML markup and a few of the Rails form helpers. This time, our form doesn't deal with a specific model object, so we're unable to use the `form_for` helper that we employed back in <u>Chapter 6</u>. Instead, we use the standard `form_tag` helper that defines the surrounding form with a `do` and `end` block:

```erb
<% form_tag session_path do %>
  : login form...
<% end %>
```

This generates the all-important form and its form HTML tags. It uses the `session_path` URL helper that we got by telling the Rails routing configuration in the last section that we want RESTful handling of the session's URLs. To check that they're being created correctly, reload the modified page in your browser and view the source of the page.

The `email_field_tag` and `password_field_tag` helpers generate HTML input elements with the type attribute set to `email` and `password` respectively:

```
<p>
  <label>Email:</label>
  <%= email_field_tag 'email' %>
</p>
<p>
  <label>Password:</label>
  <%= password_field_tag 'password' %>
</p>
```

These elements will render the text fields into which our visitors will enter their email and password. The `email` and `password` parameters that we're passing to each of these helpers assigns a name to the HTML tag that's generated; it also causes this value to show up in the `params` hash, which will prove to be very useful as we'll see later on.

Now that we've put our form in place, we can establish some functionality behind it.

Adding Functionality to the Controller

We're ready to implement the actual login functionality within the `create` controller action. You'll find the controller class in the file `app/controllers/sessions_controller.rb`. Add the following code to the `create` method of this class:

8-7. app/controllers/sessions_controller.rb *(excerpt)*

```ruby
class SessionsController < ApplicationController
  ⋮ controller code…

  def create
    @current_user = User.find_by(email: params[:email])
  if @current_user &&
↳ @current_user.authenticate(params[:password])
      session[:user_id] = @current_user.id
      redirect_to stories_path
    else
      render action: 'new'
    end
  end

    ⋮ controller code…
end
```

As Figure 8-8 shows, we've expanded the previously empty `create` action to
handle the submission of the login form. We attempt to fetch a user using the
`email` and `password` values that the visitor provided. Notice that we use one of
the `ActiveRecord` dynamic finder methods to do this:

```ruby
@current_user = User.find_by(email: params[:email)
  if @current_user &&
↳ @current_user.authenticate(params[:password])
```

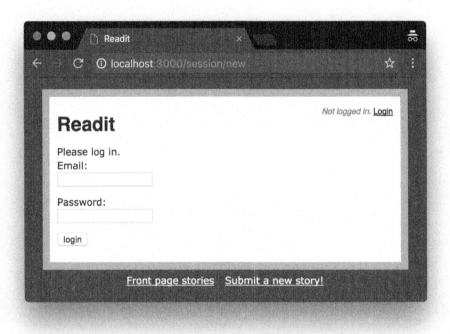

8-8. The completed login form

If we're able to locate a user whose record matches the visitor-entered email (so `@current_user` is not nil), we then use the `authenticate` method provided by `has_secure_password` to compare the supplied password value with the encrypted `password_digest` value. If everything is successful, store the ID of the `User` object retrieved within the current visitor's session. The user is then redirected to the story `index`, for which Rails gave us the shorthand `stories_path`:

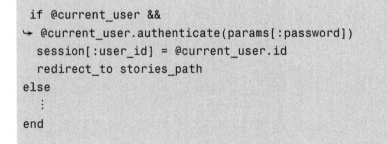

```
  if @current_user &&
↳ @current_user.authenticate(params[:password])
    session[:user_id] = @current_user.id
    redirect_to stories_path
  else
    ⋮
  end
```

If we *don't* find a corresponding user in the database, it's best to rerender the login form. Maybe the user mistyped the password or forgot the email, in which case we'd like to enable him or her to try again:

```
if @current_user &&
↪ @current_user.authenticate(params[:password])
   ⋮
else
  render action: 'new'
end
```

 Be Careful When Storing ActiveRecord Objects in a Session

Be careful when you're storing `ActiveRecord` objects in the session. `ActiveRecord` objects may change at any time, but the session container won't necessarily be updated to reflect the changes. For example, in our Readit application, a story object might be viewed by one user and modified by a second user immediately afterwards. If the entire story was stored in the session container, the first user's session would contain a version of the story that was out of date (and out of sync with the database).

To ensure that this scenario doesn't eventuate, it's best to store only the primary key of the record in question—the value of the `id` column—in the session container. Here's an example:

```
session[:user_id] = @current_user.id
```

On successive page loads, we retrieve the `ActiveRecord` object using the regular `Model.find` method, and pass in the key that was stored in the session container:

```
current_user = User.find session[:user_id]
```

This is all well and good, and if you were to try logging in at `http://localhost:3000/session/new` using the initial user that we created a few pages back, you would indeed be redirected to the story page. Go on, try it out—it works! However, something is still amiss.

Since we've stored only the user's ID in the session container, we need to ensure that we fetch the User object for that user before we hand execution control to another controller action. If we failed to fetch the rest of the user's details, we'd be unable to display the name of the currently logged-in user, which we aim to do on every page in our application.

So, before we proceed too much further, let's look at the theory behind one of the features of Rails that allows us to execute code from any controller action: filters.

Introducing Filters

A **filter** is a function that defines code to be run either before or after a controller's action is executed. Using a filter, we can ensure that a specific chunk of code is run regardless of which page the user is looking at. An example might be authenticating the current user before the action is run.

Once we've discussed how filters work, I'll show you how to use one to fetch a User object from the database when a user logs in. We'll use another filter to redirect to the login page any anonymous visitors who attempt to access a protected page.

Before Filters

The first type of filter we'll look at is the *before* filter. As you might expect, a before filter executes before the code in the controller action is executed. The method used for a before filter is `before_action`, meaning, it runs *before* the *action* runs.

Like all filters, a before filter is defined in the head of the controller class that calls it. Calling a before filter is as simple as invoking the `before_action` method and passing it a symbol that represents the method to be executed. The filter can also accept a snippet of Ruby code as a parameter, which is used as the filter code; however, this practice is discouraged, as it makes for code that's difficult to maintain.

Here's a hypothetical example in which a controller method is called using a symbol:

```
class FoosController < ApplicationController
  before_action :fetch_password
  def fetch_password
    : method body…
  end
end
```

In this example, the `fetch_password` method will be run before the actions of `FoosController`.

After Filter

Like a before filter, an after filter is defined in the controller class from which it is called. The method to use is appropriately named the `after_filter` method and, not surprisingly, these filters are executed *after* the controller's action code has been executed. Here's an example:

```
class FoosController < ApplicationController
  after_action :gzip_compression
  def gzip_compression
    : method body…
  end
end
```

Here, `gzip_compression` runs after the actions of `FoosController`.

Around Filters

A combination of before and after filters, the around filter executes both before *and* after the controller's action code.

In a nutshell, around filters are separate objects with before and after methods. These methods are automatically called by the filter framework. Despite being a combination of its simpler siblings, the around filter is significantly more advanced and, as such, won't be covered in this book.

EXTRA CREDIT: A Filter Field Trip

Do a bit of research about around filters to see how they operate. Can you think of how the code of an around filter might have to be different from a before or after filter?

A Word on Filter Methods

As we've learned, filters take a symbol as a parameter that represents the controller method to be executed. Consider the hypothetical example of our `FoosController` once more:

```
class FoosController < ApplicationController
  before_action :fetch_password
  def fetch_password
    ⋮ method body…
  end
end
```

It is best practice to make filter methods `private` or `protected`. This practice has its roots in good object oriented programming practices, specifically: don't expose more methods than necessary to your callers. Following this practice, the aforementioned code becomes:

```
class FoosController < ApplicationController
  before_action :fetch_password

  private

  def fetch_password
    ⋮ method body…
  end
end
```

Managing User Logins

Now that we've covered filter theory, let's modify our application to fetch the currently logged-in User from our database. Once we've done that, we'll display the user's name on the page and provide the ability for the user to log out again.

Retrieving the Current User

We're going to use filters to fetch the current user for each and every page of the Readit site. The phrase "each and every page" should give you a hint as to where we'll apply the filter. Filters can be inherited from parent classes and, as we want to avoid writing numerous filter declarations, we'll stick our filter in the parent class for all our controllers: ApplicationController.

Methods and filters that are defined in this class are available to all classes that inherit from ApplicationController (located at app/controllers/application_controller.rb), which is what we want:

8-9. app/controllers/application_controller.rb (excerpt)

```ruby
class ApplicationController < ActionController::Base
  ⋮ controller code…
  before_action :current_user

  protected

  def current_user
    return unless session[:user_id]
    @current_user = User.where(id: session[:user_id]).first
  end
end
```

Let's take a look at each of the lines that make up the current_user method:

```ruby
return unless session[:user_id]
```

This line is fairly straightforward. There's no point retrieving a User object if the user is yet to log in (as there's no user_id stored in the session). We can simply exit the filter method without executing the rest of the code.

The next line tries to fetch from the database a User object with an ID that's equal to the id stored in the visitor's session container:

```
@current_user = User.find(session[:user_id])
```

The fetched object will be assigned to the instance variable @current_user, which will then become available to actions in our controller, as well as our views.

We've purposely used the where method here, rather than find, even though on the surface it appears that the two would produce the same results. In fact, find displays an error if it can't retrieve a record that matches the id that's passed to it, while where exits more gracefully. It's conceivable that a user may revisit our site after his or her account has been deleted (perhaps because the user submitted the same boring stories over and over again), so we need to make sure the application will handle these cases in a user-friendly manner. Spitting out a bunch of technical-looking errors is best avoided, hence our use of where. where also returns *all* the records that satisfy the query; that is, an Array. We have to grab the first one, as we know there's only one for an ID query. If the id is not found, first will return nil.

Session Security

As we saw earlier, the value of `session[:user_id]` is stored in an encrypted fashion. This means that a user can't, for example, impersonate another user by simply changing the contents of a session.

The only way that a user could circumvent the security measures that we've put in place so far would be either to guess the session ID, or to identify it using a brute force attack.[2] Oh, apart from grabbing another user's laptop while they're in the bathroom.

As Rails uses a 128-bit hash for the session ID. as well as a secret key set in the Rails application itself (that is never exposed to the site's users) to verify the data integrity of the session container contents, it's highly unlikely that a malicious user could gain another user's ID using any of these approaches.

Our next task will be to display the name of the current user in the global application layout.

Displaying the Name of the Current User

Since we require our users to log in just once to access the entire application, let's add code that will display the name of the currently logged-in user to our global application layout. The file is located at `app/views/layouts/application.html.erb`. Make the following changes to this file:

[2.] A **brute force attack** involves looping through a list of every possible combination of alphanumeric characters (or sometimes a list of dictionary-based passwords) until a matching phrase is found.

```
<div id="content">
  <div id="login_logout">
    <% if @current_user %>
      Logged in as:
      <%= @current_user.name %>
      <em><%= link_to "(Logout)", session_path,
          method: :delete %></em>
        <% else %>
      <em>Not logged in.</em>
      <%= link_to 'Login', new_session_path %>
    <% end %>
  </div>
  <h1>Readit</h1>
  ⋮ page body…
<div>
```

Let's step through these changes. Using a simple `if` condition, we display a link to the action that's most appropriate, based on the user's login status:

```
<% if @current_user %>
```

The condition checks whether the instance variable `@current_user` evaluates to `nil`.

Once we've ensured that the user is actually logged in, we display the user's name along with a link to log out again, which we'll implement in the `SessionsController` in a moment. We indicate that we want the link to use the HTTP `DELETE` request type by passing the `method: :delete` argument to the `link_to` method. We wrap the link in an `em` tag to make it stand out:

```
Logged in as:
<%= @current_user.login %>
<em><%= link_to "(Logout)", session_path,
    method: :delete %></em>
```

If a visitor is *not* logged in, we display a link that the user can follow to the login form:

```
<%= link_to 'Login', new_session_path %>
```

As you can see, our sessions are RESTful. We've been using the bare session_path to handle both the login action (at POST /session) and the logout action (the code of which is still missing, but it will live at DELETE /session), as well as the new_session_path for the actual login form (living at GET /session/ new).

To make the page look a little nicer, let's add a snippet of CSS to the global stylesheet that's located at app/assets/stylesheets/application.css:

8-11. app/assets/stylesheets/application.css *(excerpt)*

```
#login_logout {
  float: right;
  color: #999;
  font-size: smaller;
}
```

This code dims the text colors a little, floats the container to the right, and makes the font size smaller. If you reload the page after logging in, you should see the results shown in Figure 8-12. That's much better.

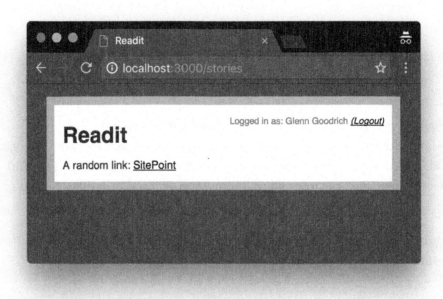

8-12. Prettying up our page

Next, we'll implement the logout functionality.

Allowing Users to Log Out

Providing our users with a manual logout function is much more user-friendly than forcing them to close their browsers to log out. We'll implement this method in our `SessionsController` class, located in `app/controllers/sessions_controller.rb`:

8-13. app/controllers/sessions_controller.rb

```
class SessionsController < ApplicationController
  ⋮ controller code…
  def destroy
    session[:user_id] = @current_user = nil
  end
end
```

Logging a user out of the application is a matter of setting two variables to nil:

- the user_id that's stored in the user's session
- the instance variable that holds the current user

Both of those tasks are completed with one line of code:

```
session[:user_id] = @current_user = nil
```

This line of code prevents our before filter (the current_user method) from retrieving anything from the database. As we're setting both the current user *and* the user id stored in the session to nil, no more User objects for this user remain in memory. The user has therefore been logged out of the system.

I've taken this opportunity to introduce another piece of shorthand syntax used often in Ruby code: we've assigned nil to two variables at once. Strictly speaking, we're assigning the result of the statement @current_user = nil (which happens to be nil) to session[:user_id].

With that code in place, adding a simple message to app/views/sessions/destroy.html.erb will confirm for the user that the logout was successful:

```
<h2>Logout successful</h2>
<%= link_to 'Back to the story index', stories_path %>
```

Let's check that this all works as we expect. Click that "Logout" link in the top right-hand corner of the page. If everything goes to plan, you should be logged out of the application and presented with a page similar to the one shown in Figure 8-14. Additionally, the name that was previously displayed in the upper right-hand corner should not be present on any successive page that you visit; you should see a *Login* link instead.

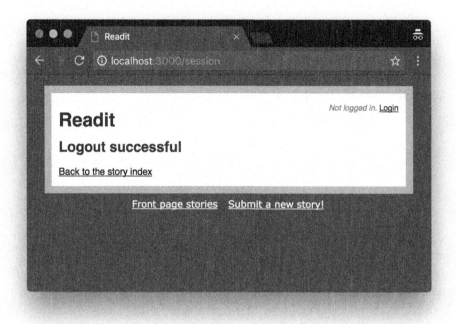

8-14. Links for logging in and logging out

Now that users are able to log in and out of the application, we're in a position to make certain actions available only to logged-in users; however, before we do this, let's add to our site an element that has been sorely lacking so far: navigation.

Adding a Navigation Menu

You're probably growing a little tired of typing `http://localhost:3000/stories/new` over and over again. Let's create a diminutive navigation menu at the bottom of every page so we can move easily between the different pages we've built.

To do so, modify the file `app/views/layouts/application.html.erb`. Above the closing body tag at the bottom of the file, place the following unordered list containing our navigation menu:

8-15. app/views/layouts/application.html.erb *(excerpt)*

```erb
<body>
  ⋮ page body…
  <ul id="navigation">
 <li><%= link_to 'Front page stories', stories_path
↪ %></li>
 <li><%= link_to 'Submit a new story!',
↪ new_story_path %></li>
  </ul>
</body>
```

We have two links in our menu at this point:

- one to the story index (which currently displays a random story from the pool)
- one to the story submission form

As usual, we'll also expand our stylesheet to make the menu look attractive. The result is shown in Figure 8-17:

8-16. app/assets/stylesheets/application.css *(excerpt)*

```css
#navigation {
  list-style: none;
  padding: 5px 0;
  margin: 0;
  text-align: center;
}
#navigation li {
  display: inline;
  padding: 0 5px;
}
#navigation li a {
  color: #fff;
}
```

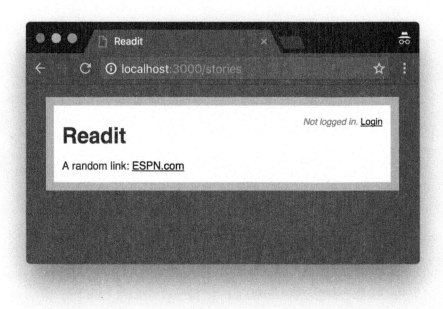

8-17. Story index with navigation

That's much better. With the navigation in place, moving around within our application becomes a lot easier.

Restricting the Application

All this login functionality would be wasted if a guest to our site had access to the same feature set enjoyed by our registered users. What would be the point of logging in?

Now that our login functionality is working, we can restrict the use of certain parts of the application by anonymous guests and users who have not logged in.

Protecting the Form

The first action to protect is the submission of stories. While we're adding this protection, we'll also check that when a new story is submitted, the application correctly saves the reference to the User who submitted it (as we defined in the relationship between a User and a Story).

The first step is to figure out how to intercept a request that comes from a user who's not currently logged in to our application. Once we've achieved this, we can direct the visitor to a login form instead of the story submission form. This sounds like a perfect job for a before filter, doesn't it?

We'll add our new filter code to the global `ApplicationController` class so that all of our controllers can benefit from this addition, since the filter is available to any of the controllers in our application.

The filter will be called `ensure_login`, which is suitably descriptive. As we're going to check from a few different places in our application whether or not a user is logged in, we'll extract this code into a separate controller method before we create our new filter. (Writing `@current_user` is not the most declarative thing in the world, anyway.)

Abstracting Code Using `helper_method`

The reason we're placing this functionality into a controller method (rather than creating a regular helper for it) is because it provides useful functionality to both controllers and views; however, regular helpers are available only to views, and controller methods are available only to controllers. We need some sort of magic bridge to make this controller method available to our views.

This magic bridge happens to be the `helper_method` statement, which makes regular controller methods available to views as if they were regular helper methods. We'll add this snippet to the `protected` area of our `ApplicationController` (in `app/controllers/application.rb`):

```
                                         8-18. app/controllers/application.rb/

class ApplicationController < ActionController::Base
  ⋮ controller code…
  protected

  def current_user
    ⋮ method body…
  end

  def logged_in?
    !@current_user.nil?
  end
    helper_method :logged_in?
end
```

Here, we've pulled our check of the current user's login status into a new method called `logged_in?`. Let's pause to examine an interesting aspect of the single-line method body:

```
!@current_user.nil?
```

The exclamation mark reverses the actual result of the `nil?` statement. If the `@current_user` variable is `nil` (`nil?` returns `true`), our visitor is *not* logged in, so `logged_in?` needs to return `false`. With the additional call to `helper_method`, we can now use `logged_in?` throughout our application to replace any usage of `if @current_user`.

Requiring Users to Log In

While we're looking at our `ApplicationController`, let's add the `ensure_login` filter to it. This will mark the first use of our new `logged_in?` helper method:

```ruby
def ensure_login
  return true if logged_in?
  session[:return_to] = request.fullpath
  redirect_to new_session_path and return false
end
```

Let's break this code down. The first line of the filter exits the method with the value `true` if the user is already logged in:

```ruby
return true if logged_in?
```

If the `logged_in?` helper method returns `false`, we need to:

1. prepare to redirect users to a location at which they can log in

2. remember where the user came from, so we can send them back to that page once the login is complete

To store the current URL, we grab it from the `request` object and add it to the user's session, so that we can retrieve it later:

```ruby
session[:return_to] = request.fullpath
```

Next, we redirect the user to the `new_session_path`, which is the new action of `SessionsController`, and return `false`:

```ruby
redirect_to new_session_path and return false
```

> **Good Coding Grammar**
>
> The **and** keyword that's used here is optional: the logic of this method would be identical if the **return** was placed on its own line; however, using **and** in this case adds to the readability of our code—and code that is more readable is more maintainable.

A return value of **false** is crucial here, because a filter that returns **false** halts the processing of any subsequent filters and exits the current controller method.

Right! Now we're armed with the protection facility, it's time to restrict access to the application's story submission capabilities to users who are logged in.

Restricting Access to Story Submission

While we want to halt anonymous visitors from submitting new stories to our site, we *do* want them to be able to view stories. Restricting user access to certain specific actions presents the perfect opportunity to use a filter condition.

Introducing Filter Conditions

A **filter condition** is simply a parameter that's passed to a filter to specify how the it is applied. The parameter can control whether the filter is applied to either:

- every method *except* those listed
- *only* the actions listed

In this case, the :only parameter is the best way for us to limit the filter to a pair of actions, new and create. Both of these actions are needed to log in a user; new to display the actual form, and create being the action to which the form is submitted.

Let's apply the ensure_login filter to the top of our StoriesController class, which is located at app/controllers/stories_controller.rb. The :only parameter accepts a symbol (or array of symbols) that represents the methods to which it should be applied:

8-20. eapp/controllers/stories_controller.rb (excerpt)

```
class StoriesController < ApplicationController
  before_action :ensure_login, only: [ :new, :create ]
  :  controller code…
end
```

```
class StoriesController < ApplicationController
  before_action :ensure_login, only: [ :new, :create ]
  :  controller code…
end
```

There, that was easy. But we've yet to make use of that `:return_to` URL that we stored in the user's session previously. Let's put it to work next.

Redirecting the User

The part of our application that redirects users after they've successfully logged in is the `create` method of the `SessionsController` class. This is located in `app/controllers/sessions_controller.rb`.

Let's modify the redirection code to specify the location to which a user is redirected based on whether or not the user's session actually contains a `:return_to` URL:

8-21. app/controllers/sessions_controller.rb (excerpt)

```
def create
  session[:user_id] = @current_user.id
  if session[:return_to]
    redirect_to session[:return_to]
    session[:return_to] = nil
  else
    redirect_to stories_path
  end
end
```

What's really worth a mention about this code is that we reset the `:return_to` URL to `nil` after a successful redirect. After all, there's no point in carrying around old baggage.

Now, fire up your web browser and execute the following steps to test out this new feature:

1. Log out of the application, if you're currently logged in.
2. Click the "Submit a new story!" link, and confirm in your browser's address bar that you're redirected to `/session/new`.
3. Log in using the login form, and verify that you're redirected back to the story submission form.

All good? Great!

Associating Stories with Users

The last enhancement that we'll add in this chapter is to associate a story with the ID of the user who submitted it. This will give us a record of who submitted what to Readit.

Storing the Submitter

As we established the association between stories and user `ids` at the beginning of the chapter, we simply need to tell Rails *what* we want to store. Change the first line of the create action of the `StoriesController`, located at `app/controllers/stories_controller.rb`:

```
def create
  @story = @current_user.stories.build story_params
    ⋮
end
```

Storing the submitter is as simple as that. We know that the currently logged-in user is stored in `@current_user`, because we set it using the `current_user` method before filter. We're using the declared stories association (or, more specifically, its build method) to get us a `Story` object that comes preset with the ID of the current user.

To illustrate, here's another example of this in action, performed straight in the Rails console (`rails c`):

```
$ rails c
>> u = User.first
=> #<User id: 1, …>
>> s = u.stories.build
=> #<Story id: nil, …>
>> s.user_id
=> 1
```

As you can see, the story that is *built* using the build method is completely unsaved. Yet it has a value set for its `user_id` attribute that is identical to the ID of the `User` object we created.

But of what use is storing information without it being displayed? You guessed it—displaying the submitter's details is our final task here.

Displaying the Submitter

We're going to modify each story's display page to show the name of the user who submitted it. This page corresponds to the `show` action of our `StoriesController` class displaying the submitter, the template for which is located at `app/views/stories/show.html.erb`:

8-22. app/views/stories/show.html.erb *(excerpt)*

```
<ul id="vote_history">
  : vote history list items…
</ul>
<p class="submitted_by">
  Submitted by:
  <span><%= @story.user.name %></span>
</p>
<p>
  <%= link_to @story.link, @story.link %>
</p>
```

Here we're using `@story.user` to fetch the user object that's associated with the currently displayed story. We then display the value of the user's name attribute to produce the result shown in Figure 8-23.

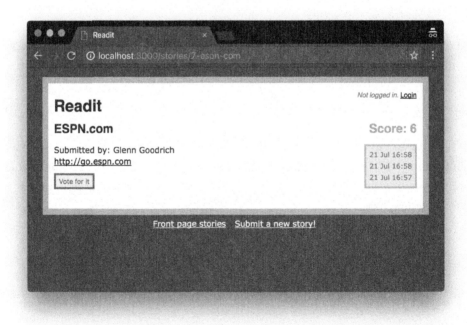

8-23. The name of a story's submitter displays with the story

Complete Data

One of the downsides of using an iterative approach to development is that our data is not necessarily complete at each stage of the development process. For example, unless you've specifically added **user_id** values to every **Story** object in your database, you're probably seeing the odd page error. You could use either of these approaches to rectify this issue:

- Manually add the missing values to your objects from the Rails console, remembering to use the **save** method so that the value is stored permanently.

- Delete all data in your database (via the Rails console), and begin to add your data from scratch via the application.

We need only two or three objects at this stage of development, so neither of these options should be too onerous for you.

One Last Thing: Associate Votes to Users

Just like we did with the stories, the votes need to be associated with the current user as well. This is a simple change to the **create** method in **VotesController**, as shown here:

8-24. app/controllers/vote_controller.rb (excerpt)

```
def create
  @story = Story.find(params[:story_id])
  @story.votes.create(user: @current_user)
  respond_to do |format|
 format.html { redirect_to @story, notice: 'Vote was
↪ successfully created.' }
    format.js {}
  end
end
```

There, now the vote will be attributed to the user.

We've accomplished quite a lot in this chapter, both in theory and in code. Being professional Rails coders, our next step is to add tests for all of these cool features.

Testing User Authentication

To develop our testing suite, we'll create unit tests to cover changes to the application's model, followed by functional tests for each of our controllers.

Testing the Model

We've extended our models very little in this chapter, so our unit tests will be straightforward. Basically, we have:

- created a new model (User)
- added a relationship between the User and Story model
- added a relationship between the User and Vote model

Before we can write any tests, though, we need to make sure that our test data is up to date.

Preparing the Fixtures

The User model didn't come with very meaningful fixture data, so let's address that now. Replace the contents of the model's fixture file (located at test/fixtures/users.yml) with the following data:

```
glenn:
  password_digest: <%= BCrypt::Password.create("sekrit",
↪ cost: 4) %>
    name: Glenn Goodrich
    email: glenn.goodrich@sitepoint.com
john:
  password_digest: <%= BCrypt::Password.create("passwrd",
↪ cost: 4) %>
    name: John Doe
    email: john@doe.com
```

Whoa, that's different. Remember when I went on about not storing plain-text passwords in the database? As a result, the `users` table has a field called `password_digest` that stores an encrypted version of the password. Our user fixtures, therefore, have to store the encrypted version of the password that we'll use in our tests, or authentication will fail. `has_secure_password` uses the `BCrypt` library to create the secure hash. `BCrypt` has a `Password` class that creates the hash using the password value and a `cost`, which simply tells `BCrypt` how long to take to generate the hash. BCrypt defaults `cost` to 10, which is fine for web authentication. Encryption is well beyond the scope of this book, but you know what that means ...

 EXTRA CREDIT: Break the Code on Encryption

Doing some basic research on encryption and how Rails uses it to keep your data and users secure is a good idea. There are many articles out there, including a great series by Engine Yard on password security[3].

To test the associations between the three models properly, we'll need to modify the fixtures for both our `Story` and `Vote` models. Only a small change is required: the addition of some data for the `user_id` attribute that we inserted at the start of this chapter.

Make the following changes in `test/fixtures/stories.yml`:

[3.] https://blog.engineyard.com/2014/password-security-part-1

```
                                      8-26. test/fixtures/stories.yml (excerpt)

one:
  ⋮ YAML data…
  user: glenn
two:
  ⋮ YAML data…
  user: glenn
```

And make these alterations in `test/fixtures/votes.yml`:

```
                                      8-27. test/fixtures/votes.yml (excerpt)

one:
  ⋮ YAML data…
  user: glenn
two:
  ⋮ YAML data…
  user: john
```

Now that our fixtures contain appropriate data, we can start writing some unit tests.

Testing a User's Relationship to a Story

The unit tests for our User belong in `test/models/user_test.rb`. First, we'll test the relationship between a User and a Story. Make the following changes to this file:

```
                                      8-28. test/models/user_test.rb (excerpt)

class UserTest < ActiveSupport::TestCase
  test "has a story association" do
assert_equal 2, users(:glenn).stories.size
assert users(:glenn).stories.includes stories(:one)
  end
end
```

We use two assertions to test the association between the `Story` and `User` models. The first assertion confirms that the total number of `Story` objects associated with the user `glenn` is indeed 2:

```
assert_equal 2, users(:glenn).stories.size
```

The second assertion identifies whether or not the `:one` `Story` is associated with `glenn`:

```
assert users(:glenn).stories.includes stories(:one)
```

With this in place, let's add a test for the inverse of this relationship.

Testing a `Story`'s Relationship to a `User`

By now, you're no doubt very familiar with the directory and filenaming conventions we're using. The complementary unit test for the relationship between a `User` and a `Story` tests the `Story`'s relationship to a `User`, and belongs in `test/models/story_test.rb`. Make the following changes to this file:

8-29. test/models/story_test.rb *(excerpt)*

```
class StoryTest < ActiveSupport::TestCase
  ⋮ test methods…
  test "is associated with a user" do
assert_equal users(:glenn), stories(:one).user
  end
end
```

The assertion we've written here simply confirms that the user associated with the first story is the user we expect, based on our fixture data (that is, `glenn`):

```
assert_equal users(:glenn), stories(:one).user
```

Let's add some similar tests for the other relationship that our `User` model has: its relationship with a `Vote`.

Fixing Broken Story Tests

Now that a story must be related to a user, the following test will fail:

```
test "is valid with required attributes" do
  s = Story.create(
    name: 'My test submission',
    link: 'http://www.testsubmission.com/')
  assert s.valid?
end
```

This is because we haven't given the story a user and `belongs_to` associations are required by default. Thus, `s.valid?` is `false`. To fix it, change it as follows:

8-30. test/models/story_test.rb (excerpt)

```
test "is valid with required attributes" do
  s = users(:glenn).stories.create(
    name: 'My test submission',
    link: 'http://www.testsubmission.com/')
  assert s.valid?
end
```

Here's another story test that now fails for the same reason:

```
test "return 3 latest votes" do
  10.times { stories(:one).votes.create }
  assert_equal 3, stories(:one).votes.latest.size
end
```

The change is easy (can you figure it out before I show you?):

```ruby
test "return 3 latest votes" do
  10.times { stories(:one).votes.create(user: users(:glenn)) }
  assert_equal 3, stories(:one).votes.latest.size
end
```

All better now.

Testing a User's Relationship to a Vote

While we've yet to add anything to our application's user interface to store or display the details of users associated with votes, we've put the infrastructure in place to do so. For this reason, we can test the relationship between a User and a Vote with a similar approach to what we took with the unit tests created for the relationship between a Story and a User.

To test a User's relationship to a Vote, add the following test to test/models/user_test.rb:

```ruby
test "has a votes association" do
  assert_equal 1, users(:glenn).votes.size
  assert users(:john).votes.includes votes(:two)
end
```

On the first line, the assert_equal assertion compares the number of Vote objects associated with a test user with the number of votes that the same user was assigned in our fixture data:

```ruby
assert_equal 1, users(:glenn).votes.size
```

The second assertion makes sure that the second Vote object is associated with the user john:

```
assert users(:john).votes.includes votes(:two)
```

Now there's only one more unit test to write: a test for the inverse of this relationship.

Testing a `Vote`'s Relationship to a `User`

The test that confirms a `Vote`'s relationship to a `User` belongs in `test/models/vote_test.rb`. Add the following test to this file:

8-33. test/models/vote_test.rb *(excerpt)*

```ruby
class VoteTest < ActiveSupport::TestCase
  ⋮ test methods…
  test "is associated with a user" do
    assert_equal users(:john), votes(:two).user
  end
end
```

This last test confirms that the user associated with the second vote of a story is indeed the second user who voted for the story, as defined by our fixture data.

Clever Cloning by Rails

You may be wondering how migrations are applied to the test database on which we're running our tests. As you'll recall, this database is quite separate from the development database to which our migrations are applied.

Rails is smart enough to figure out that testing should occur on a database with a structure that's identical to the one used for development. So Rails clones the structure of your development database, and applies it to the test database every time you execute your unit or functional tests.

Running the Unit Tests

We can now run our updated suite of unit tests using the following code, the results of which are also shown:

```
$ rails test:models
Running via Spring preloader in process 49271
Run options: --seed 64460

# Running:

..........

 Finished in 0.097536s, 102.5260 runs/s, 143.5364
↪ assertions/s.

10 runs, 14 assertions, 0 failures, 0 errors, 0 skips
```

Testing the Controllers

The majority of the functional code that we wrote in this chapter was in the SessionsController, although we also made a few changes to the StoriesController. Consequently, we have quite a few tests to write to ensure that all of this new functionality is covered.

Testing the Display of the Login Form

The first test we'll add to our functional test file (test/controllers/ sessions_controller_test.rb) is a simple HTTP GET operation that looks for the display of our login form:

8-34. test/controllers/sessions_controller_test.rb *(excerpt)*

```
class SessionsControllerTest <
↪ ActionDispatch::IntegrationTest
  test "new shows a login form" do
    get new_session_path
    assert_response :success
    assert_select 'form p', 4
  end
end
```

We've encountered before most of what we can see here. The test asserts that:

- the page request was successful
- a form tag is contained in the result, with four <p> tags nested below it

Testing a Successful Login

The following test, to be added to the same file, will attempt an actual login:

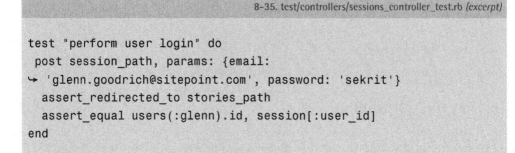

```
8-35. test/controllers/sessions_controller_test.rb (excerpt)

test "perform user login" do
  post session_path, params: {email:
↪ 'glenn.goodrich@sitepoint.com', password: 'sekrit'}
  assert_redirected_to stories_path
  assert_equal users(:glenn).id, session[:user_id]
end
```

Let's look at each line of this test in more detail.

As was the case when we tested the submission of stories, here we need to pass additional arguments to the `create` action—values for the `email` and `password` parameters:

```
  post session_path, params: {email:
↪ 'glenn.goodrich@sitepoint.com', password: 'sekrit'}
```

The values we've used here match the values in our `users.yml` fixture file. If you added your own user to that file, you'll need to change this test accordingly.

If you think about how our `create` method works, you'll recall that we redirect the user after they've logged in successfully; however, the URL to which a user is redirected varies depending on whether or not the user's session contains a URL. In this test, the user's session is empty, so we expect the user to be sent to the `/stories` page. The `assert_redirected_to` method comes in handy here:

```
assert_redirected_to stories_path
```

Lastly, a successful login means that:

- the id of the user will be stored in the user's session
- the instance variable @current_user will be set

Within the test, we have access to the session of the hypothetical user who just logged in, so we can compare both the session value and the instance variable with the corresponding details that we set for the user in our fixture data:

```
assert_equal users(:glenn).id, session[:user_id]
```

In a perfect world, this would be the last of the tests that we need to write. But in the *real* world, not every login attempt is successful.

Testing a Failed Login

Login attempts fail for various reasons: users may type their passwords incorrectly, or try to guess another person's login details. When a login attempt fails, the application should not reveal any content that's intended for users who have logged in. As such, login failures need to be tested too.

Here's the test:

8-36. test/controllers/sessions_controller_test.rb *(excerpt)*

```
test "bad login fails" do
  post session_path, params: {email: 'noone@nowhere.com',
↳ password: 'user'}
  assert_response :success
  assert_nil session[:user_id]
end
```

If a user tries to log in to our application using a non-existent username, the login form should redisplay. Our first assertion confirms that the page loads correctly:

```
assert_response :success
```

The last assertion checks the `user_id` value that's stored in the user's session to make sure it's `nil`:

```
assert_nil session[:user_id]
```

Okay, we've tested all our code that relates to our login procedures. But what happens *after* a user logs in?

Testing Redirection After Login

To trial the redirection of users who log in to their original destination, we'll add a test that ensures users are redirected to the protected path once they login:

8-37. test/controllers/sessions_controller_test.rb *(excerpt)*

```
test "redirects after login with return url" do
  get new_story_path
  assert_redirected_to new_session_path
  post session_path,
    params: {
      email: 'glenn.goodrich@sitepoint.com',
      password: 'sekrit'
    }
  assert_redirected_to new_story_path
end
```

This is an ideal time to point out that these controller tests are **integration tests**. This means that code is "behind the curtain" and we don't manipulate it. We simply do what the user does and test outcomes–the purpose of this test. The user tries to access the `new_story_path`, which is the New Story form:

```
get new_story_path
```

If it goes the desired way, this unauthenticated user will be redirected to the new_session_path, which is just the login form:

```
assert_redirected_to new_session_path
```

Now, the user logs in:

```
post session_path,
  params: {
    email: 'glenn.goodrich@sitepoint.com',
    password: 'sekrit'
  }
```

And we test that the user is redirected to their original, preferred destination:

```
assert_redirected_to new_story_path
```

You, as the developer, understand that we are putting the original URL into session[:return_to] and then checking that value on login; however, an integration test is for *behavior*, not internal details. If, for some reason, you change how the redirection occurs in the future behind the scenes, you still want the same behavior. This test accomplishes this.

Integration testing can sometimes feel like an art—it is certainly the next level up for a new Rails developer. Pat yourself on the back, you've done well.

Testing a Logout

The last part of the SessionsController that we test is the destroy action. To emulate a user logging out, we actually need to create what resembles an integration test. Why? Because before we can log out, we must log in:

8-38. test/controllers/sessions_controller_test.rb (excerpt)

```
test "logout and clear session" do
  post(
    session_path,
  params: { email: 'glenn.goodrich@sitepoint.com', password:
↳ 'sekrit' }
  )
  assert_not_nil session[:user_id]

  delete session_path
  assert_response :success
  assert_select 'h2', 'Logout successful'

  assert_nil session[:user_id]
end
```

This test is longer than most of our previous tests, but with the number of tests you have under your belt at this stage, you should be able to comprehend each line without much trouble.

First, we ensure that the `user_id` stored in the session is populated before the user logs out:

```
assert_not_nil session[:user_id]
```

Without this step, we can't guarantee that the `destroy` action is really doing its job.

The crux of this test lies in its last line:

```
assert_nil session[:user_id]
```

Here we're confirming that the all-important variable that we populated when the user logged in is set to `nil` once the user has logged out.

Phew, that was quite a number of tests. We're not done with functional testing just yet, though. You may like to fortify yourself with a strong coffee before tackling the rest of the functional tests—we'll be testing the changes we've made to our `StoriesController` and `ApplicationController` classes.

Testing the Display of the Story Submitter

The following test checks that the name of the user who submitted a story is displayed correctly on a story's page. Add it to `test/controllers/stories_controller_test.rb`:

8-39. test/controllers/stories_controller_test.rb *(excerpt)*

```ruby
class StoriesControllerTest <
↳ ActionDispatch::IntegrationTest
  ⋮ test methods…
  test "show story submitter" do
    get story_path(stories(:one))
    assert_select 'p.submitted_by span', 'Glenn Goodrich'
  end
end
```

We've seen all this before: confirming that an element containing our submitter's name is present is simply a matter of scanning the HTML code for a p element of class `submitted_by`, which contains the name of the submitter inside a span.

Testing the Display of Global Elements

To test the global elements that we added to the `application.html.erb` layout file, we'll add two tests. For the sake of convenience, both tests will utilize the index action of our `StoriesController`:

```
test "indicates not logged in" do
  get stories_path
  assert_select 'div#login_logout em', 'Not logged in.'
end

test "show navigation menu" do
  get stories_path
  assert_select 'ul#navigation li', 2
end
```

We've covered these `assert_select` statements several times already, so we'll skip going over old ground. Instead, let's move on to test that our Readit application displays the name of the logged-in user at the top of every page.

Testing the Display of the User's Name

The `div` element in the top-right corner of the browser window displays the name of the user who's currently logged in. We've checked the contents of this element when a user *hasn't* logged in; we still need to add a test to check whether the login has been successful.

Before we do so, though, let's add two methods that will make the authoring of this test (and others related to it) a whole lot easier. Since it's likely that we'll access this functionality in more than one place, we'll put these new methods inside the file `test/test_helper.rb`. This file is to tests what `ApplicationController` is to our controllers: every method added to that file is available to all of our test cases.

8-41. test/test_helper.rb (excerpt)

```ruby
class ActiveSupport::TestCase
  : class body...
  def login_user
  post session_path, params: { email: users(:glenn).email,
↪ password: 'sekrit'}
  end

  def logout_user
    delete session_path
  end
end
```

As you can see, the utility methods handle logging the user in and out of the application. Using this approach, we can test an action that was previously only available to users who were logged in, just by calling `login_user` before we call the authenticated action and `logout_user` when done. This is inline with the integration test approach I mentioned earlier. We are simply logging in just like the user would, then calling the action we want to test with the logged in user.

Let's see them in action. Before that little detour, we were on the way to writing a test that confirms the contents of the `login_logout` div. These contents should include a (`Logout`) link as well as the user's name, which is set by our before filter in the `current_user` method:

```ruby
test "indicates logged in user" do
  login_user
  get stories_path
  assert_select 'div#login_logout em a', '(Logout)'
end
```

By employing our new utility method `login_user` to login, requesting the `stories_path` route of our `StoriesController` class is the same as it ever was:

```
get stories_path
```

Once we've gained access to the index page, it's easy to use some assertions (in which we're now absolutely proficient) to confirm that the contents of the `div` are as we expect.

Testing Redirection After Logout

Our next few tests will cover the changes we made to the new action of our `StoriesController`.

First, we'll check that users who aren't logged in are correctly redirected to the login page if they try to access our story submission form:

```
test "redirects if not logged in" do
  get new_story_path
  assert_response :redirect
  assert_redirected_to new_session_path
end
```

This is a fairly straightforward test: the `get` statement tries to request the story submission form without first logging in:

```
get new_story_path
```

The remainder of the test confirms that the request results in the user being redirected to the new action of our `SessionsController`:

```
assert_response :redirect
assert_redirected_to new_session_path
```

Our test suite is certainly expanding. We have just two more tests to write in this chapter.

Testing Story Submission

If you've been particularly eager and tried executing your functional test suite
prematurely, you'll have noticed that a few tests that worked previously now fail.
These failures occur because we modified our story submission form; it now
requires that a user_id is present in the session before a page request can be
successful. Our old tests didn't account for this change, so they now fail.

We need to modify the four tests that are affected so that each of them includes a
user id in the session. At this point, it should become obvious that it was well
worth the effort for us to create the login_user and logout_user utility methods:

```ruby
class StoriesControllerTest <
↳ ActionDispatch::IntegrationTest
  ⋮ class methods…
  test "gets stories" do
    login_user
    get stories_path
    ⋮ method body…
  end

  test "gets new story form" do
    login_user
    get new_story_path
    ⋮ method body…
  end

  test "adds a story" do
    login_user
    assert_difference 'Story.count' do
      post stories_path, params: {
        ⋮ story attributes…
      }
    ⋮ method body…
  end

  test "rejects when missing story attribute" do
    login_user
    assert_no_difference 'Story.count' do
```

```
    post stories_path, params: {
      ⋮ story attributes…
    }
  ⋮ method body…
  end
  ⋮ class methods…
end
```

As you can see, the changes are very small. The `login_user` method is added before each action that performs the request. Easy.

Testing Storage of the Submitter

The last test we'll add checks that users who are currently logged in are correctly associated with any stories that they submit:

```
test "stores user with story" do
  login_user
  post stories_path, params: {
    story: {
      name: 'story with user',
      link: 'http://www.story-with-user.com/'
        }
  }
  assert_equal users(:glenn), Story.last.user
end
```

If you've made it this far, you're probably itching to see the results of executing our rapidly expanding test suite.

Fixing VotesController Tests

Just like stories, votes belong to a user. So, it's very likely your votes controller tests are failing now because we are authenticating before we submit the votes. Time to fix that. Before we do, however, I want to briefly introduce a common convention of unit tests.

Programmers have been writing tests for a long time, so some patterns and conventions have cropped up and are used to make test writing a bit more concise. A couple of these conventions deal with **setup** and **teardown** methods.

Let's start with the setup methods first. A setup method is run *before* every test in it's *context*. The context, in our case, is the current test class. As such. The same is true of teardown methods, except they are run *after* each test. An example will clear this up.

We need to authenticate a user for every test in the `VotesControllerTest` class. Minitest provides `setup` and `teardown` methods that allow us to prepare for and cleanup after our tests, respectively. This is perfect for logging in and logging out. Check it out:

8-42. test/controllers.votes_controller_test.rb (excerpt)

```
class VotesControllerTest <
↳ ActionDispatch::IntegrationTest
  setup do
    login_user
  end

  teardown do
    logout_user
  end

  test "creates vote" do
    assert_difference 'stories(:two).votes.count' do
      post story_votes_path(stories(:two))
        end
  end

  test "create vote with ajax" do
    post story_votes_path(stories(:two)), xhr: true
    assert_response :success
  end

  test "redirect after vote with http post" do
    post story_votes_path(stories(:two))
    assert_redirected_to story_path(stories(:two))
  end
end
```

Neat, eh? The tests are exactly the same, but we've added `setup` and `teardown` blocks to handle logging in and logging out. I know what you're thinking: Why didn't we log out of the `StoryControllerTests`? Why didn't we use setup and teardown for them, too? Well, we didn't want to run the login for *every* test in that file. As for not logging out, Rails will clean up the session for you, so it isn't *strictly* required. However, it is a good practice, so you know what's coming...

> ### EXTRA CREDIT: Exploring Other Ways to Run Tests
>
> There are other ways to run tests that allow for creating nested contexts in a test class, but I won't cover them here. I advise you to lookup `Minitest::Spec` to start or checkout RSpec, a very popular Ruby gem for test specifications. Each of these items have their own language and idioms for defining contexts and other items. Exploring them will raise your test game to the next level. Oh, and go back and logout of each `StoriesControllerTest` that needs it. It'll build character.

Running the Full Test Suite

Run the full test suite with our trusty `rails` command. If everything has gone well, you should see results similar to the following:

```
$ rails test
Running via Spring preloader in process 34312
Run options: --seed 60092

# Running:

............................

Finished in 1.062286s, 28.2410 runs/s, 49.8924 assertions/s.

29 runs, 53 assertions, 0 failures, 0 errors, 0 skips
```

If any of your tests failed, the error message that's displayed should help you determine where it went wrong. The error will direct you to the location of the erroneous class and method, and the exact line number within that method. And before you start pulling your hair out, remember that you can double-check your code against the code archive for this book. It went through considerable testing before release, so you can count on the code in it to work.

Even more rewarding than seeing the number of tests and assertions that our test suite now covers is looking at the output of the **stats** task. This command displays a number of statistics relating to the architecture of our application, including the ratio of lines of application code to lines of test code. We've been extremely busy writing tests in this chapter, so let's see the results:

```
$ rails stats
```

My application reports a code-to-test ratio of 1:1.6, as the screenshot below indicates.

```
+----------------------+-------+-------+---------+---------+-----+-------+
| Name                 | Lines |  LOC  | Classes | Methods | M/C | LOC/M |
+----------------------+-------+-------+---------+---------+-----+-------+
| Controllers          |    90 |   75  |    4    |   12    |  3  |    4  |
| Helpers              |     8 |    8  |    0    |    0    |  0  |    0  |
| Models               |    22 |   21  |    3    |    2    |  0  |    8  |
| Mailers              |     0 |    0  |    0    |    0    |  0  |    0  |
| Javascripts          |    27 |    1  |    0    |    0    |  0  |    0  |
| Libraries            |     0 |    0  |    0    |    0    |  0  |    0  |
| Controller tests     |   140 |  119  |    3    |    0    |  0  |    0  |
| Helper tests         |     0 |    0  |    0    |    0    |  0  |    0  |
| Model tests          |    64 |   53  |    3    |    0    |  0  |    0  |
| Mailer tests         |     0 |    0  |    0    |    0    |  0  |    0  |
| Integration tests    |     0 |    0  |    0    |    0    |  0  |    0  |
+----------------------+-------+-------+---------+---------+-----+-------+
| Total                |   351 |  277  |   13    |   14    |  1  |   17  |
+----------------------+-------+-------+---------+---------+-----+-------+
  Code LOC: 105     Test LOC: 172      Code to Test Ratio: 1:1.6
```

8-43. My code-to-test ratio

This means we've written one-and-a-half times the amount of code to test our application than we've written for Readit itself. This is a good thing: it means that we can be confident that our application is of high quality.

Summary

In this chapter, we explored an approach for sectioning off the parts of a Rails application. This was so that some features are available to everyone, while others are available only to users who have logged in.

First, we discussed some theory about sessions and cookies. We then created a new model—the `User`—and built a login form that allows users to log in to Readit. We stored the login functionality in a new `SessionsController` class, which made extensive use of the session container. The end result was that we were able to restrict access to the story submission form to users who were logged in, and direct other visitors to the login form. And to top it all off, we verified that the changes to our code are free of bugs by writing a number of tests.

The next chapter, in which we'll add the last of the features to our Readit application, will cover more complex `ActiveRecord` associations. Though we're moving into more advanced territory, we'll keep moving through each task step by step, so don't be nervous. Let's go add the finishing touches to Readit.

Chapter

Advanced Topics

As we enter the final quarter of this book, we'll implement the last of the features that we listed back in Chapter 1, in preparation for Readit's much anticipated first release.

Along the way, we'll cover some of the more advanced topics that are involved in developing web applications with Ruby on Rails, such as writing your own helpers, using callbacks, and creating complex associations.

Promoting Popular Stories

To start, we'll make a change to the way our users view our application. We'll separate the display of our stories into two pages: one for stories with a score *above* a certain threshold, and one for stories with a score *below* that threshold.

This will encourage readers to push stories to the front page by voting for them. This functionality will replace the story randomizer that currently appears on the index page of our `StoriesController`—it's becoming boring and falling short of meeting the needs of our application.

Before we can start hacking away at these new pages, we should refine our existing models. In particular, we need an easy way to select stories on the basis of their voting scores.

Using a Counter Cache

We've already seen how we can count the number of votes associated with a given story by calling the `size` method on the associated `Vote` object:

```
>> Story.first.votes.size
=> 3
```

Behind the scenes, this snippet performs two separate SQL queries. The first query fetches the first story from the `stories` table; the second query counts the number of `Votes` whose `story_id` attributes are equal to the `id` of the `Story` object in question.

This approach to counting records isn't usually a problem in small applications that deal with only a handful of records; however, when an application needs to deal with several thousand or more, these double queries can significantly impede the application's performance.

One option for tackling this issue is to use more advanced SQL commands, such as `JOIN` and `GROUP BY`; however, like you, I don't really enjoy writing SQL queries. Instead, I'll introduce you to another funky Rails feature: the counter cache.

Introducing the Counter Cache

The **counter cache** is an optional feature of `ActiveRecord`, and makes counting records fast and easy. The use of the word "counter" here is as in "bean counter," not as in "counter-terrorism." The name "counter cache" is intended to reflect the caching of a value that counts records. You can enable the counter cache by including the parameter `counter_cache: true` when defining a `belongs_to` association.

From a performance point of view, the counter cache is superior to an SQL-based solution. When we're using SQL, the number of records for an object associated with the current object needs to be computed by the database every time that object is requested. The counter cache, on the other hand, stores the number of records of each associated object in its own column in the database. This value can be retrieved as often as is needed, without requiring potentially expensive computation to take place.

When It Almost Doesn't Count

The counter cache doesn't actually go through the database to calculate the number of associated records every time an object is added or removed, effective from the point at which it was turned on. Instead, it increases the counter for every object that's added to the association, and decreases it for every object that's removed from the association, from the point at which it's enabled.

As the counter cache needs to be stored somewhere, we'll create room for it in our `Story` model with the help of a migration.

Making Room for the Cache

We'll make a new migration template using the `rails generate migration` to generate the counter cache:

```
$ rails generate migration AddCounterCacheToStories
↳ votes_count:integer
Running via Spring preloader in process 10833
    invoke  active_record
  create
↳ db/migrate/20160420164312_add_counter_cache_to_stories.rb
```

As expected, our new migration template is stored in the file db/migrate/
xxx_add_counter_cache_to_stories.rb. This migration will be used to add a
new column to the stories table, where the column will store a value that
represents the number of Vote objects associated with each Story. The name of
the column should match the method that we would normally call to retrieve the
object count, so we'll call it votes_count. Modify the migration file so that it
looks like this:

```
class AddCounterCacheToStories <
↪ ActiveRecord::Migration[5.0]
  def change
    add_column :stories, :votes_count, :integer, default: 0
    Story.find_each do |s|
      Story.reset_counters s.id, :votes
    end
  end
end
```

Let me explain what's going on here. Columns that store the counter cache need a
default value of 0 in order to operate properly. This default value can be provided
to add_column using the :default argument, as we've done in the first line of our
change method:

```
add_column :stories, :votes_count, :integer, default: 0
```

In the past, we've used migrations to make schema changes, but migrations can
also be used to migrate data. As mentioned before, the number of objects
associated with the model using the counter cache is never actually calculated by
Rails—values are just incremented and decremented as records are modified.
Consequently, the next line in our migration loops through the Story objects in
the database, and manually resets each Story's initial voting score:

```
Story.find_each do |s|
  Story.reset_counters s.id, :votes
```

```
end
```

`Story.find_each` loops over of all stories in the database in batches of 1000. The block resets the voting score for the current story (which is held in the variable s) by calling the class method `Story.reset_counters` and passing in the story ID and the association name. In effect, this is the same as counting all of the `Vote` objects associated with the current `Story`. We have to update the counter this way because, by default, `votes_count` is read-only. ActiveRecord supplies `reset_counters` for just this purpose.

Right, let's make use of this migration.

Applying the Migration

Go ahead and apply this migration using the `rails` command:

```
$ rails db:migrate
```

Once that's completed, there's just one more small change to make to ensure that our association between a `Vote` and a `Story` uses the counter cache we've just set up. Change the `belongs_to` association in `app/models/vote.rb` to the following:

```
belongs_to :story, counter_cache: true
```

It should be noted that Rails will, from this point forward, automatically refer to the value stored in the `votes_count` column, even if we actually call `votes.size`. Because of this behavior, none of the existing code in our project needs to change.

Let's now make that new front page happen!

Implementing the Front Page

Let's implement a simple algorithm for Readit: stories with a voting score above a certain threshold will appear on the front page, while stories with a score below that threshold will display on a voting page.

First, we'll make all the changes required to get our front page running smoothly, utilizing standard templates and partials. We can then make use of these templates to implement our voting bin.

Modifying the Controller

The first change we'll make is to our `StoriesController`. We need to replace the current `index` action (which displays a random story) with one that retrieves the list of stories that have received enough votes to appear on the front page. Modify the index method of the `StoriesController` class located in `app/controllers/stories_controller.rb` so that it looks like the following:

```
def index
  @stories = Story.where('votes_count >= 5').order('id
↳ DESC')
end
```

Let's examine the code.

`Story.where`, as you already know, fetches from the database all stories that match a specified criterion. To implement the voting threshold, we've specified a condition that the total `votes_count` must be greater than or equal to five, using the counter cache that we've jsut created. The result of the `where` operation will then be stored in the `@stories` instance variable.

In addition, we're specifying that our records be ordered by descending `id` here, which will ensure that the newest stories appear at the top of the results, and the older ones at the bottom.

> ### 💡 Ordering by `id`
>
> We could also use `created_at DESC`, which might be better in the long run. Ordering by `id` means we're dependent on the `id` field being of type `integer`, or something that's ordered sequentially. This is not always the case, especially as you start doing more complicated work. For now, though, using `id` works for us.

Modifying the View

Now that we've retired the story randomizer, we also have to rip apart the `index.html.erb` template, which was formerly responsible for rendering a single story link. Our new template will render a collection of stories, each displaying its current voting score and the name of the user who submitted it.

Modify the corresponding index template (located at `app/views/stories/index.html.erb`) so that it resembles this:

```
<h2>
  <%= "Showing #{ pluralize(@stories.size, 'story') }"
↪ %>
</h2>
<%= render partial: 'story', collection: @stories %>
```

The first line of ERb code outputs the number of stories being displayed:

```
  <%= "Showing #{ pluralize(@stories.size, 'story') }"
↪ %>
```

To display this value, we're making use of the `pluralize` helper provided by Rails. `pluralize` displays the noun that is passed in as an argument, either in singular or in plural form. If there's only one story to show, the header will read "Showing 1 story"; in all other cases it will read "Showing x stories", where x is the number of stories available.

Most of the time, Rails is smart enough to correctly pluralize the most common English nouns automatically. If this fails to work for some reason, you have the option of passing both singular *and* plural forms, like so:[1]

```
<%= "Showing #{ pluralize(@stories.size, 'story',
↪ 'stories') } %>
```

To render each story in the collection that we retrieved, we're using a partial. We first encountered these when displaying voting history back in Chapter 7:

```
<%= render partial: 'story', collection: @stories %>
```

As this is the advanced topics chapter, here's another tip. The above line can be abbreviated as follows:

```
<%= render partial: @stories %>
```

How would this work? Given a call like this, Rails looks at the type of object you pass in by checking the class of the first object in the array, which happens to be a Story object. It then assumes a straight mapping between models and controllers, and looks for a partial template in app/views/stories/_story.html.erb. Had we passed in a collection of votes, as we did back in Adding Voting History in Chapter 7, Rails would look for a template in app/views/votes/_vote.html.erb. See the pattern?

The next item on our list is the creation of the partial.

---

[1] If you need to "train" Rails to correctly pluralize a noun in more than one spot, it may be worth adding your own pluralization rules to the Rails Inflector. See the config/initializers/inflections.rb file for an example.

Creating the Partial

Create the file `app/views/stories/_story.html.erb`, and edit it to appear as
follows:

```
                                              9-1. app/views/stories/_story.html.erb

<div class='story'>
  <h3><%= link_to story.name, story %></h3>
  <p>
    Submitted by: <%= story.user.name %> |
    Score: <%= story.votes_count %>
  </p>
</div>
```

This partial is responsible for displaying the core facts of a story in the listings on
the application's front page (and, as you'll see later, in the voting bin). It's a fairly
straightforward template that you should have no trouble understanding. We
wrap our story in `div` tags and automatically assign a `class` of "story".

Apart from the `div` tag, the title of the story is displayed in an `h3` element, which
links directly to the story page using the `link_to` helper; the original submitter of
the story and current voting score are displayed underneath.

We'll now use the assigned element `class` of "story" to apply some CSS styling.

Styling the Front Page

Now that we have some new elements on the front page, let's add style rules for
those elements to our stylesheet, which is located at `app/assets/stylesheets/`
`stories.scss`:

9-2. app/assets/stylesheets/stories.scss (excerpt)

```scss
.story {
  float: left;
  width: 50%;
}


.story h3 { margin-bottom: 0; }
.story p  { color: #666; }
```

While we're giving our front page an overhaul, let's also remove the default Rails welcome page that's displayed when a user accesses `http://localhost:3000/`, and make our new front page the default page instead.

Setting the Default Page

To set the default page, we once again need to alter Rails' routing configuration, which is located in the file `config/routes.rb`. If you look closely, you'll notice a commented line (if you deleted it earlier, don't worry—you can just type out the line you need in a moment):

```ruby
# root 'welcome#index'
```

By removing the first # character (which uncomments the line) and making a slight change to the route, we can set the destination for requests for the address `http://localhost:3000/` to be the index action for our `StoriesController`:

9-3. config/routes.rb (excerpt)

```ruby
root "stories#index"
```

Before you jump into your browser to test this new route, you should be aware of one small caveat: the default Rails welcome page is a simple HTML page (it contains no ERb code at all). It will be displayed if the `root` route is not defined in the `config/routes.rb` configuration file. So in order to display our story index as the default page, this route has to be defined.

Let's take a peek at our new front page (after making sure our web server is running); mine is shown in Figure 9-4. How many stories you have listed will depend on how many votes you've given your stories.

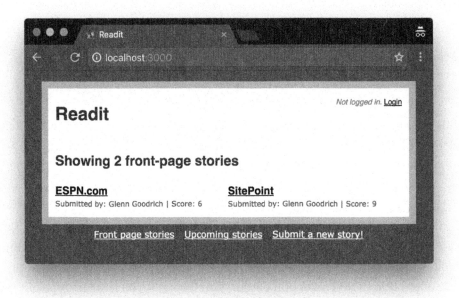

9-4. Scoring stories

If, like mine, your front page is looking rather empty, you're probably keen to start voting! Right now, none of our stories have five votes, so they're sitting in the bin (as in "container of refuse"). Let's briefly cover the implementation of the voting bin, so that you can use it to start voting on stories in the queue.

Implementing the Voting Bin

To create a voting bin, create a new method called bin in the file /app/controllers/stories_controller.rb:

```
class StoriesController < ApplicationController
  ⋮ controller code…
  def bin
    @stories = Story.where("votes_count < 5").order("id
```

```
↪ DESC")
    render action: "index"
  end
end
```

Most of this code looks straightforward enough—but what about that `render` call hiding in there?

Before I explain this, let me point something out, in case you haven't spotted it already: this code is almost identical to what we wrote for our `index` action—it just applies a different condition to the collection of stories.

This fact should trigger the realization that this is a good opportunity to reuse some code. Let's extract most of the code used in these two controller methods (`index` and `bin`) and place it in a protected controller method called `fetch_stories` method, which we'll then use from both locations within our code.

As we discussed earlier, protected methods are only accessible from within a class and its subclasses; they're not accessible from anywhere outside the class.

Here's that extracted method:

```
def fetch_stories(conditions)
  @stories = Story.where(conditions).order('id DESC')
end
```

As the only part that differs between the `index` and `bin` actions is the condition, we'll allow the condition to be passed to the new protected method as an argument.

Our `StoriesController` should now look as follows (only the code relevant to this section is shown):

```
class StoriesController < ApplicationController
  ⋮ controller code…
```

```ruby
  def index
    @stories = fetch_stories "votes_count >= 5"
  end

  def bin
    @stories = fetch_stories "votes_count < 5"
    render action: "index"
  end
  ⋮ controller code…
  protected

  def fetch_stories(conditions)
    @stories = Story.where(conditions).order("id DESC")
  end
end
```

This is one way to approach this scenario. A second and quite common way is to use ActiveRecord scopes[2]. **Scopes** are a means to define common queries for a model that can be called in the same way as methods. As with anything, an example will make it clear.

In this controller code, we have two scopes: let's call them "upcoming" and "popular". Now, open up app/models/story.rb and add the following:

```ruby
class Story < ApplicationRecord
  ...associations...
  scope :upcoming, -> { where("votes_count <
↳ 5").order("id DESC") }
  scope :popular, -> { where("votes_count >=
↳ 5").order("id DESC") }
  ...methods...
end
```

With our scopes in place, return to the controller and change the index and bin actions:

[2.] http://guides.rubyonrails.org/active_record_querying.html#scopes

```
class StoriesController < ApplicationController
  : controller code…
  def index
    @stories = Story.popular
  end

  def bin
    @stories = Story.upcoming
    render action: "index"
  end
  : controller code…
  protected
  ...removed fetch_stories...
end
```

Refresh the page, and the app looks just the same. Except that now we're using scopes. So, you're probably wondering which approach you should use, right? Well, at the end of the day, it's a matter of preference. If you think you'll use the upcoming and popular scopes in future development, scopes probably make sense. If the controller is the only place we'll ever fetch stories in this way, a small controller method is no big sin. I prefer my controllers to just route requests to models (and other objects). However, I've done it both ways in my Rails life.

Now, back to that peculiar render call in the bin action:

```
render action: "index"
```

I mentioned earlier that the two actions we have for listing stories (index and bin) are almost identical; well, they also have in common the template they use. The aforementioned line of code makes sure of that. It specifies that the view template for the index action should also be used by the bin action. As such, we're rendering the same template for a slightly different set of stories.

Before we go ahead and give our two pages sufficient visual distinction—such as headings that tell our users where they are in the application—let's digress to add yet another piece to our routing configuration.

Adding Custom Actions to RESTful Routes

RESTful routes, as you may remember from Mapping a New Resource in Chapter 6, give us a defined set of routes and route generation helpers to refer to routes (or URLs). We've just implemented a new controller action not contained in that set of default routes, so we have to tell Rails what we'd like to do with this new action, how users will reach it, and how we want to refer to it.

Back in `config/routes.rb`, here's the line that gives us all the RESTful goodness for performing regular operations on stories, as well as votes:

```
resources :stories do
  resources :votes
end
```

You may be able to tell from our use of helpers such as `stories_path` and `story_path` in the past couple of chapters that there are routes operating on the stories in general (without referring to a specific one by `id`, such as `stories_path`, for instance) and those that operate specifically on a story (for example, `story_path`). These latter ones need an actual story object to be passed in to operate properly.

We need to discuss this distinction in order to add a custom action to our set of defined routes at the right spot. Since our `index` and `bin` actions are so similar in function, we can safely presume that `bin` would be another action that will operate on the entire collection of stories, since it displays an arbitrary set of stories based on their vote count.

To include a new custom route that operates on a collection of objects, add the following to the routing configuration file:

```
resources :stories do
  collection do
    get "bin"
  end
  resources :votes
end
```

In addition to the name of the custom action, Rails wants us to tell it the actual HTTP method used to talk to this action, which in this case is GET. By changing our routing configuration in this way, we obtain a newly defined helper method: `bin_stories_path`, which refers to the stories in our submission bin. We'll use this helper in a moment, when we modify the site navigation menu to include a link to the bin.

Next up, though, we'll deal with the missing distinction between our two story-listing pages by adding headings to the `index.html.erb` template, all with a little assistance from some `ActionView` helpers.

Breaking the RESTful Rules

The RESTful interface that our Rails app exposes is now non-standard. REST is an architectural style and it evokes many, many opinions—some pedantic, some pragmatic. There are those who argue that adding a non-standard operation, such as `bin`, breaks the RESTful nature of the application. In my view, it gives us what we need when we need it. If you feel differently (many do), another great approach is described in Jerome Dalbert's post[3] about how DHH himself organizes his controllers.

Abstracting Presentation Logic

In this section, we'll look at a way to abstract any presentation logic that you happen to add to your view templates. First, let's discuss why we need to bother extracting Ruby code from our views, even though view templates may appear to be the easiest place to implement presentation logic.

[3.] http://jeromedalbert.com/how-dhh-organizes-his-rails-controllers/

Avoiding Presentation Logic Spaghetti

Recall that our intention is to display a heading that's appropriate in the index template, depending on whether the list of stories being displayed contains front-page stories or upcoming stories.

Of course, we could implement this functionality by adding the logic directly to the app/views/stories/index.html.erb template as shown in this code (we're only *looking* at this stage—avoid *doing* anything just yet):

```
<h2>
  <% if controller.action_name == 'index' %>
    <%= "Showing #{ pluralize(@stories.size,
        'front page story') }"%>
  <% else %>
  <%= "Showing #{ pluralize(@stories.size, 'upcoming
↪ story') }" %>
  <% end %>
</h2>
```

You'll notice that this solution entails a fair amount of duplication; all we're changing in the **else** block is a single word. Additionally, that Ruby code is always wrapped in ERb tags (<% %> and <%= %>) in view templates means that these templates can begin to look like a dish of spaghetti containing chained method calls, nested levels of parentheses, **if** clauses, and other complexities.

When your own code starts to look like spaghetti, it may be time to consider extracting some of that code into an **ActionView** helper.

Introducing ActionView Helpers

As you've heard countless times now, a view should contain presentational code only. In order to adhere to the MVC paradigm as strictly as possible, you should aim to place all logic outside the views: in a controller (for application logic) or a model (for business logic). A third option for presentation-related logic not quite belonging in a controller or a model is the **ActionView** helper.

We talked about making helper methods available to views in <u>Protecting the Form</u> in Chapter 8, when we implemented the `logged_in?` helper method; however, back then we implemented this functionality as a protected controller method, then made available to our views using the `helper_method` statement.

Native `ActionView` helpers differ from protected helper methods in that they're *not* available to controllers, hence the name. An `ActionView` **helper** is a function that helps to reduce the clutter in your view templates.

Writing an `ActionView` **Helper**

`ActionView` helpers are available in two basic forms.

The first is the global helper, which is stored in the file `app/helpers/application_helper.rb`. You can think of a global `ActionView` helper as being the "view" equivalent to the `ApplicationController` class in the "controller" world. Any helper that you add to this file will be available from every view of every controller.

The second form of `ActionView` helper is specific to the views of a particular controller. We'll use this approach for our `ActionView` helper, where we'll create a new helper method for our `StoriesController` in the file `app/helpers/stories_helper.rb`. That way, it will be clear that it's related to `StoriesController`.

Here's the helper method to add:

```
                                                    9-6. app/helpers/stories_helper.rb

module StoriesHelper
  def story_list_heading
    story_type = case controller.action_name
      when "index" then "front-page story"
      when "bin" then "upcoming story"
      end
    "Showing #{ pluralize(@stories.size, story_type) }"
  end
end
```

Let's step through this code. Its first task is populate a variable `story_type` using a Ruby `case` statement:

```
story_type = case controller.action_name
  when "index" then "front-page story"
  when "bin" then "upcoming story"
  end
```

This statement compares the value of `controller.action_name` (which contains the text value of the controller action being executed, exactly as it appears in the URL) with a couple of predefined values–namely, the values `'index'` and `'bin'`.

Next, we display the same "Showing ..." string with the `pluralize` helper that we used in our previous attempt at writing this view:

```
"Showing #{ pluralize(@stories.size, story_type) }"
```

This time, however, we're passing `story_type` as the part of the string that's being pluralized. This string is either set to `front-page story` or `upcoming story`.[4] While this isn't necessarily a shorter solution than the previous one, it certainly removes a lot of clutter from our view, which we now reduce to a single line!

```
<h2><%= story_list_heading %></h2>
  <%= render partial: @stories %>
```

Now we just add our voting bin page to the navigation menu in the footer of each page, and we're done with abstracting presentation logic.

---

[4] If we wanted to be pedantic about reducing code duplication, we could even extract the word "story" from that string, and simply set the `story_type` variable to "front page" or "upcoming." But you have to draw the line somewhere!

Expanding the Navigation Menu

To add a link to our navigation menu, we simply add another list item to the unordered list at the bottom of the application layout. The layout is stored in app/views/layouts/application.html.erb:

9-7. app/views/layouts/application.html.erb

```
<ul id="navigation">
  <li><%= link_to 'Front page stories', stories_path
↳ %></li>
  <li><%= link_to 'Upcoming stories',
↳ bin_stories_path %></li>
  <li><%= link_to 'Submit a new story!',
↳ new_story_path %></li>
</ul>
```

Now we can finally give our changes a whirl. Point your browser to http://localhost:3000/ and click the *Upcoming stories* link at the bottom of the page.

The resulting page, an example of which is depicted in Figure 9-8, should contain all the stories in your database that have a voting score below five.

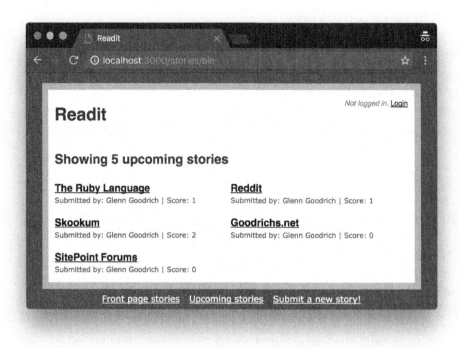

9-8. The story voting bin

Before you use this unique opportunity to promote the first story to Readit's front page, we'll require that users be logged in before they can vote. This will give us the ability to check a user's voting history later on.

Our application is looking much more like a story-sharing site. Onto the next feature!

Requiring a Login to Vote

The next enhancement we'll make will ensure that users log in before they're able to vote. First, we modify `VotesController` so that the `create` method responds only to users who are logged in. We then store the `id` of the current user as part of the new vote.

The first step is to add a new `before_action` method in `app/controllers/votes_controller.rb`, like so:

```
class VotesController < ApplicationController
  before_action :ensure_login
  :  controller code...
end
```

Since the `VotesController` only contains a single action at this stage, there's no need to limit the `before_action` by using the `:except` or `:only` options.

Now, it only makes sense to display a feature to visitors if they can make use of it. Let's add a little login teaser to the story page, to suggest visitors log in if they want to vote for stories. Make the following changes to `app/views/stories/show.html.erb`:

9-9. app/views/stories/show.html.erb *(excerpt)*

```
><% if logged_in? %>
  <div id="vote_form">
    <%= form_for [@story, Vote.new], remote: true do %>
      <%= submit_tag 'vote' %>
        <% end %>
  </div>
<% else %>
  <p>
    <em>
      You would be able to vote for this story if you were
      <%= link_to 'logged in', new_session_path %>!
    </em>
  </p>
<% end %>
```

This `if` clause decides whether or not to display the vote link to visitors, depending on their login status. If the user isn't logged in, that person is presented with a teaser and a link to log in, as shown below.

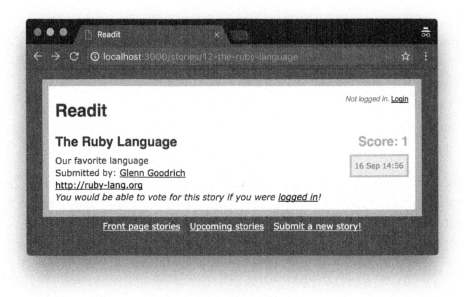

9-10. The front page with a teaser

To complete this feature addition, we'll modify the create action of our VotesController so that it stores the current user with each vote. By the way, if you fixed the tests in the last chapter as recommended, you've already done this:

```ruby
class VotesController < ApplicationController
  : controller code…
  def create
    @story = Story.find(params[:story_id])
    if @vote = @story.votes.create(user: @current_user)
      respond_to do |format|
 format.html { redirect_to @story, notice: 'Vote was
↪ successfully created.' }
        format.js {}
          end
        end
  end
end
```

This new line saves the reference to the current user with each vote.

It's now time to create some additional stories and start submitting votes, if you're yet to do so already.

Visit the voting bin by selecting the *Upcoming stories* link from the navigation menu, and click on a story's title to visit the story page. From there, click the vote link a few times until the story has five or more votes. Visit the front page, and you should see your story appear. The result of my serial voting is shown below.

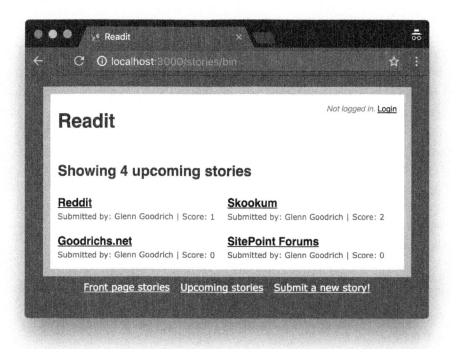

9-11. The front page with some upvoted stories

That's another feature crossed off the list. Next!

Auto-voting

Our next task is to hop into the `Story` model and remedy a piece of functionality that will indisputably aid in the promotion of stories to the front page. New stories will be automatically voted for by yourself as soon as you submit them. To implement this feature, I'll introduce you to a feature of Rails models that we've yet to touch on: callbacks. **Callbacks** are little snippets of code that are triggered by model events—for example, when a model is created, updated, or destroyed.

Introducing Model Callback

Callbacks in models can be called before or after certain actions, such as the creating, updating, or destroying of a model. The concept of a callback may sound similar to the filters we applied to our controllers in Introducing Filters earlier—that's because they *are* similar.

We've already encountered a callback in our application. It was used to apply the validation we implemented in Applying Validations in Chapter 6. Internally, `ActiveRecord` prefixes validation methods before calling the `save` method that writes a model to the database. If the callback result allows the request to continue—meaning the request has passed the defined validations—the `save` operation is executed.

The names of the available callback methods are fairly intuitive: `before_create`, `before_save`, and `before_destroy` are called before the model in question is created, saved, and deleted respectively. There are also a number of `after_` callbacks that, as expected, are called after the operation.

A Combo of Callbacks

There are also `around_` callbacks and `before/after_validation` callbacks. For all the available callbacks, check out the Rails Guides[5].

As with filters in controllers, callbacks in models are usually defined as protected methods. The callback resides in a model class, and is referred to by the class method via a symbol. Here's an example:

```
class Story < ApplicationRecord
  after_create :create_initial_vote
  ⋮ model code…
  protected
    def create_initial_vote
```

[5.] http://guides.rubyonrails.org/active_record_callbacks.html

```
      : callback method…
    end
end
```

We'll use `after_create`, because we'd like to create votes for newly submitted stories only, and not for every update of an existing story (which would require the use of the `after_save` callback).

 Defining Callbacks

In your experimentation with Rails, you may come across the following syntax for model callbacks. Here the code that's to be executed when an event occurs is defined as an instance method named after the callback:

```
class MyModel < ApplicationRecord
  after_save do
    : callback method…
  end
end
```

While this approach is technically correct, I prefer to define my callbacks using descriptive method names, and to refer to them using the `after_save` `:my_method` syntax instead. This is because it's much easier to see what's going on: you can glance at the header of the model class in which the callbacks are declared, then look at each of the callback methods separately.

The reason we're using `after_create` instead of `before_create` should be obvious: if we were to create the vote *before* the model itself had been saved to the database, we'd risk the model's failure to pass the validation checks–hence, we'd have created a vote for an invalid record!

Adding a Callback

Let's add a callback to our `Story` model. Add the following code to the file `app/models/story.rb`:

```ruby
class Story < ApplicationRecord
  after_create :create_initial_vote
  ⋮ model code…
  protected
    def create_initial_vote
      votes.create user: user
    end
end
```

Once again, just one line of Ruby code is sufficient to accomplish the task at hand. Let's dissect what this line actually does.

First, you'll notice that we're able to directly use two of the attributes of the story: the votes association and the user attribute. As long as a method doesn't carry variables of the same name, executing votes or user will refer to the methods of the story object. We know the submitter of the story is stored in user, so we can refer to that attribute in order to create the initial vote:

```ruby
votes.create user: user
```

Before we try out our newly implemented callback that creates the initial vote, let's add an item that's been missing from our stories.

Adding a Description to Stories

In the next enhancement to our application, we'll add an extra attribute to our Story model: a description column that allows users to write a few paragraphs about their submissions.

Adding a Model Attribute

Since we're talking about adding an attribute, you've probably assumed there's a new migration ahead, and indeed there is. Let's generate the migration file that will store the code we'll use to add the description column:

```
$ rails generate migration AddDescriptionToStories
↳ description:text
```

The contents of this migration (stored in db/migrate/
xxx_add_description_to_stories.rb) are straightforward, so only a limited
explanation is needed:

9-13. db/migrate/xxx_add_description_to_stories.rb

```
class AddDescriptionToStories <
↳ ActiveRecord::Migration[5.0]
  def change
    add_column :stories, :description, :text
  end
end
```

As you can see, we're adding a single column to the stories table. We've
specified that the new description column must be of type text, because a
column of type string can only store up to 255 characters, and it's possible that
story descriptions will exceed this limit.

The final step is to apply this migration using the rails command:

```
$ rails db:migrate
Running via Spring preloader in process 48184
 == 20160422175022 AddDescriptionToStories: migrating
↳ ===========================
-- add_column(:stories, :description, :text)
   -> 0.0010s
 == 20160422175022 AddDescriptionToStories: migrated
↳ (0.0010s) ==================
```

Expanding the Submission Form

Another change we'll make before we test our initial vote creation code is to add another field to the story submission form (in the file /app/views/stories/ new.html.erb). This field will accept the description column that we just created:

9-14. /app/views/stories/new.html.erb (excerpt)

```
.footer {
  background-color: #CCC;
  border-top: 1px solid #333;
}
```

```
<%= form_for @story do |f| %>
  ⋮ form HTML…
<div>
  <p><%= f.label :description %></p>
<%= f.text_area :description %>
</div>
<div>
  <p><%= submit_tag %></p>
</div>
<% end %>
```

Figure 9-15 shows the form after we apply this change.

9-15. Enabling users to add a story description

We've given our users plenty of room by making the `description` column of type `text`. To accommodate this larger story description, we're using a `textarea` element instead of a one-line input field:

```
<%= f.text_area :description %>
```

We'll also display the description on the story's page, just above the `submitted_by` paragraph in the file `/app/views/stories/show.html.erb`:

```
                                    9-16. /app/views/stories/show.html.erb (excerpt)

<ul id="vote_history">
  ⋮ vote history…
</ul>
<p>
  <%= @story.description %>
</p>
<p class="submitted_by">
  ⋮ submitted by…
</p>
```

White-listing the New Attribute

There's one final item on the to-do list before we can test our new form: white-listing the `description` attribute. If you remember from Chapter 6, Rails uses Mass Assignment Protection as a security measure, so we have to add our new attribute to the list of permitted attributes in `StoriesController` (found in /app/controllers/stories_controller.rb). Change the `story_params` method to this:

```
                              9-17. /app/controllers/stories_controller.rb (excerpt)

def story_params
  params.require(:story).permit(:name, :link, :description)
end
```

Okay, now we should be in business. Let's hop over to our browser and submit a new story to see whether the automated submission of the first vote works as expected. And sure enough, it does—as Figure 9-18 shows!

9-18. Automated submission working as expected

Adding User Pages

To track the history of our site's usage on a per-user basis, we'll create a place where this information can be displayed.

We're going to add a user page, which will list the six stories most recently submitted by the logged-in user, and the six stories for which that person most recently voted. To select the most recently voted-for stories, we'll make use of another type of relationship: the join model.

Introducing the Join Model Relationship

A **join model relationship** is a relationship between two models that relies upon a third. Without the third model, there's no direct relationship between the two models that are being linked.

In our Readit application, an association only exists between our `Story` and `User` models when we talk of who *submitted* each story. Currently, we lack the ability to find out who *voted* for each story. This is where the join model comes into play: the `Vote` model is already associated with both the `User` and the `Story` models; with the addition of the `has_many :through` statement, the `Vote` can serve as the connecting element in this new relationship. This relationship is illustrated in Figure 9-19.

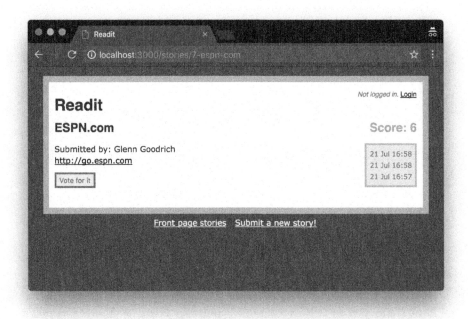

9-19. The name of a story's submitter displays with the story

The `Vote` model is the join model because it joins the `User` and the `Story` models.

Introducing the `has_many :through` Association

The code that implements a join model relationship is the line `has_many :through`. Let's use it to add a join model relationship to our `User` model. Open the file `/app/models/user.rb` and make the changes in bold:

9-20. /app/models/user.rb (excerpt)

```ruby
class User < ApplicationRecord
  has_secure_password
  has_many :stories
  has_many :votes
  has_many :stories_voted_on,
      through: :votes,
      source: :story
end
```

Normally, Rails is smart enough to figure out associated class names on its own, so long as the association class names are given a name that matches the plural form of the class name (for instance, :stories); however, because our User model already has a has_many relationship (has_many :stories), we must assign this new association a different name (:stories_voted_on). We also need to specify the model with which we're associating the users, which is exactly what the source: :story argument does.

The code that defines this relationship as a join model relationship is the through: :votes argument, which can be read as: "a User *has many* Stories *through* the Vote model."

With this association in place, we find that several new instance methods are available to every User object:

```ruby
>> u = User.first
=> #<User id: 1, …>
>> u.stories_voted_on.size
=> 1
>> u.stories_voted_on.first
=> #<Story id: …>
```

As you can see, this association behaves like a regular has_many association, and if you were none the wiser, you'd never actually know that three models were involved in retrieving the associated data.

Adding Another Controller

Before we implement our user page, we need to generate another controller, since we're yet to deal with User objects to date.

By now, you should be ever so familiar with the procedure to generate a controller with the `rails generate` command, so I'll spare you the details. Enter the following command to create a new `UsersController`:

```
$ rails generate controller Users show
```

Additionally, we'll add a resource declaration to the routing configuration stored in `config/routes.rb`, like so:

```
resources :users
```

Here, we use the plural for both `resources` and `:user`. Can you remember why? (Hint: The answer is in Chapter 8 where we added sessions.)

The actual implementation of the show action in `UsersController` is as follows:

9-21. /app/controllers/user_controller.rb

```ruby
class UsersController < ApplicationController
  def show
    @user = User.find(params[:id])
    @stories_submitted = @user.stories.
      limit(6).order("stories.id DESC")
    @stories_voted_on  = @user.stories_voted_on.
      limit(6).order("votes.id DESC")
  end
end
```

Let's look at this code. Remember that the `params` hash stores the various parts of the current URL, as defined in the application's routing configuration. To retrieve the requested user from the database, we employ the `find` method:

```
@user = User.find(params[:id])
```

The data we'll display on the user page is fetched by the associations that are available via the `User` object. We then populate a couple of instance variables, calling methods to sort the items in the desired order and limit the number of items retrieved:

```
@stories_submitted = @user.stories.
  limit(6).order("stories.id DESC")
@stories_voted_on  = @user.stories_voted_on.
  limit(6).order("votes.id DESC")
```

Since multiple tables are involved in retrieving the data in which we're interested, we have to be more explicit with our ordering instructions. Here we're using `stories.id` and `votes.id` in the order clause respectively. The part before the period actually specifies the table that contains the `id` column by which to sort. Since most (if not all) of our tables *have* an `id` column, this is a necessary evil.

The next task on our list is to create the view template for this page.

Creating the View

The view template for our user page has been generated (with fairly non-spectacular content) in `/app/views/users/show.html.erb`. This template will use the instance variables that we created in our controller to display the recently submitted stories and votes. It does so by rendering a collection of partials:

```
                                            9-22. /app/views/users/show.html.erb
 <h2>Stories submitted by <%= @user.name
 ↪ %></h2>
<div id="stories_submitted">
  <%= render partial: @stories_submitted %>
</div>
 <h2>Stories voted for by <%= @user.name
 ↪ %></h2>
<div id="stories_voted_on">
  <%= render partial: @stories_voted_on %>
</div>
```

The partial we're rendering with this code already exists. We're reusing the `story` partial from `StoriesController`, which Rails will know to use because we're passing in a collection of `Story` objects using the shorthand notation of the render call:

```
<%= render partial: @stories_submitted) %>
```

Next, we'll add a link to the user page by linking the name of the submitter as it's displayed on the story page (`/app/views/stories/show.html.erb`):

```
<p class="submitted_by">
  Submitted by:
 <span><%= link_to @story.user.name, @story.user
 ↪ %></span>
</p>
```

Now we'll make a small addition to our stylesheet (`stories.scss`) for the sake of some visually pleasing cosmetic treatment:

9-23. /app/assets/stylesheets/stories.scss (excerpt)

```scss
.story p {
  color: #666;
  font-size: 0.8em;
}
h2 {
  clear: both;
  margin: 0;
  padding: 10px 0;
}
```

Lastly, we'll add the login of the user in question to the links generated for the user page by overriding the `to_param` method of `User`, just as we did with the `Story` class:

9-24. /app/models/user.rb (excerpt)

```ruby
class User < ApplicationRecord
  ⋮ model code…
  def to_param
    "#{id}-#{name}"
  end
end
```

In practice, you should probably ensure that the name attribute contains only alphanumeric characters. You can accomplish this little exercise with some help from the `format` option of the `validates` method.

There we go! As Figure 9-25 shows, we now have a user page that makes use of our newly added `has_many :through` association, listing both the stories that were submitted by a given user and the stories for which that person recently voted.

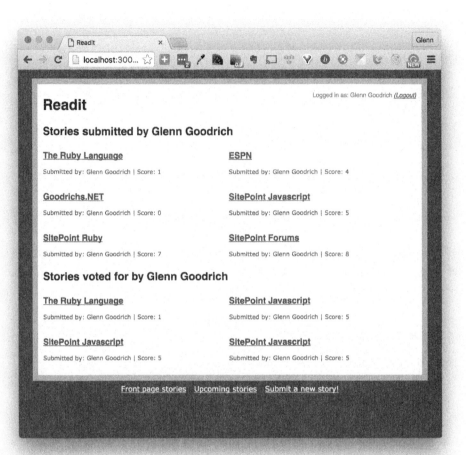

9-25. Telling stories

Testing the New Functionality

As is standard practice, we'll add test coverage by writing unit tests and then adding functional tests for all the enhancements we've made.

Testing the Model

We made a number of changes to our model in this chapter, including utilizing the counter cache and introducing the join model relationship. Let's write some unit tests for those changes now.

Testing Additions to the Counter Cache

The first change we made in this chapter was to modify the `Story` model so that it uses the counter cache to track the number of votes associated with any given `Story`. To test this feature, we'll have to pull a few tricks out of the box, as there are numerous conditions to take into account.

To begin with, let's add a test to the test case for a scenario in which a vote is cast. The test case is located in `/test/models/story_test.rb`:

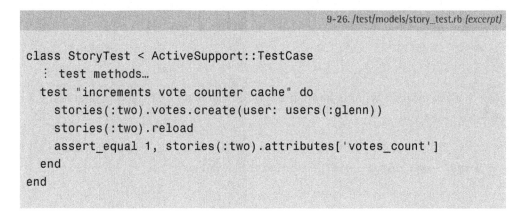

9-26. /test/models/story_test.rb (excerpt)

```
class StoryTest < ActiveSupport::TestCase
  : test methods...
  test "increments vote counter cache" do
    stories(:two).votes.create(user: users(:glenn))
    stories(:two).reload
    assert_equal 1, stories(:two).attributes['votes_count']
  end
end
```

This contains a method we've yet to encounter (`reload`), so let's dissect the code.

The purpose of this test is to verify that the cached votes count is properly incremented hen a new vote is added; however, there's a gotcha when using counter caches and fixtures. The fixtures counter cache attributes will be incorrect when you first grab the fixture. This is due to fixtures being created without going through ActiveRecord, instead being thrown straight into the database with SQL. So we need to set the counters for the records we want to use in the fixtures file. Change the stories fixtures (in `/test/fixtures/stories.yml`) to:

```
one:
  name: My old weblog
  link: http://ruprict.net/
  user: glenn
  votes_count: 2

two:
  name: SitePoint Forums
  link: http://community.sitepoint.com
  user: glenn
  votes_count: 0
```

Now we can explain what is happening in the test. The first step we take is to create a new vote:

```
stories(:two).votes.create(user: users(:glenn))
```

The second line is where it becomes interesting. We're forcibly reloading the model from the database:

```
stories(:two).reload
```

We do this because once a new vote has been added, the number of stories that are cached in each model's attributes is suddenly out of sync with the database.

If we were to check the log file when we come to run our tests later, we'd find lines such as the following:

```
UPDATE stories SET votes_count = votes_count + 1 WHERE (id =
↪ 2)
```

This is the SQL statement that Rails generates to update the counter cache. You'll notice that the statement doesn't bother to check the current value of votes_count—it just tells the database to increment votes_count by one. And with good reason.

You see, in a live application many users may be using the site at the same time, and some of them might even be casting votes in parallel. The value of votes_count would be negated if the SQL for each vote submission relied upon its own copy of votes_count at the time the statement was executed.

As such, you have to reload the model if you ever require access to the current number of votes after a new vote is added. This situation is unlikely to occur often; normally you'd redirect your user to a new page anyway. But when we're writing tests that simulate user behavior, it's important to be mindful of this issue.

There's also something special about the assertion in this test: instead of comparing the return value of the votes_count instance method, we access the "raw" attribute as it comes out of the database:

```
assert_equal 1, stories(:two).attributes['votes_count']
```

If we had used the instance method, there'd have been no need to enable counter caching in order for our test to pass; votes_count would simply have issued a second database query to count the votes. By using the attribute itself, we're asserting that the counter cache is doing its job.

Testing Deletions from the Counter Cache

With that first test out of the way, this second test covering the deletion of votes should be straightforward. Our application is yet to allow users to delete votes, but we'll include this test for the sake of completeness:

```
class StoryTest < ActiveSupport::TestCase
  ⋮ test methods…
  test "decrements votes counter cache" do
    stories(:one).votes.first.destroy
    stories(:one).reload
    assert_equal 1, stories(:one).attributes['votes_count']
  end
end
```

This test is basically the opposite of the previous one. Again, we need to reset the counters for our record. Then we destroy the first vote from the first story and then reload the model to reflect this change:

```
stories(:one).votes.first.destroy
stories(:one).reload
```

Finally, we compare the cached `votes_count` value to the value we expect it to have:

```
assert_equal 1, stories(:one).attributes['votes_count']
```

Testing the Creation of the Initial Vote

The next test covers the new functionality that we added to our model for the automatic creation of a vote when submitting a story:

```
class StoryTest < ActiveSupport::TestCase
  ⋮ test methods…
  test "casts vote after creating story" do
    s = Story.create(
      name: "Vote SmartThe 2008 Elections",
      link: "http://votesmart.org/",
      user: users(:glenn)
    )
    assert_equal users(:glenn), s.votes.first.user
  end
end
```

You should be able to follow the twists and turns of this test quite easily. To test the creation of a vote after a story has been saved to the database, a new story is created (don't forget to pass in a user):

```
s = Story.create(
  name: "Vote SmartThe 2008 Elections",
  link: "http://votesmart.org/",
  user: users(:glenn)
)
```

The assertion confirms that the user of the first vote attached to the newly created story is indeed the user we passed in when we created the story in the first place:

```
assert_equal users(:glenn), s.votes.first.user
```

This establishes that there's at least a single vote, and that the user has been properly inherited from the story.

Testing the Join Model Relationship

Lastly, we need to add a test to deal with the new `has_many :through` association that we added to our `User` model. Expand the test cases (located in `/test/models/user_test.rb`) as follows:

9-30. /test/models/user_test.rb (excerpt)

```
class UserTest < ActiveSupport::TestCase
  ⋮ test methods…
  test "voted on association" do
    assert_equal [ stories(:one) ],
      users(:glenn).stories_voted_on
  end
end
```

`<`

This test relies on fixture data, so we can assert immediately that the list of stories for which our test user voted is equal to the list that we expect:

```
  assert_equal [ stories(:one) ],
↪ users(:glenn).stories_voted_on
```

Now we've got some controller tests to write.

Testing the `StoriesController`

In this chapter, we've added quite a bit of functionality to `StoriesController` that needs testing. This is a little more complicated than in previous chapters, so the corresponding tests will be more complex. Additionally, we've added a new `UsersContoller` with a relatively simple action, which also needs testing.

Testing the Story Index Pages

As a next step, we're confirming that each of the story-listing actions (index and bin) picks the proper records from the database. To do this, let's add another story to the fixtures in /test/fixtures/stories.yml:

```
                                           9-31. /test/fixtures/stories.yml (excerpt)

promoted:
  name: What is a Debugger?
  link: http://en.wikipedia.org/wiki/Debugger/
  user: john
  votes_count: 5
```

As you can see, we're cheating a bit and hardcoding the votes_count to five.

We'll start by changing an existing test (test "gets index") and adding one more basic test to cover correct template rendering:

```
                                9-32. /test/controllers/stories_controller_test.rb (excerpt)

  class StoriesControllerTest <
↪ ActionDispatch::IntegrationTest
    ⋮ test methods…
    test "gets stories" do
      get stories_path
      assert_response :success
      assert response.body.include?(stories(:promoted).name)
    end

    test "gets bin" do
      get bin_stories_path
      assert_response :success
      assert response.body.include?(stories(:two).name)
    end
    ⋮ test methods…
  end
```

Both tests are similar in nature and neither exposes any new functionality. Each calls its respective action, checks that the request was responded to successfully, and confirms that an appropriate story is rendered (remember, we're using exactly the same template for both the `index` and `bin` actions). It also ensures the `@stories` instance variable doesn't wind up being `nil`.

Testing the Routing Configuration

We also altered the routing configuration in this chapter, so let's add a test to confirm that our changes are working properly:

```
test "story index is default" do
  assert_recognizes({ controller: "stories",
  action: "index" }, "/")
end
```

The `assert_recognizes` assertion confirms that a given request is translated into an expected set of parameters, mostly consisting of a controller and an action name:

```
  assert_recognizes({ controller: "stories", action: "index"
↪ }, "/")
```

Our assertion here confirms that a request for "/" (the front page of our domain) is indeed routed to the `index` action of `StoriesController`.

Testing Page Headings

The next pair of tests deals with the view side of the `index` action, and confirms that the header tag contains a proper heading, complete with the expected number of stories:

9-33. /test/controllers/stories_controller_test.rb *(excerpt)*

```
test "shows story on index" do
  get stories_path
  assert_select 'h2', 'Showing 1 front-page story'
  assert_select 'div#content div.story', count: 1
end

test "show stories in bin" do
  get bin_stories_path
  assert_select 'h2', 'Showing 2 upcoming stories'
  assert_select 'div#content div.story', count: 2
end
```

The second `assert_select` assertion tests for an appropriate number of `div` elements with a class attribute of `story`. These divs come out of the `_story.html.erb` partial and, as such, we're looking for one `div` per story. Each story `div` is contained in the all-encompassing `div` that has an `id` of `content`.

Testing the Story Submission Form

We added to the story submission form a new field that allows users to submit story descriptions. To test this functionality, change the existing `test "new shows new form"` test to match the following:

```
test "new shows new form" do
  login_user
  get :new
  assert_select 'form p', count: 3
end
```

In this test, the `assert_select` call counts the number of `p` elements below the `form` tag, and checks the total against our expected number of 3—three form fields plus a Submit button.

Testing the Story Display Page

Since users who are not logged in no longer see the vote button, we need to revise an existing test and add a new one. (Again, if you worked ahead last chapter as recommended, these are likely to be fixed):

9-34. /test/controllers/stories_controller_test.rb *(excerpt)*

```
test "show story vote elements" do
  login_user
  get story_path(stories(:one))
  ⋮ method body…
end

test "does not show vote button if not logged in" do
  get story_path(stories(:one))
  assert_select 'div#vote_link', false
end
```

We pass `false` to `assert_select` to confirm that there are *no* elements on the page that match the given CSS selector.

Testing the Navigation Menu

We added an item to our navigation menu, so we should increase the number of list items that we check for in the following test from two to three:

9-35. /test/controllers/stories_controller_test.rb *(excerpt)*

```
test "show navigation menu" do
  get stories_path
  assert_select 'ul#navigation li', 3
end
```

Testing the Story Submitter Link Text

Lastly, let's change our existing test for the story submitter on the story page
(test "shows_story_submitter") ensuring that it now links to the story
submitter's user page:

9-36. /test/controllers/stories_controller_test.rb (excerpt)

```ruby
test "show story submitter" do
  get story_path(stories(:one))
  assert_select 'p.submitted_by span a', 'Glenn Goodrich'
end
```

Phew! That was quite a litany of tests. Let's now turn our attention to the tests of
the other controllers affected by the goings-on in this chapter.

Testing the VotesController

Since we've modified the voting procedure to be available for logged-in users
only, we have to modify some existing tests, as well as add a new one to cover
storage of the user for every vote cast.

Testing User Voting History

Additionally, we'll add a test to confirm that the vote action indeed stores the
current user with the submitted vote:

9-37. /test/controllers/votes_controller_test.rb (excerpt)

```ruby
test "stores user with vote" do
  post story_votes_path(stories(:two))
  stories(:two).reload
  assert_equal users(:glenn), stories(:two).votes.last.user
end
```

Testing the UsersController

Without further ado, we'll add three tests to cover the functionality encapsulated within the user page we added to UsersController:

9-38. /test/controllers/users_controller_test.rb *(excerpt)*

```ruby
class UsersControllerTest < ActionController::TestCase
  test "show user" do
    get user_path(users(:glenn))
    assert_response :success
    assert response.body.include?(users(:glenn).name)
  end

  test "show submitted stories" do
    get user_path(users(:glenn))
    assert_select 'div#stories_submitted div.story', count: 2
  end

  test "show stories voted on" do
    get user_path(users(:glenn))
    assert_select 'div#stories_voted_on div.story', count: 1
  end
end
```

All three tests use basic assertions to confirm that the proper user is found by the show action, and that the user's story submissions and votes are displayed properly on the page.

Running the Complete Test Suite

We've made a massive number of additions to our suite of tests in this chapter, so it should be especially rewarding to run the full suite now using:

```
$ rails test
Running via Spring preloader in process 44037
Run options: --seed 14835
```

```
# Running:

.............................................

 Finished in 0.675667s, 65.1209 runs/s, 125.8017
↳ assertions/s.

40 runs, 67 assertions, 0 failures, 0 errors, 0 skips
```

Summary

Wow, what a journey! In this chapter, we've added a stack of features to Readit, such as the display of popular story listings on the front page, and the implementation of a voting bin containing stories on which people can vote.

Along the way, we learned that the counter cache offers an easy way to store the number of records associated with any given model, and we used `ActiveRecord` callbacks as a means to hook into certain events occurring on our models. We used a `after_create` callback to cast an initial vote for submitted stories, and we also tackled `ActionView` helpers to reduce clutter in our shared view.

Lastly, we covered an additional type of association: the join model relationship. It was used to implement a user page showing the story submissions and voting history of each registered user.

After numerous tests and assertions, we can attest that Readit is in very good shape indeed. Of course, there are countless enhancements that we could make to our little application; some of the functionality that comes to mind includes:

- creating a form that enables new users to register
- sending an email to new users to notify them of their passwords
- allowing users to comment on stories
- restricting users to vote for each story once only

I'm sure your mind is racing with ideas for a number of spectacular features that could set your application apart from the pack! While the addition of all these features is more than we could possibly cover in this book, you now have a solid grounding—both in theory and in practice—on which you can build to further develop Readit on your own. Remember to keep expanding your test suite to include all the cool new features that you add.

In the next chapter, we'll take a quick look at the Rails plugin architecture, and use one of the existing plugins to expand Readit's feature set: implementing tagging functionality for our story submissions.

Chapter

Rails Plugins

While this book is unable to cover all of the built-in functionality that ships with Rails—and there's plenty of functionality for you to discover and experiment with once you're beyond the last chapter—the plugins architecture of Rails warrants our attention.

What is a plugin?

A plugin is a component that you can add to your application to extend its functionality. While you can certainly write your own plugins[1], we'll limit our discussion here to using existing plugins. Plugins have been developed for various parts of the Rails framework, adding functionality such as:

[1.] http://guides.rubyonrails.org/plugins.html

- extensions to ActiveRecord functionality
- helper methods
- new template engines (for coding a view using an alternate templating language)

The number of existing Rails plugins is enormous and grows every day. Programmers in the Ruby and Rails communities are excellent about sharing code and creating useful plugins based on extensions they need. A good resource of existing Rails plugins can be found by searching for "Rails" on the Rubygems site[2] or on the Ruby Toolbox[3] site.

Plugins are distributed as gems, which we covered in Chapter 2. Plugins can be pulled into an existing Rails application by adding them to the `Gemfile` and running `bundle install`. You probably remember our discussion about Bundler from Chapter 4, where its job is to manage application dependencies. Bundler makes including existing plugins into our app a breeze.

Finding a plugin that does what you require is usually just a Google or RubyGems search away. As seen in Figure 10-1, searching for "rails tagging" brings up a few gems that have been created, including one called `acts-as-taggable-on`[4].

[2.] https://rubygems.org/search?utf8=%E2%9C%93&query=Rails

[3.] https://www.ruby-toolbox.com/

[4.] https://github.com/mbleigh/acts-as-taggable-on

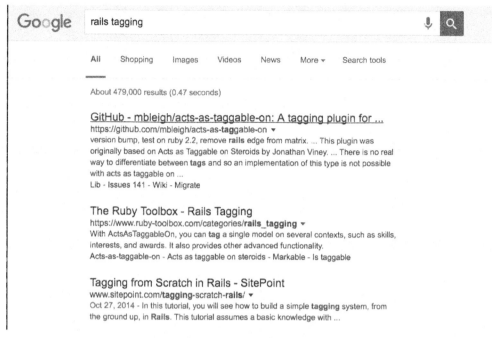

10-1. Searching for a plugin on "rails tagging"

The overwhelming majority of gems keep their source on GitHub[5], including `acts-as-taggable-on` from the first link in our search above. Following that link leads to the source on GitHub, as shown in Figure 10-2.

[5.] https://github.com

10-2. The GitHub repository for 'acts-as-taggable-on'

Most GitHub source repositories have a `README` or `README.md` file that explains what the gem does, how to install and use it, and so on. `acts-as-taggable-on` follows this convention, which can be seen in Figure 10-3. It explains the object of the gem, the supported versions of Rails, as well as how to install and configure the gem.

ActsAsTaggableOn

`gem version` `3.5.0` `build failing` `code climate` `2.7` `docs`

This plugin was originally based on Acts as Taggable on Steroids by Jonathan Viney. It has evolved substantially since that point, but all credit goes to him for the initial tagging functionality that so many people have used.

For instance, in a social network, a user might have tags that are called skills, interests, sports, and more. There is no real way to differentiate between tags and so an implementation of this type is not possible with acts as taggable on steroids.

Enter Acts as Taggable On. Rather than tying functionality to a specific keyword (namely `tags`), acts as taggable on allows you to specify an arbitrary number of tag "contexts" that can be used locally or in combination in the same way steroids was used.

Compatibility

Versions 2.x are compatible with Ruby 1.8.7+ and Rails 3.

Versions 2.4.1 and up are compatible with Rails 4 too (thanks to arabonradar and cwoodcox).

Versions >= 3.x are compatible with Ruby 1.9.3+ and Rails 3 and 4.

For an up-to-date roadmap, see https://github.com/mbleigh/acts-as-taggable-on/milestones

Installation

To use it, add it to your Gemfile:

```
gem 'acts-as-taggable-on', '~> 3.4'
```

and bundle:

```
bundle
```

10-3. A standard README file

After reading through the `README.md`, we now know how to pull the gem into our application and use its functionality. You may feel that walking through the topic of "how to find and learn about gems" is a bit tedious, but you will find yourself spending loads of time doing just that—so I figured it was tedium well spent.

No Time for Name-calling

There are many ways to extend Rails; for example, by using a "plugin", "engine", and "railtie", to name a few. While there are technical differences between these items, they are often (incorrectly) used interchangeably. Defining these terms and their differences is beyond the scope of this book, so I'm going to stick to the word "plugin" for now. As you grow in your Rails-fu, you'll no doubt want to do some research around Rails extensibility. Boom—I just turned this note into an EXTRA CREDIT!

Okay, enough theory! Let's go ahead and install our first plugin.

Adding Tagging to Readit

Tagging is the process by which content creators attach simple textual labels to their data, be it a photo, a link, or a restaurant review. These tags vary widely in their nature; they may be related to location or content, for instance. This results in everyone seeming to have a unique system for tagging data. Currently, the hashtag (#) is probably the most popular form of tagging content with metadata, thanks to Twitter!

Tags are definitely more flexible than a category tree, as they allow you to assign as many or as few tags as you like to any item of data. The convention that has evolved is for the user to enter tags for a content item into a text field. Multiple tags should be separated by a space or a comma.

Introducing the `acts-as-taggable-on` Gem

Instead of reinventing the wheel and implementing our own tagging system for Readit, we'll use one of the available Rails plugins for this job, the aforementioned `acts-as-taggable-on`. You may be wondering what kind of name the developer originally chose for his plugin. At some point, David Heinemeier Hansson himself actually developed a plugin named `acts_as_taggable` as a proof of concept for some then-new features for Rails. It wasn't intended for production use, and has since been deprecated, but was picked up again because tagging is such an essential component of today's websites with user-generated content. Jonathan Viney, a Rails core contributor and all-round guru, took up where Heinemeier Hansson left off and created his work under the name of `acts_as_taggable_on_steroids`. Yet development waned, so *another* developer name Michael Bleigh formed `acts-as-taggable-on`, and has been developing it ever since. With that bit of family history out of the way, let's have a look at what this plugin can do for us.

A History of `acts_as_*`

As this is far being from an obvious name for a plugin, allow me to explain the background of the `acts_as_*` naming convention.

In Rails' own plugin repository can be found a number of acts, which are functional extensions to an `ActiveRecord` model. These acts equip models with certain functionality that usually can be enabled using a single line of code.

As this functionality enables models to "act as something else," the convention of calling these functional additions "acts" arose, and the code that enables the functionality `acts_as_something` shortly followed.

At the time of writing, many "acts as" gems are available on Rubygems.org: `acts_as_list`, `acts_as_tree`, and `acts_as_paranoid`, to name a few. While some are more complex than others, each of these acts apply a hierarchy to a set of model objects. In the case of `acts_as_list`, objects are positioned in a flat list; with `acts_as_tree`, the resulting hierarchy is a sophisticated tree system, such as that used in a threaded forum, for example.

But what about `acts-as-taggable-on`? As the name suggests, this plugin provides a simple yet effective means by which you can make your models taggable. It ships with its own `ActiveRecord` model class called `ActsAsTaggableOn::Tag`, as well as functionality for parsing a list of tags divided by spaces into separate model objects of class `ActsAsTaggableOn::Tag`.

Namespacing Safety Measures

You probably noticed that the `Tag` class is namespaced under `ActsAsTaggableOn`. Namespacing classes inside a gem is a Ruby community best practice based on years of class names stomping all over each other from different gems and libraries. `Tag` is a fairly common name, so putting it in the `ActsAsTaggableOn` namespace ensures we avoid loading another gem that clobbers the class.

Of course, before we can play with this plugin, we'll need to install it.

Installing the `acts-as-taggable-on` Gem

To install the gem, change directory to the application root folder and add the
following line to the `Gemfile`:

```
gem "acts-as-taggable-on", "~> 4.0"
```

The ~> tells Bundler that we want any version in the 4.x series. If 4.2 is the latest,
that's what we'll get; however, if the versions went 4.2, then 5.0, we'd *still* end up
with 4.2. Make sense?

Now run the following:

```
$ bundle install
Fetching gem metadata from https://rubygems.org/...........
Fetching version metadata from https://rubygems.org/...
Fetching dependency metadata from https://rubygems.org/..
Resolving dependencies...
Using rake 10.5.0
Using i18n 0.7.0
Using json 1.8.3
Using minitest 5.8.4
...
Installing acts-as-taggable-on 4.0.0.pre
...
 Bundle complete! 14 Gemfile dependencies, 56 gems now
↪ installed.
 Use `bundle show [gemname]` to see where a bundled gem is
↪ installed.
Post-install message from acts-as-taggable-on:
When upgrading
```

As you can see, Bundler runs through all the dependencies of our app, including
installing the `acts-as-taggable-on` into the application "bundle". There's even a
post-install message from the `acts-as-taggable-on` gem telling us what to do
next.

Creating a Migration for the Plugin

Our plan is to allow users of our application to add tags to stories submitted to Readit, so our Story model needs to be taggable. Both the tags themselves and the relationships between tags and stories need to be stored somewhere, so we'll use a migration to create new tables. And while this plugin makes use of a new model (the ActsAsTaggableOn::Tag model provided by the acts-as-taggable-on plugin), the model wasn't created by the rails generate command, so we're yet to have a migration to go with it. Luckily, the plugin does come with a convenient generator method to create a fitting migration:

```
$ rails acts_as_taggable_on_engine:install:migrations
Running via Spring preloader in process 64781
 Copied migration
↳
201...7_acts_as_taggable_on_migration.acts_as_taggable_on_engine.rb
↳ from acts_as_taggable_on_engine
 Copied migration
↳ 201...8_add_missing_unique_indices.acts_as_taggable_on_engine.rb
↳ from acts_as_taggable_on_engine
 Copied migration
↳
2_add_taggings_counter_cache_to_tags.acts_as_taggable_on_engine.rb
↳ from acts_as_taggable_on_engine
 Copied migration
↳ 201...0_add_missing_taggable_index.acts_as_taggable_on_engine.rb
↳ from acts_as_taggable_on_engine
 Copied migration
↳
201...1_change_collation_for_tag_names.acts_as_taggable_on_engine.rb
↳ from acts_as_taggable_on_engine
 Copied migration
↳ 201...2_add_missing_indexes.acts_as_taggable_on_engine.rb
↳ from acts_as_taggable_on_engine
```

Rake'n'rails

The message received after we bundled instructed you to use `rake` instead of `rails`. Welcome to the bleeding edge. In previous versions of Rails, `rake` was used to run tasks like this, but Rails 5 added `rails` as an alias. This was to allow devs to use `rails` for all generators and tasks.

This task copied five migrations into our `db/migrate` directory. These files produce the tables used by `acts-as-taggable-on`, along with creating some database indexes and other database artifacts. The `acts-as-taggable-on` plugin uses two tables:

- The `tags` table stores the `ActsAsTaggableOn::Tag` model, which is just a regular `ActiveRecord` model. This table contains one entry for each tag. So, for example, if you tagged two or more `Story` models with the tag `ruby`, only one `ActsAsTaggableOn::Tag` object (`ruby`) would be stored in the database. This approach makes it easy for our application's users to find content; if users were interested in finding stories about Ruby, they could browse through all the stories to which the `ruby` tag was applied.
- The `taggings` table stores the actual mappings between the `ActsAsTaggableOn::Tag` model and those models that make use of the `acts-as-taggable-on` functionality.

Following is the migration code that was generated for us. It is ready to use as is, and is stored in the `db/migrate/xxxx_acts_as_taggable_on_migration.rb` file:

```ruby
class ActsAsTaggableOnMigration < ActiveRecord::Migration
  def self.up
    create_table :tags do |t|
      t.string :name
    end

    create_table :taggings do |t|
      t.references :tag

      # You should make sure that the column created is
      # long enough to store the required class names.
      t.references :taggable, polymorphic: true
```

```
    t.references :tagger, polymorphic: true

    # Limit is created to prevent MySQL error on index
    # length for MyISAM table type: http://bit.ly/vgW2Ql
    t.string :context, limit: 128

    t.datetime :created_at
  end

  add_index :taggings, :tag_id
 add_index :taggings, [:taggable_id, :taggable_type,
↳ :context]
  end

  def self.down
    drop_table :taggings
    drop_table :tags
  end
end
```

This migration starts out simply enough. It creates the tags table that contains just one column: name (in addition to the id column belonging to every table).

While it may appear straightforward on the surface, the taggings table is a little more complex than a mere list of objects and their tags. As mentioned, it's possible to make more than one model in your application taggable; however, the mappings between the ActsAsTaggableOn::Tag model and those models to which tagging functionality has been added use a single table.

acts-as-taggable-on uses each of the columns created in the taggings table as follows:

- tag_id is created by t.references :tag and stores the id of the ActsAsTaggableOn::Tag
- taggable_id is created by t.references :taggable, polymorphic: true and stores the id of the object that is *being tagged* (for example, the ID of a Story)

- `taggable_type` is created by `t.references :taggable, polymorphic: true` and stores the class of the object that is being tagged (for example, `Story`)
- `tagger_id` is created by `t.references :tagger` and stores the `id` of the user that created the tag (for example, the ID of a `User`)
- `tagger_type` is created by `t.references :tagger` and stores the class of the object that is doing the tagging (for example, `User`)

You may be asking what "polymorphic" means in our migration. Hold tight, I'll cover that soon enough.

Before we can give our `Story` model a little `acts-as-taggable-on` goodness, we need to apply the migration just generated, as shown below.

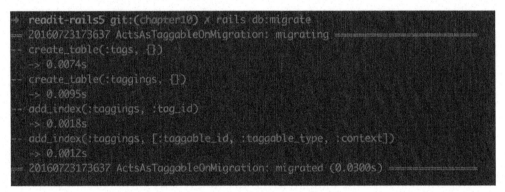

10-4. Applying the generated migration

Great! Now we can make our `Story` model taggable. Let's chat about polymorphic associations.

Understanding Polymorphic Associations

We've looked at the underlying tables utilized by the `acts-as-taggable-on` plugin, and we know what's stored in which columns. But what kind of association is this?

It's not a one-to-many relationship, because one tag may be applied to many items *and* one item may have many tags. It's a kind of bidirectional, one-to-many relationship. In fact, it's often called a "many-to-many" relationship. Rails features a type of relationship that's just for this type of situation. It's called a *polymorphic association*.

In a polymorphic association, a model is associated with objects of more than one model class, as Figure 10-5 illustrates. In order to store this relationship in the database accurately, the object's class name (or "type") *and* ID must be stored. Check out the migration that we just created, and you'll see this is exactly what's achieved by the schema created.

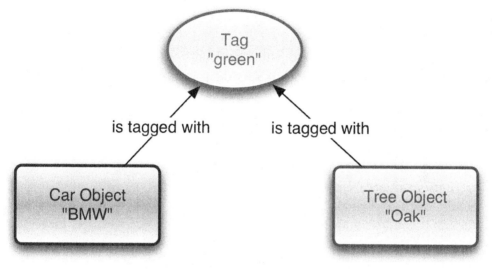

10-5. Two models are assigned the same tag

If the schema didn't save both the class name and ID of the object, we potentially face a situation in which a tag is applied to both a `User` object with an ID of 1 and a `Story` object also with an ID of 1. The chaos that would result!

Fortunately, Rails automatically and transparently handles most of the details that implement this relationship for you.

Making a Model Taggable

To use `acts-as-taggable-on`, modify the `Story` class definition located in `/app/ models/story.rb` as follows:

```
class Story < ApplicationRecord
  acts_as_taggable
  : Story model…
end
```

Yes, that *is* it! With the plugin in place, it takes just 16 characters to make a model taggable. Please note that the function name is still `acts_as_taggable` as opposed to the plugin name, which is `acts-as-taggable-on`.

Next, we'll hop into the Rails console to play with our `Story` model's new functionality. The `acts-as-taggable-on` plugin has added various extra methods to our model. Let's take a look at some of them.

First, retrieve a story from the database:

```
>> s = Story.first
=> #<Story id: 2, name: "SitePoint Forums", …>
```

We can look at the tags already assigned to this story by using the `tag_list` instance method:

```
>> s.tag_list
=> []
```

By simply assigning a new value to the `tag_list` attribute, we have the ability to tag an object. In its simplest form, this value can be a comma-separated list of tags to apply:

```
>> s.tag_list = 'sitepoint, forum, community'
=> "sitepoint, forum, community"
```

When the model is then saved to the database, we can use the `tag_list` method again to fetch an array of tags assigned to the model:

```
>> s.save
=> true
>> s.tag_list
=> ["sitepoint", "forum", "community"]
```

The `tag_list` method is in fact a shortcut to the association data, which is available through the `tags` instance method. This method provides access to an array of the `ActsAsTaggableOn::Tag` objects with which this particular story is associated:

```
>> s.tags.size
=> 3
```

As mentioned earlier in the chapter, we can also use methods of the `ActsAsTaggableOn::Tag` class to retrieve a list of stories tagged with a particular word. We load up an existing tag (which we've just created through the assignment of a comma-separated list of tags to the `tag_list` attribute of the `Story` model) using a standard `ActiveRecord` method:

```
>> t = ActsAsTaggableOn::Tag.find_by(name:
↪ "sitepoint")
=> #<ActsAsTaggableOn::Tag id: 1, name:
↪ "sitepoint">
```

Each `ActsAsTaggableOn::Tag` instance collects a list of all the objects to which it has been assigned—information that's available through the `taggings` instance method. Let's request the size of the array:

```
>> t.taggings.size
=> 1
```

Based on the value returned by the size method, we can hazard a guess that the object available in this array is the Story object we tagged earlier. Let's use the first method to be sure:

```
>> t.taggings.first
 => #<ActsAsTaggableOn::Tagging id: 1, tag_id: 1,
↪ taggable_id: 2,
taggable_type: "Story", …>
```

Yes, we were right!

The objects contained in this taggings array are the fully functional model objects of class ActsAsTaggableOn::Tagging. This is like an intermediate model between the Tag and the object *being tagged*, such as a Story object. If we want to access the actual tagged model, we have to go through yet another association that the acts-as-taggable-on plugin defined for us: taggable.

```
>> t.taggings.first.taggable
=> #<Story id: 2, name: "SitePoint Forums", …>
```

This property retrieved for us the actual story object to which we applied the tag. We're now free to invoke the same methods and access the same attributes that we would when dealing straight with a Story object. Let's request the name of the story that we've tagged with the sitepoint tag:

```
>> t.taggings.first.taggable.name
=> "SitePoint Forums"
```

Straightforward stuff, no? I have to admit, there are a lot of chained method calls there. Didn't we learn about a new type of association that connects a model *through* another model in the previous chapter. Feel free to implement that on your own.

One last point: because it's conceivable that a tag may be applied to more than one type of model, each model is equipped with a new dynamic finder that fetches only objects of that object's class assigned a certain tag. That dynamic finder is `tagged_with`:

```
>> s = Story.tagged_with("sitepoint")
 => #<ActiveRecord::Relation [#<Story id: 2, name:
↳ "SitePoint Forums", ...>
>> s.size
=> 1
>> s.first.name
=> "SitePoint Forums"
```

Okay, enough with the console. Let's now give users the ability to tag stories through our application's web interface.

Enabling Tag Submission

Before we get all fancy *displaying* tags all over our site, we need a way for users to *submit* tags with a new story. Let's add a new form field to the story submission form.

Modifying the View

To add the form field, modify the submission form located in the file `app/views/stories/new.html.erb`:

```
                                    10-7. app/views/stories/new.html.erb (excerpt)

<% form_for @story do |f| %>
  : form HTML...
  <p>
    Tags (comma separated):<br />
        <%= f.text_field :tag_list %>
  </p>
  <%= submit_tag %>
<% end %>
```

Users will be separating each tag with a comma, so a simple text field for tag
entry will do the job nicely:

```
<%= f.text_field :tag_list %>
```

The only mind-bending aspect about this line is the use of a regular `text_field`
method. This would have us believe that our `Story` object somehow gained a
database column for `tag_list`, which it most certainly did not. In fact, this is
exactly why the `acts-as-taggable-on` uses a pragmatic approach for the
implementation of tagging for specific objects. It provides the `tag_list` and
`tag_list=` methods for objects of classes that have been tag-enabled with
`acts_as_taggable`, thus closely resembling what `ActiveRecord` provides us with
for regular database-backed attributes. Behind the scenes, the plugin intercepts
what's being set for this attribute and transparently handles creating new `Tag`
objects and `Taggings` relationships. Cool, huh?

Modifying the Controller

To assign the submitted tags to the new story, you probably expected to modify
the `story_params` method of the `StoriesController` class to allow `tag_list` to
be passed to the model. Well, you're right! Open up `app/controllers/`
`stories_controller.rb` and change the `story_params` method like so:

```
                                 10-8. app/controllers/stories_controller.rb (excerpt)
```

```ruby
def story_params
  params.require(:story).permit(:name, :link, :description,
↳ :tag_list)
end
```

Now our users can submit tags with their stories. Let's display them, shall we?

Enabling Tag Display

We want our tags to appear in a few places. First of all, they should be visible on the story page itself. It would also be nice to see them in the story listings on the front page, as well as on the page showing stories in the voting bin.

Modifying the View

To display the assigned tags on the story page, modify the `show` template located at `app/views/stories/show.html.erb`. Add the following code between the containers of the story link and the voting form (`vote_form`):

```erb
<% unless @story.tag_list.empty? %>
  <p class="tags">
    <strong>Tags:</strong>
    <%= @story.tag_list %>
  </p>
<% end %>
```

Once again, if a story has an empty list of tags, we don't bother listing them; so we'll wrap the logic in an `unless` clause:

```erb
<% unless @story.tag_list.empty? %>
  ⋮ tag HTML…
<% end %>
```

If tags *are* associated with a story, we go ahead and render the list of tags for now:

```
<%= @story.tag_list %>
```

Updating the story Partial

Now we'll display tags for each story that appears in the story listings on the front page and in the voting bin. To add this information to the display, we modify the `app/views/stories/_story.html.erb` partial:

10-9. app/views/stories/_story.html.erb *(excerpt)*

```
<% div_for(story) do %>
  <h3><%= link_to story.name, story %></h3>
  <p>
    Submitted by: <%= story.user.name %> |
    Score: <%= story.votes_count %><br />
    Tags: <%= story.tag_list %>
  </p>
<% end %>
```

This code also prints a comma-separated list of the tags assigned to a story using the `tag_list` instance method.

Assigning Our First Tags

With a solid foundation in place for the assignment and display of tags in the application, you can now start experimenting with this exciting new piece of functionality. Submit a new story from your browser using the story submission form, this time including a few tags as I've done in Figure 10-10. If your web server is still running from the previous chapter, you may need to restart it before it will recognize the new plugin.

10-10. Submitting a story with tags

When you view the front page, upcoming page, or individual story listings, you should see the tags display nicely below your story, as in Figure 10-11.

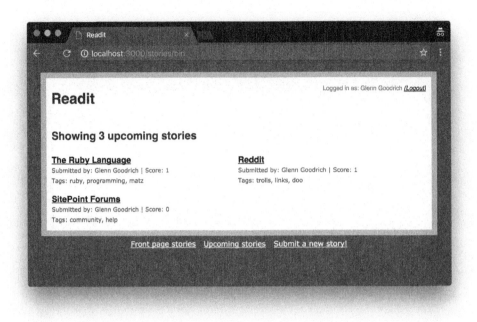

10-11. Tags on display

(Remember, you won't have any tags yet for the existing stories.)

Everything looks good; however, we'd like to link those tags to a page showing all stories with this tag in common. That's our next task.

Viewing Stories

At this stage, it may seem we're taxing ourselves by having to create a separate controller to implement the view-by-tag feature; however, as you've made it to the final third of the book, creating a new controller shouldn't impose too much on your Rails development skills. Besides, this will work nicely with the RESTful approach we're applying to Readit's development.

Creating the Controller

Our new controller is supposed to deal with objects of class `Tag`, so `TagsController` will be an excellent fit. You can create it as follows:

```
$ rails generate controller Tags show
Running via Spring preloader in process 67691
  create  app/controllers/tags_controller.rb
  route   get 'tags/show'
  invoke  erb
  create    app/views/tags
  create    app/views/tags/show.html.erb
  invoke  test_unit
  create    test/controllers/tags_controller_test.rb
  invoke  helper
  create    app/helpers/tags_helper.rb
  invoke    test_unit
  invoke  assets
  invoke    coffee
  create      app/assets/javascripts/tags.coffee
  invoke    scss
  create      app/assets/stylesheets/tags.scss
```

To make our new controller adhere to RESTful principles, we require another
entry in `config/routes.rb`:

10-12. config/routes.rb *(excerpt)*

```
Rails.application.routes.draw do
  resources :tags
  : other routes…
end
```

Now go ahead and open `app/controllers/tags_controller.rb`, and adjust the
`show` action to this:

```ruby
class TagsController < ApplicationController
  def show
    @stories = Story.tagged_with(params[:id])
  end
end
```

There's nothing too fancy here; we simply retrieve all the stories tagged with a particular tag using a method we played with in the `console` earlier in this chapter—`tagged_with`:

```ruby
@stories = Story.tagged_with(params[:id])
```

The last task required by this page is the creation of an appropriate heading to distinguish it from our other story lists.

Filling in the View Template

The view template for the `show` action is really very simple. We could almost reuse the `app/views/stories/index.html.erb` template, but it's a little awkward to reuse action templates between two separate controllers, so we won't do that. What we will do, however, is reuse the partial to render a list of stories.

To do so, open `app/views/tags/show.html.erb` and adjust it as follows:

```erb
<h2>Stories tagged with <%= params[:id]
 ↳ %></h2>
<%= render partial: @stories %>
```

This ends up being similar to the aforementioned `index` template, but retains the flexibility of dragging in additional models we can equip with tagging functionality in the future.

Displaying Tagged Stories

We could now simply construct a URL to a tag page of our own, seeing we know what kind of tag we've used in our story submissions; however, we want our users to be able to click on tags displayed in the story listings, so as to reach the respective page listing all stories with that tag.

To do this, we'll change the `app/views/stories/show.html.erb` template slightly to render a partial instead:

10-14. app/views/stories/show.html.erb *(excerpt)*

```erb
<% unless @story.tag_list.empty? %>
  <p class="tags">
    <strong>Tags:</strong>
  <%= render partial: "tags/tag", collection: @story.tags
  %>
  </p>
<% end %>
```

We can't use here the shorthand syntax we first met a couple of chapters ago because of the namespacing of the `Tag` class. So we explicitly tell Rails to render the `tag` partial in the `tags` view directory. This render call will search for a partial in `app/views/tags/_tag.html.erb`, so let's create that partial now.

Creating a `tag` Partial

To render a collection of tags assigned to a story, we need a `tag` partial. Create the file `app/views/tags/_tag.html.erb`, and edit the contents to contain this single line:

10-15. app/views/tags/_tag.html.erb

```erb
<%= link_to tag, tag_path(id: tag.name) %>
```

This `link_to` call departs slightly from the oh-so-comfortable convention-laden form that we've grown to love. It's because we actually want the URL for our tag pages to look like this:

```
http://localhost:3000/tags/sitepoint
```

While we could certainly go ahead and modify the `to_param` method of the `Tag` class, this would require changing the contents of the `acts-as-taggable-on` plugin. Although this is certainly possible, it's best discouraged, as a future update to the plugin could break our changes. This is the reason why I opted to construct the URL by explicitly assigning the `name` value of the tag to the `id` part of the URL.

Updating the Stylesheet

To give our tag links a little room to breathe on the page, we'll add the following snippet of CSS to our stylesheet, located at `app/assets/stylesheets/tags.scss`:

10-16. app/assets/stylesheets/tags.scss *(excerpt)*

```
.tags a { padding: 0 3px; }
```

Excellent. Let's see how it's all looking now, shall we? Loading up a page of a story with tags assigned should look similar to Figure 10-17.

10-17. Story page with tags

Clicking on any of the provided tags should reveal a list of stories that share this tag, an example of which can be found in Figure 10-18. Lovely!

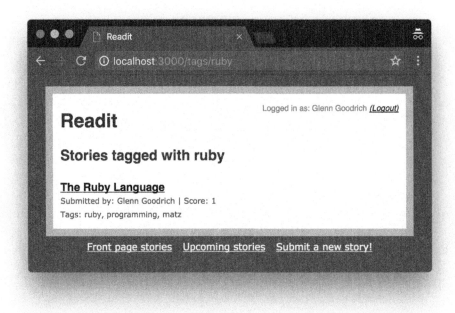

10-18. Testing the Tagging Functionality

Testing the Tagging Functionality

Some plugins come bundled with complete test coverage, while others do not. The original `acts_as_taggable` was quite bare-bones in that regard. The makeover, however, is extensive in its test coverage. Still, it's good practice to add to your test suite to ensure that you're testing *your usage* of the plugin, which definitely isn't covered by the standard test suite for the plugin.

Testing the Model

To test the tagging functionality that our `Story` model has inherited, we're going to add two more unit tests to the `StoryTest` test case.

Before we commence, we need to ensure that Rails has applied all our new migrations to the test database. This is done with the same `db:migrate` command, but we set the `RAILS_ENV` variable to `test`, which tells Rails to use the test environment:

```
rails db:migrate RAILS_ENV=test
```

A Conventional Environment

There are a few environment variables that Rails will use by convention (you should be used to the idea of convention by now). RAILS_ENV is one of them, and it determines which environment is current. You'll recall that by default, there are three possible environments: development, test, and production.

Testing the Assignment of Tags

The first test we'll add to the /test/models/story_test.rb file is as follows:

10-19. /test/models/story_test.rb *(excerpt)*

```
class StoryTest < ActiveSupport::TestCase
  ⋮ test methods…
  test "is taggable" do
    stories(:one).tag_list = 'blog, ruby'
    stories(:one).save
    assert_equal 2, stories(:one).tags.size
    assert_equal [ 'blog', 'ruby' ], stories(:one).tag_list
  end
end
```

This test uses the tag_list attribute accessor to apply two tags to one of the stories in our fixture data:

```
stories(:one).tag_list = 'blog, ruby'
```

To reflect the newly added tags, we save the object in question:

```
stories(:one).save
```

The two assertions in this test confirm that the number of tags assigned to the story meets expectations, and that the list of tags returned by the `tag_list` method contains the correct tags in the form of an array:

```
assert_equal 2, stories(:one).tags.size
assert_equal [ 'blog', 'ruby' ], stories(:one).tag_list
```

Testing the Finding of a Story by Tag

The next unit test we add for our `Story` model is this:

10-20. /test/models/story_test.rb (excerpt)

```
test "finds tagged with" do
  stories(:one).tag_list = 'blog, ruby'
  stories(:one).save
  assert_equal [ stories(:one) ],
    Story.tagged_with('blog')
end
```

This test confirms that the functionality for finding stories by tag works as expected. After tagging a story, the test uses the `tagged_with` class method to retrieve a list of stories with the `blog` tag, comparing it with the list of stories that we expect to be returned.

Great, we're done! Let's go do some functional testing.

Testing the Controller

We're now going to add a few tests to our `StoriesControllerTest` to confirm that our tagging feature works correctly from a controller perspective.

Testing the Submission of a New Story with Tags

The first test confirms that the process of adding a new story with tags works:

10-21. /test/controllers/stories_controller_test.rb *(excerpt)*

```
class StoriesControllerTest <
↪ ActionDispatch::IntegrationTest
  : test methods…
  test "add story with tags" do
    login_user
    post :create, story: {
      name: "story with tags",
      link: "http://www.story-with-tags.com/",
      tag_list: "rails, blog"
    }
    assert_equal [ 'rails', 'blog' ], assigns(:story).tag_list
  end
end
```

In this test, we specify the tags as part of the :story hash. Remember, tags are submitted just like any other attribute in the story submission form:

```
post stories_path, story: {
  name: "story with tags",
  link: "http://www.story-with-tags.com/",
  tag_list: "rails, blog"
}
```

The assertion then ensures the tag_list method of the newly added Story returns the tags that we submitted:

```
assert_equal [ 'rails', 'blog' ], assigns(:story).tag_list
```

Testing the Display of Tags on a Story Page

The next test checks whether a story's individual page displays its tags properly:

10-22. /test/controllers/stories_controller_test.rb (excerpt)

```
class StoriesControllerTest <
↪ ActionDispatch::IntegrationTest
  ⋮ test methods…
  test "show story with tags" do
    stories(:promoted).tag_list = 'apple, music'
    stories(:promoted).save
    get story_path(stories(:promoted))
    assert_select 'p.tags a', 2
  end
end
```

In this test, we confirm that the container element on the story page contains an appropriate number of elements. We do this by counting the number of links within the p element that have a class of tags:

```
assert_select 'p.tags a', 2
```

Testing the Display of the Story Submission Forms

Because we added a new field to the story submission form, we have to edit our StoriesControllerTest class so that the "shows new form" test counts an additional paragraph element:

```
class StoriesControllerTest <
↪ ActionDispatch::IntegrationTest
  ⋮ test methods…
  test "shows new form" do
    login_user
    get new_story_path
    assert_select 'form p', count: 4
  end
end
```

Let's now move on and write some tests for our `TagsController`.

Testing the show Action of `TagsController`

To test our newly created `TagsController`, add the following to the `TagsControllerTest` test case stored in `test/controllers/tags_controller_test.rb`:

```
                                        10-23. test/controllers/tags_controller_test.rb
test "renders tagged stories" do
  stories(:one).tag_list = 'blog, ruby'
  stories(:one).save
  get tag_path("ruby")
  assert_response :success
  assert_select 'div#content div.story', count: 1
end
```

In this test, we put the template code through its paces. The `assert_select` assertion call confirms that the resulting page contains the expected number of div elements with a class of `story`:

```
assert_select 'div#content div.story', count: 1
```

And that, dear reader, is the last test I'll make you write! Well, for this chapter, anyway.

Running the Test Suite ... Again!

To assure ourselves that all of these new tests pass (as well as our existing ones), we'll run the whole suite again using `rake`.

```
$ rails test
Running via Spring preloader in process 60620
Run options: --seed 20795
```

```
# Running:

. . . . . . . . . . . . . . . . . . . . . . . . . . . . . . . . . . . . . . . . . . . . . . . . . . . . . . .

Finished in 1.056509s, 49.2187 runs/s, 90.8653 assertions/s.

45 runs, 73 assertions, 0 failures, 0 errors, 0 skips
```

If all of your tests passed, give yourself a congratulatory pat on the back. And if there are any errors or failures, double-check your code against the code in the book and the book's code archive to see where you might have gone wrong. The error messages displayed in your console will help, of course. And if you get truly stuck, you could jump ahead to the next chapter to read about debugging your Rails application.

Summary

In this chapter, we looked at using an existing Rails plugin to extend our application's functionality without reinventing the wheel. After installing the plugin and applying the necessary migrations, we only had to add a single line of code to make use of the rich functionality provided by the plugin. When we'd ascertained how the plugin worked, we expanded the story submission form to take a comma-separated list of tags, and expanded several views to display the tag data.

Our work is not done yet, though—we still have a bit to learn about debugging our application, running integration tests, and configuring our environment for production. These topics will be the focus of the remaining chapters.

Chapter

Debugging, Testing, and Benchmarking

Welcome to a chapter devoted to the very topics nobody likes to talk about: errors, bugs, flaws, and exceptions. These topics, however dismaying, are *de rigeur* for any comprehensive hands-on technical guide—let's not pretend that development is perennially easy and always results in perfect, error-free code!

Once you begin developing applications on your own, the first lesson you'll learn—probably the hard way—is that bugs arise all the time, regardless of how proficient you are as a developer. It's your job to find and fix them, so you'd better be good at it!

Of course, the fun doesn't stop at bugs and errors. It may be that your finished application is not as speedy as you'd like. If this is the case, you'll need tools on hand to profile your application, so that you can locate the bottlenecks responsible for slowing things down.

In this chapter, we'll explore all of these issues.

Debugging Your Application

When you're building a web application, there are times when you immediately know the exact cause of a problem and how to fix it. For example, a broken image on your website instantly indicates that you've forgotten to upload it, or that the path to the image is incorrect. With other bugs, however, you may fail to have the merest ghost of an idea what's happened. It's at times like these that knowing how to debug your code comes in *very* handy.

There are various approaches to debugging. The simplest involves printing out the values of some of the variables that your application uses while it runs, to gain a better idea of what's going on at each step in your code. A more complex approach involves complicated but powerful techniques: setting breakpoints, hooking into the running application, and executing code in the context in which you suspect it's misbehaving.

We'll begin our discussion with something simple: we'll look at the `debug` statement that's available within `ActionView` templates. Over the course of the next two sections, we'll work to squash a real live bug in our Readit application; I've gone against the developer grain and deliberately introduced problems into our existing, perfectly working application code so that we can get our hands dirty with a practical application. As you follow along, try to think of the potential causes for problems we encounter.

Are you ready? Let's try our hand at a little debugging.

Debugging within Templates

I've deliberately broken our application by changing a specific line of code (obviously, I'll avoid telling you which—that's the whole point of this exercise!). The result of this code change is that the story page for a newly submitted story throws an exception and no longer displays the story. Figure 11-1 shows how this bug appears in the browser.

11-1. A mystery bug causing an error to display when we view a story

To complete this exercise, you'll first need to follow these steps to set up the purposefully buggy version of Readit:

1. Copy the folder named `readit-debug-01` from the code archive, and place it alongside your existing `readit` application folder.
2. Move into the `readit-debug-01` folder and run `rails db:migrate` to run the migrations.
3. Start up your broken version of the Readit application using the now familiar `rails s` command.
4. Open up a Rails console (`rails c`) and add a new user as follows:
   `User.create(name: "Glenn Goodrich", email: "glenn.goodrich@sitepoint.com", password: "password", password_confirmation: "password")`
5. Log in and add a new story to Readit. I've given my story the name "All About Debuggers."

6. Once you've submitted your new story, point your browser to
   `http://localhost:3000/stories/1-all-about-debuggers`.

When your browser has finished loading the page, you should see a similar sight
to Figure 11-1. The line number may not match exactly, but as long as the error is
the same, everything's working as expected.

How should we approach such an error? Let's begin by taking a closer look at the
error message:

```
Showing
↳ /Users/ggoodrich/projects/sitepoint/readit/app/views/stories/
show.html.erb
↳ where line #20 raised:

undefined method `name` for nil:NilClass
```

The obvious deduction is that our application tried to call the `name` method on a
`nil` object in our `show.html.erb` template. Understandably, Rails could not
perform such an action, as the object `nil` is without a `name` method.

The error message also includes an excerpt of the code that Rails believes was
responsible for the exception:

```
Extracted source (around line #20):

18: <p class="submitted_by">
19:    Submitted by:
 20:      <span><%= link_to @story.user.name,
↳ @story.user %></span>
21: </p>
22: <p>
23:    <%= link_to @story.link, @story.link %>
```

The error message directs us to line 20 of the template, which is where the
`link_to` helper tries to assemble a link to the user page associated with the user

who originally submitted the story. This line also contains the call to the `name` method that raised the exception. We're calling the `name` method on the `user` object associated with the story that's currently being viewed:

```
20:    <span><%= link_to @story.user.name,
↪ @story.user %></span>
```

Rereading the error message, we're under the impression that `@story.user` must actually be `nil`. But what good are impressions in web application programming? No good at all. We require cold, hard facts!

Let's put two tasks on our to-do list:

- Confirm that `@story.user` is indeed `nil`.
- Find out *why* it is `nil`.

To tackle the first item on our list, let's alter the parts of the template that raised the exception, in order to inspect the contents of `@story.user`. To do so, open the `app/views/stories/show.html.erb` template and change the following sections:

```
<p class="submitted_by">
  Submitted by:
  <%= @story.user.class %>
 <span><%# link_to @story.user.name, @story.user
↪ %></span>
</p>
```

I made two changes to the template. First, I added a statement to print the class of the `@story.user` variable to our browser. Then, I used the `<%# %>` syntax to comment out the `link_to` statement. If we fail to do this, the application will continue to raise an exception when we reload the page, and we won't receive the output of the line we added. This line is now considered a comment rather than part of the working code, and as such it won't be executed.

When we reload the page, we see that `@story.user` is indeed `NilClass`, which is the class of `nil` and explains the exception we're seeing. Figure 11-2 shows the results of our work. The first item on our to-do list is done.

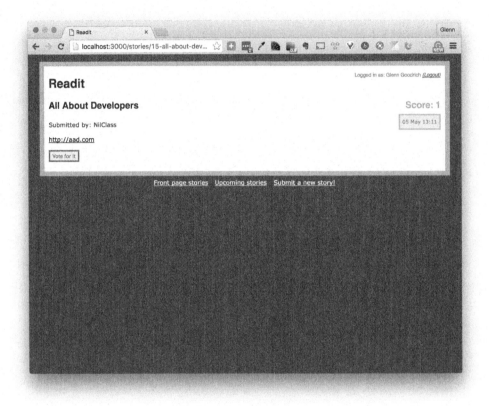

11-2. Confirmation of our `nil` user

To find out *why* `@story.user` is `nil`, we'll have to follow the steps that led to the user assignment when submitting new stories. Before we proceed, though, we should revert the changes that we just made to the `show.html.erb` template. Remove the statement that prints the class name, and make the `link_to` statement active again:

```
<p class="submitted_by">
  Submitted by:
  <span><%= link_to @story.user.name, @story.user
↳ %></span>
```

```
</p>
```

When we implemented user authentication in <u>Chapter 8</u>, we populated this variable with the currently logged-in user available in the `@current_user` instance variable. Let's check the contents of this variable using the `debug` helper.

Add the following statement to the template that's being rendered for the new action—it's located in `app/views/stories/new.html.erb`:

```
<% if @story.errors.any? %>
  ⋮ error HTML…
<% end %>
<%= debug @current_user %>
<%= form_for @story do |f| %>
  ⋮ form HTML…
<% end %>
```

The code I added between the `@story.errors.any?` block and the `form_for` statements is the `debug` helper provided by Rails:

```
<%= debug @current_user %>
```

The `debug` statement instructs Rails to output a YAML representation of the object that we pass as a parameter. In this case, because we're working from a view template, this output will be sent directly to the browser. Load the story submission form (`http://localhost:3000/stories/new`) with this debugging code in place, and you should see a resemblance to Figure 11-3.

11-3. Looking at a YAML representation of `@story`

The output should remind you of our test fixtures—it's formatted in YAML, after all. The debugging content that's shown in addition to our regular template output is a representation of `@current_user`, which contains the currently logged-in user.

The `debug` helper automatically wraps its output in a `pre` element. By default, the contents of a `pre` element are displayed by the browser as preformatted text in a monospace font.

Within the YAML representation, you can tell that what we're being shown is indeed a fully fledged user object appropriately stored in the referenced instance variable. This indicates the part of our code that fetches the user from the database via the ID stored in the session is indeed working fine.

Web Console

Another debugging option that ships with Rails is **web console**. The web_console gem, included in the `development` group of our application's bundle, enables us to create a Rails console in some really interesting places. In this example, instead of using `debug` to print out the value of the `@current_user`, we can use web_console to create a Rails console *right on the page* and execute arbitrary Ruby in the context of the page.

In order to use web_console, we'll add a call to `console` to our new controller action:

```
def new
  console
  @story = Story.new
end
```

Now refresh the page and you'll see a >> prompt in the area at the bottom, which resembles a terminal, as shown in Figure 11-4.

11-4. A web console–right on the page

As I mentioned, you can execute Ruby commands in this console in the context of the page. So we can check the value of `@current_user` by simply typing `@current_user` as seen in Figure 11-5.

11-5. Checking the value of `@current_user`

The value of `@current_user` is clearly printed in our web console. We can check the value of anything that's in the current scope, such as `session[:user_id]` or `@story` (which is set to a new, empty `Story`). Pretty cool, eh? Incidentally, the console is also available, by default, on any error pages in development.

Using web_console can be a lifesaver—it's a very quick way to figure out what is happening without having to add `debug` statements and refresh the page several times.

The last place to check is where it actually makes use of `@current_user` and the association between the `User` and `Story` classes to instantiate `Story` object with a prepopulated `user_id`: the `create` action of our `StoriesController`.

At this point, it's time to come clean about what causes our application bug. Here's what the aforementioned controller action looks like:

```
def create
  @story = Story.new story_params
  # @story = @current_user.stories.build story_params
  : method body…
end
```

As you can see, the line that instantiates the new `Story` object has been replaced by one that uses the `Story` class directly, instead of going through the association available via the `@current_user` object. As a result, no user will be assigned to the newly submitted story.

A slight change to the `Story` model was also necessary to make this work. I set the `belongs_to :user` association to `optional` in `/app/models/story.rb`:

```
belongs_to :user, optional: true
```

It's an ideal time to point out that, by default, `belongs_to` associations are mandatory. This is a change in Rails 5 from previous versions to protect us from unknowingly creating a bunch of orphaned objects.

"But wait!" you might be thinking. "Wouldn't a test have caught this problem?"

Of course it would have.

Running the functional tests (using `rails test:controllers`) with the modified controller action in place, as just seen, would reveal a test failure::

```
$ rails test:controllers
Run options: --seed 38543

# Running:

..............F
```

```
Failure:
 StoriesControllerTest#test_stores_user_with_story
↳ [/Users/ggoodrich/projects/sitepoint/readit-debug-01/test/
controllers/stories_controller_test.rb:106]:
--- expected
+++ actual
@@ -1 +1 @@
 -#<User id: 61347656, password_digest:
↳ "$2a$04$YF6ypVtUFIzFiJCgZNkCI.4GIn/OuDBus41OlcqN.IW...",
↳ name: "Glenn Goodrich", email:
↳ "glenn.goodrich@sitepoint.com", created_at: "2016-07-29
↳ 12:54:34", updated_at: "2016-07-29 12:54:34">
+nil



 bin/rails test
↳ test/controllers/stories_controller_test.rb:99


...............

Finished in 1.915820s, 16.7030 runs/s, 29.2303 assertions/s.

32 runs, 56 assertions, 1 failures, 0 errors, 0 skips
```

The test that fails verifies that the submission of a new story stores the current user; obviously, it doesn't. The error messages from the test even tell us that it expected a User object with a name of Glenn Goodrich; instead, it received a nil object.

What lesson can we take from this exercise? Well, if you equip your code with proper test coverage from the beginning, you'll have an easy and efficient way to spot an error in your code later on.

If you've been following along (you *have* been following along, right?), you'll need to either remove the story with the broken user association, or fix the user association through the console by changing its user_id to 1.

Debugging A Slightly Trickier Bug

In the next example, we'll look at another problem that I've secretly introduced to our existing code. If you take a look at Figure 11-6, you'll notice that although we've provided a description for the new story we submitted, it's missing from the final story page.

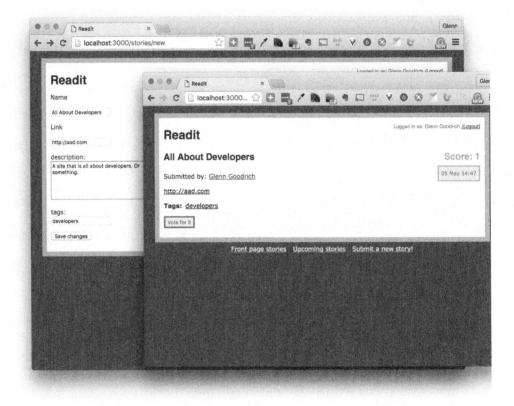

11-6. Story description missing from a newly submitted story

If you'd like to follow along with this example, copy the `readit-debug-02` from the code archive, and set it up using the steps for setting up `readit-debug-01` (I'll even wait for you!).

"Ha!" I hear you laugh. "I learned in the last section that I just need to run the test suite and it'll tell me what's wrong!"

While that's a great idea, the reality is that when we run the full test suite with `rails test` from the application root, every single test passes, as if nothing were wrong. Here are the results of running the test suite:

```
$ rails test
Running via Spring preloader in process 3965
Run options: --seed 63168

# Running:

.......................................................

Finished in 1.021801s, 49.9119 runs/s, 92.9731 assertions/s.

48 runs, 77 assertions, 0 failures, 0 errors, 0 skips
```

What happened here? We'll need to find out. While we used statements to investigate specific objects and attributes in the previous example, in this case, it's unclear where to begin.

Meeting byebug

When the first edition of this book was published, this section talked about a gem called ruby-debug and walked through how to set up it up in Rails. ruby-debug is still a viable option, but the Rails guides now talk about a new gem called byebug. Rails includes byebug in the `development` group of every Gemfile, so it's already in our bundle, so no installation is required.

While it would be beyond the scope of this chapter to explain how byebug works its magic, suffice to say that byebug uses a natively compiled Ruby extension that's written in C. The result is that it performs amazingly well, even with very large Ruby scripts. For further reading on byebug and many helpful articles and links to Ruby resources, I thoroughly recommend reading the Rails Guides on debugging[1] along with byebug's markdown guide[2]. There are also writings about byebug[3] on the SitePoint Ruby channel, which is worth checking out.

byebug provides you with a more advanced shell, similar to that provided by GDB[4], the GNU debugger for the C programming language.

In this shell you can:

- step forward and backward in your code
- execute and skip lines of code without copying and pasting them from your code editor window
- list the actual source context at which you've stopped your application
- edit the current code while it's running
- step into irb mode and make use of the same shell used by byebug (if you find old habits difficult to shake)

Debugging an Application with byebug

Let's crack the byebug whip at this problem. First, add the byebug keyword to the new action in app/controllers/stories_controller.rb:

```ruby
def create
  @story = @current_user.stories.build story_params
  if @story.save
    byebug
    flash[:notice] = 'Story submission succeeded'
    redirect_to stories_path
  else
    render action: 'new'
  end
end
```

---

1. http://guides.rubyonrails.org/debugging_rails_applications.html
2. https://github.com/deivid-rodriguez/byebug/blob/master/GUIDE.md
3. https://www.sitepoint.com/the-ins-and-outs-of-debugging-ruby-with-byebug/
4. http://sourceware.org/gdb/

If you try to submit a new story now, you'll experience "hanging browser syndrome," indicating that your byebug statement has kicked in and you're ready to debug.

Bundler byebug Boo-boo

For you Windows users out there, you may see an error stating "undefined local variable byebug", which means that byebug has not been installed properly by Bundler. It seems that in the Rails 5 default Gemfile, the line that pulls in byebug looks like:

```
gem "byebug", platform: "mri"
```

This is unfortunate, because the Windows platform is "mingw32", so byebug is not loaded by Bundler. To fix this, remove the , platform: "mri" from the Gemfile, stop your Rails server, and bundle install again. That should clear it right up.

Instead of firing up a separate client to connect to the inner workings of your application, byebug has opened this debugger shell right inside the terminal window with your application server, as Figure 11-7 indicates.

```
Started POST "/stories" for 127.0.0.1 at 2016-05-05 11:07:55 -0400
Processing by StoriesController#create as HTML
  Parameters: {"utf8"=>"✓", "authenticity_token"=>"tCzk79iUU6Z7EGXriInb0MDel76EJkq6u8SALk/zEu8ZI2krv/Ziezs1sbFhGlHTpOe/I8DEVM0dr/YwhiNdbQ==",
"=>"rails, debugging"}, "description"=>"Debugging guide for Rails", "commit"=>"Save changes"}
  User Load (0.2ms)  SELECT  "users".* FROM "users" WHERE (1) ORDER BY "users"."id" ASC LIMIT 1
   (0.1ms)  begin transaction
  SQL (1.3ms)  INSERT INTO "stories" ("name", "link", "user_id", "created_at", "updated_at") VALUES (?, ?, ?, ?, ?)  [["name", "Rails Guides
-05 15:07:55.695484"], ["updated_at", "2016-05-05 15:07:55.695484"]]
  SQL (0.1ms)  INSERT INTO "votes" ("user_id", "story_id", "created_at", "updated_at") VALUES (?, ?, ?, ?)  [["user_id", 1], ["story_id", 2],
  Story Load (0.1ms)  SELECT  "stories".* FROM "stories" WHERE "stories"."id" = ? LIMIT 1  [["id", 2]]
  SQL (0.3ms)  UPDATE "stories" SET "votes_count" = COALESCE("votes_count", 0) + 1 WHERE "stories"."id" = ?  [["id", 2]]
  ActsAsTaggableOn::Tag Load (0.1ms)  SELECT "tags".* FROM "tags" WHERE (LOWER(name) = LOWER('rails') OR LOWER(name) = LOWER('debugging'))
  ActsAsTaggableOn::Tag Exists (0.1ms)  SELECT  1 AS one FROM "tags" WHERE "tags"."name" = 'rails' LIMIT 1
  SQL (0.2ms)  INSERT INTO "tags" ("name") VALUES (?)  [["name", "rails"]]
  ActsAsTaggableOn::Tag Exists (0.1ms)  SELECT  1 AS one FROM "tags" WHERE "tags"."name" = 'debugging' LIMIT 1
  SQL (0.1ms)  INSERT INTO "tags" ("name") VALUES (?)  [["name", "debugging"]]
  ActsAsTaggableOn::Tag Load (0.2ms)  SELECT "tags".* FROM "tags" INNER JOIN "taggings" ON "tags"."id" = "taggings"."tag_id" WHERE "taggings"
d", 2], ["taggable_type", "Story"]]
  ActsAsTaggableOn::Tagging Exists (0.1ms)  SELECT  1 AS one FROM "taggings" WHERE ("taggings"."tag_id" = 2 AND "taggings"."taggable_type" =
r_type" IS NULL) LIMIT 1
  SQL (0.2ms)  INSERT INTO "taggings" ("tag_id", "context", "taggable_id", "taggable_type", "created_at") VALUES (?, ?, ?, ?, ?)  [["tag_id",
  ActsAsTaggableOn::Tag Load (0.1ms)  SELECT "tags".* FROM "tags" WHERE "tags"."id" = ? LIMIT 1  [["id", 2]]
  SQL (0.1ms)  UPDATE "tags" SET "taggings_count" = COALESCE("taggings_count", 0) + 1 WHERE "tags"."id" = ?  [["id", 2]]
  ActsAsTaggableOn::Tagging Exists (0.1ms)  SELECT  1 AS one FROM "taggings" WHERE ("taggings"."tag_id" = 3 AND "taggings"."taggable_type" =
r_type" IS NULL) LIMIT 1
  SQL (0.0ms)  INSERT INTO "taggings" ("tag_id", "context", "taggable_id", "taggable_type", "created_at") VALUES (?, ?, ?, ?, ?)  [["tag_id",
  ActsAsTaggableOn::Tag Load (0.0ms)  SELECT "tags".* FROM "tags" WHERE "tags"."id" = ? LIMIT 1  [["id", 3]]
  SQL (0.0ms)  UPDATE "tags" SET "taggings_count" = COALESCE("taggings_count", 0) + 1 WHERE "tags"."id" = ?  [["id", 3]]
   (1.3ms)  commit transaction

[16, 25] in /Users/ggoodrich/projects/sitepoint/book-rails3/code/new_code/chapter11/readit-debug-02/app/controllers/stories_controller.rb
   16:
   17:   def create
   18:     @story = @current_user.stories.build story_params
   19:     if @story.save
   20:       byebug
=> 21:       flash[:notice] = "Story submission succeeded"
   22:       redirect_to stories_path
   23:     else
   24:       render action: 'new'
   25:     end
(byebug)
```

11-7. The ruby-debug interactive prompt appears within the server console

From this prompt, you can use a variety of commands to explore your application while it's paused mid-execution. Throughout this example, I'll indicate the byebug shell prompt using the characters (`bb`), while commands typed at this prompt will appear in bold, as follows:

```
(bb) list
```

The byebug Commands

What follows is a quick rundown of the most important byebug commands, along with a brief description of what they do. Don't worry too much about remembering every last detail—the built-in `help` command will list all the available commands for you. You can also type `help <commandname>` for help with a specific command.

where	Displays a trace of the execution stack, similar to that displayed when your application raises an exception.
info breakpoints	Displays a trace of the execution stack, similar to that displayed when your application raises an exception.
break	Sets new breakpoints in the source code from within the byebug shell.
delete	Deletes existing breakpoints from within the byebug shell.
continue	Leaves the current debugger shell and resumes execution of the application until the next breakpoint is encountered.
irb	Invokes an interactive Ruby interpreter—similar to the shell used by the breakpoint library—at the current point of execution.
list	Displays the code fragments surrounding the current point of execution. (We'll make use of this command in a moment.)
methods	Explores the available class methods and instance methods respectively.
next/step	Continues execution one step at a time. next will step *over* the next line of execution, while step will step *into* the next line of execution.
var **all/global/const**	all will show all variables and their values within the current context. global will show the global variables, and const will show the constants.
quit	Exits the debugger. Note that this command will also exit the application server if it was invoked from the command line, as has been demonstrated. To exit just the current debugging session, use finish.

For a list of all available commands and options, use the help command.

Moving Around in the Shell

Now that we've been dropped into a shell, it's time to make use of some of these commands to zero in on the root of our problem—that is, our stories displaying without descriptions.

First of all, let's find out exactly what point we're at in the execution of our story submission. This is the job of the list command, as shown below.

11-8. The `list` command displaying the current location in a paused application

As you can see, the `list` command displays a source code listing showing the current location in a paused application.

At this point, we can examine parts of the working environment, such as the `@story` instance variable or the `params` hash, from the shell. Let's investigate the `description` attribute of the `Story` object stored in our `@story` variable:

```
(bb) @story.description
=> nil
```

Hmph. I wonder if we're passing `description` in the `params` hash. Let's check:

```
(bb) params[:story][:description]
=> nil
```

As you can see, this also returns `nil`: an empty object. So as a last resort, let's take a peek at the full `params` hash, which contains the values of all the form fields that have been submitted, no matter which scope they reside in.

The section highlighted in Figure 11-9 is the root of the problem. As you can see, the `description` is indeed present in the `params` hash, but it's not part of our story. While the `Story`'s `name` and `link` attributes are sitting nicely together in the `params[:story]` hash, `description` sits separately in `params[:description]`.

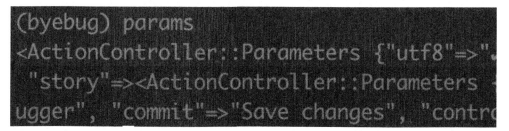

11-9. Description is present, but apart

How did that happen? If we look at our form template (located at `app/views/stories/new.html.erb`), you'll see that I've "accidentally" used the wrong form field helper:

```
# Wrong:
<p>
  description:<br />
  <%= text_area_tag :description %>
</p>
```

Instead of going through the `FormBuilder` object that the `form_for` helper provides and using the `text_area` helper, my code was calling `text_area_tag`. This resulted in the description becoming a separate entry in the `params` hash, and our story never received its value. This is what it should look like:

```
# Right:
<p>
  description:<br />
  <%= f.text_area :description %>
</p>
```

Discovering All the Fancy Tools in byebug

Admittedly, we haven't had to use any of byebug's more advanced features to debug this example problem. But when we're forced to debug more complicated code, byebug's fancy features become really handy.

Let's first take a look at the stepping methods, which allow us to step through the code, one line at a time. To do so, we'll move our byebug statement into a method that contains more code than the previous example, so we can actually step through each line. The best candidate for this task is the create action of our VotesController found in readit-debug-02/app/controllers/ votes_controller.rb. Here's a version of this method to which I've added the byebug statement (remember to remove it from our StoriesController):

```
def create
  byebug
  @story = Story.find(params[:story_id])
  @story.votes.create(user: @current_user)
  respond_to do |format|
  format.html { redirect_to @story, notice: 'Vote was
↳ successfully created.' }
    format.js
  end
end
```

To invoke the debugger in this new location, exit your current debugging session using the cont command. This will resurrect your stalled browser and enable you to continue browsing the Readit application. Select a story from the Upcoming Stories queue and click the *Vote for it* button to engage the debugger once more.

Previously, we saw that the list command could give us an indication of where in the source code our application was currently paused. When it's paused, we can use the next command to advance to the next line of code. Typing next will display the regular Rails log output for the following line, then return you to the byebug prompt. From here, you can once again use list to check your new location in the application, as I've done in Figure 11-10.

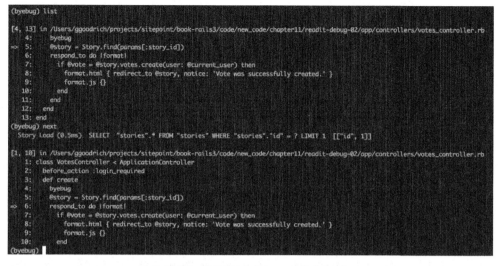

```
(byebug) list
[4, 13] in /Users/ggoodrich/projects/sitepoint/book-rails3/code/new_code/chapter11/readit-debug-02/app/controllers/votes_controller.rb
     4:     byebug
=>   5:     @story = Story.find(params[:story_id])
     6:     respond_to do |format|
     7:       if @vote = @story.votes.create(user: @current_user) then
     8:         format.html { redirect_to @story, notice: 'Vote was successfully created.' }
     9:         format.js {}
    10:       end
    11:     end
    12:   end
    13: end
(byebug) next
Story Load (0.5ms)  SELECT "stories".* FROM "stories" WHERE "stories"."id" = ? LIMIT 1  [["id", 1]]

[1, 10] in /Users/ggoodrich/projects/sitepoint/book-rails3/code/new_code/chapter11/readit-debug-02/app/controllers/votes_controller.rb
     1: class VotesController < ApplicationController
     2:   before_action :login_required
     3:   def create
     4:     byebug
     5:     @story = Story.find(params[:story_id])
=>   6:     respond_to do |format|
     7:       if @vote = @story.votes.create(user: @current_user) then
     8:         format.html { redirect_to @story, notice: 'Vote was successfully created.' }
     9:         format.js {}
    10:       end
(byebug)
```

11-10. Using **next** to advance one line of code

To explore the methods provided by an object that you're curious about, you can use the `methods` method, just as you would in irb. When executed with the optional i argument, it will produce a list of the instance methods provided by the object you pass to it, sorted alphabetically:

```
(bb) @story.methods
```

An example using the `@story` object is shown below.

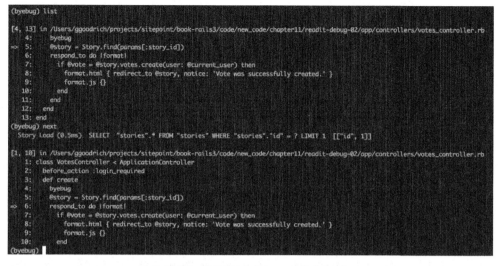

11-11. Using the **method** command to display an object's instance methods

Setting Breakpoints Mid-execution

While the `next` command can be useful if you know exactly where to go poking around in your application, it can be less practical in a Rails application. The level at which the stepping occurs can in some circumstances be far too granular, resulting in stepping through multiple lines of core library files instead of your own code.

To gain a little more control over where the debugger halts execution, you can manually set breakpoints without having to edit any files or stop the server. Breakpoints can be set by specifying either:

- a combination of filename and line number
- a class name and the name of an instance method or class method

As an example, we're going to set a manual breakpoint a few lines from the current location (inside the create action of `VotesController`). We'll do all of this without having to open a text editor, or step over every line between the current point of execution.

Typing `list` at our current position (you may need to "vote" again to retrieve a byebug prompt) shows:

```
1: class VotesController < ApplicationController
2:   before_action :login_required
3:   def create
4:     byebug
=> 5:     @story = Story.find(params[:story_id])
6:     respond_to do |format|
 7:       if @vote = @story.votes.create(user: @current_user)
↳ then
 8:         format.html { redirect_to @story, notice: 'Vote
↳ was successfully created.' }
9:         format.js {}
10:       end
(byebug)
```

We can manually set a breakpoint using the `break` command:

```
(byebug) break app/controllers/votes_controller.rb:7
Successfully created breakpoint with id 1
(byebug)
```

By specifying the file and line number, byebug creates a breakpoint. It's worth noting that in this case, specifying the file is superfluous because we are in the same file; however, I included it for completeness.

You can now let go of the current breakpoint by typing the `continue` command in the byebug shell. Execution will resume until line 7 is reached, at which point the application will pause again, as shown below.

11-12. Stopping at a breakpoint that was set by specifying class and method name

A list of active breakpoints can always be obtained via the `info breakpoints` command.

Using the Rails Logging Tool

Rails comes with an internal logging tool for writing custom event-triggered entries to your application's log file.

While logging events can be useful for debugging purposes—especially in a production environment, where you want to avoid scaring your users with the output of debugging code—event logging can also be of general interest. For instance, log entries can reveal usage patterns for your application such as the times at which maintenance jobs start and end, or the frequency with which external services are accessed.

We'll use the Rails logging tool to implement an **access log** for our application: a log of the pages requested by users who are logged in. While web server logs allow for comprehensive analysis, they lack any details of the specific user requesting the page; such information can come in handy, either to the marketing department (for their mysterious purposes), or for when you're trying to diagnose a problem reported by a particular user.

To implement the access log, we need to:

1. Create a call to the Rails internal logging system.

2. Place this call in an appropriate location in our application code so that it's executed for every page. This location must allow the code to determine whether or not a user is logged in.

We have a location that meets both of these requirements: the `current_user` before filter, which lives in the `ApplicationController` class.

To document the page requests of our users, we use the `Rails.logger` object, which is available at any point in a Rails application. `Rails.logger` is used to write a new entry to the environment-specific log file. By default, we operate in the development environment, so the `Rails.logger` object will write new entries to the bottom of the log file `log/development.log`.

As with logging functionality in Java or other platforms, Rails logging can deal with a variety of severity levels. When you log an entry, it's up to you to decide how severe is the event you're logging. The most common severity levels are `debug`, `info`, `warn`, and `error`. It's really up to you how you use each level.

Each of the Rails environments has different default settings for the severity levels written to the log file. In the production environment, which we'll cover in depth in the final chapter, the default is the `debug` level.

Here's the `current_user` action in `app/controllers/application_controller.rb` with an added `Rails.logger` statement:

```
def current_user
  return unless session[:user_id]
```

```
@current_user = User.where(session[:user_id]).first
Rails.logger.info "#{@current_user.name} requested
↳ #{request.fullpath} on #{Time.now}"
end
```

EXTRA CREDIT: Six Degrees of Severity

There are six severity levels: unknown, fatal, error, warn, info, and debug. We won't dig too far into the logger, but you can use the Internet to learn more. Adam Hawkins' post on using the logger[5]

As you can see in the `Rails.logger` call, we're using the `info` severity level to log these statements in all environments, including production. Specifying the severity level is simply a matter of calling the appropriately named instance method of the `logger` object.

The string written to the log file is actually a composite of three Ruby statements. First, we log the value of the name attribute for the current user:

```
Rails.logger.info "#{@current_user.name} requested
↳ #{request.fullpath} on #{Time.now}"
```

Then we add the URL that the user requested (without the host and port; you'll see an example in a second), which is available from the `request` object that Rails provides:

```
Rails.logger.info "#{@current_user.name} requested
↳ #{request.fullpath} on #{Time.now}"
```

Lastly, the current date and time are added to the string:

---

[5] http://hawkins.io/2013/08/using-the-ruby-logger/ is a great start.

```
Rails.logger.info "#{@current_user.name} requested
↳ #{request.fullpath} on #{Time.now}"
```

With these details in place, every page in our application will make an entry to the application log file. Here's a sample session, with all the clutter from the development log removed:

```
Started GET "/stories" for 127.0.0.1 at 2016-05-05 13:10:16
↳ -0400
Processing by StoriesController#index as HTML
  User Load (0.1ms)  SELECT  "users".* FROM "users" WHERE
↳ "users"."id" = ? ORDER BY "users"."id" ASC LIMIT ?  [["id",
↳ 1], ["LIMIT", 1]]
  Glenn Goodrich requested /stories on 2016-07-31 14:04:38
↳ -0400
  Rendering stories/index.html.erb within layouts/application
```

The current_user method exits immediately if the current user hasn't logged in; as a result, our log file displays only log entries from pages requested by users who were logged in when they used Readit. Of course, you can customize log output to your heart's content if this format fails to suit your needs. For example, you could modify it to be more readable for humans, or more easily parsed by a Ruby script.

Overcoming Problems in Debugging

While we've added a considerable number of tests to our application code so far, we certainly have yet to cover *every* aspect of the application.

Whenever you fix a problem during the development of your application, take a moment to add a test to your test suite verifying that the problem has been fixed—just as we did in the last section. Following this approach will ensure that you never receive another bug report for the same problem.

Another approach is to write a test to verify the problem *before* you attempt to fix it. This way, you can be sure that as long as your test fails, the problem still exists. It's up to you to determine your own approach to the task of debugging, but aim to not move on from any problem without having added a new test for it to your test suite.

Testing Your Application Using Integration Tests

The test code that we've written so far for Readit has dealt mostly with the isolated testing of controller actions and model functionality. To test scenarios that involve multiple controllers and models, Rails also comes with a more thorough testing feature called integration testing.

An **integration test** verifies the behavior of a number of controllers and models as a user interacts with the application. Integration tests tell a story about a fictitious user of our application: the user's login process, the links that person follows, and the actions taken by that user. I briefly mentioned integration tests in Chapter 8. As of Rails 5, all controller tests are integration tests by default.

Integration tests are aimed at testing behavior of a use case. In some cases, a use case may be more than just one controller action (again, we did this for one of our chapter eight tests). Consider these examples:

- A visitor wants to submit a story, and tries to access the story submission form. As he is yet to log in, he is redirected to the login form. Once logged in, he's presented with the submission form and submits a story.
- A given user is the fifth user to vote for a particular story. She knows that the threshold for stories to appear on the front page is five votes, so once she's voted, she visits the front page to check that the story just voted for appears there.
- A user submits a new story with a number of tags. After sending in her submission, she proceeds to the tag page for a particular tag used on her submission, checking that the story does indeed appear in the list.

As you can see, integration tests can be quite specific and detailed; writing Ruby test code to match the level of detail specified by the aforementioned scenarios is perfectly achievable.

Let's write a slightly more involved integration test from scratch, shall we?

Creating an Integration Test

Returning to our rocking Readit application (meaning, stop using the readit-debug-0x versions we've been playing with in this chapter), the first step we'll take is to generate a new integration test. Then, we'll set up a test case to implement the first of the scenarios that we just discussed: a user who is not logged in tries to submit a story. This scenario will be translated into Ruby code.

Every integration test class is stored in the readit/test/integration/ directory. Generate a new integration test called StoriesTest using the Rails generator. Can you guess the syntax?

```
$ rails g integration_test stories
Running via Spring preloader in process 74846
      invoke  test_unit
      create    test/integration/stories_test.rb
```

As you can see, the generator created a file for our test at test/integration/stories_test.rb. Let's create a test for our scenario:

```
require "test_helper"

class StoriesTest < ActionController::IntegrationTest
  test "story submission with login" do
    get new_story_path
    assert_response :redirect
    follow_redirect!
    assert_response :success
    post session_path, params: {
      email: 'glenn.goodrich@sitepoint.com', password: 'sekrit'
    }
    follow_redirect!
    assert_response :success
    post stories_path, params: {
      story: {
```

```
      name: 'Submission from Integration Test',
      link: 'http://test.com/'
    }
  }
  assert_response :redirect
  follow_redirect!
  assert_response :success
  end
end
```

On the surface, this resembles a regular functional test: the test performs an action, then asserts that the results of that action are as expected. In this case, the first action is to request a page; the test then verifies that the response code and the template used to render the page are as expected, then continues with the rest of its actions.

However, instead of the get and post calls being based on specific controllers and their respective actions, page requests in an integration test take standard URLs (we use the path helpers that come with Rails routes). Why? Well, an integration test such as this doesn't test a controller in complete isolation from its environment. Instead, it views the application as a whole, so other elements of the application–such as routing and the handover of control from one controller to another–are tested as well. The first step of our test is to request the new Story form by using the appropriate URL and testing the response:

```
get new_story_path
assert_response :redirect
follow_redirect!
```

At this point, the test assumes that a redirect was issued after the last get call, which we're asserting using assert_response. It also assumes that the URL to which a user is redirected—the story submission page—is followed in the test. This introduces another new tidbit in this test code: the follow_redirect! statement.

Other than that, the test consists of plain old functional test code.

Running an Integration Test

Let's run this test to make sure it passes as expected. As with model and controller tests, integration tests are run with a `rails` command:

```
$ rails test:integration
```

Integration tests are executed along with your unit and functional tests when running the `rails test` command. Here's the outcome of our test:

```
$ rails test:integration
Running via Spring preloader in process 84542
Run options: --seed 59044

# Running:

.

Finished in 0.395582s, 2.5279 runs/s, 20.2234 assertions/s.

1 runs, 5 assertions, 0 failures, 0 errors, 0 skips
```

As you can see from this basic example, an integration test gives you the assurance that your application behaves independently of your functional and unit tests, and that all of your application's components are put through their paces in an automated manner.

Using Breakpoints in a Test

Just as we used byebug to jump into the running application at a predefined point, we can also jump into the application from within a test. This technique can be useful for determining why a test is failing, or for gaining insight into the resources available when we're writing tests.

Using breakpoints in tests is equally as straightforward as using them in regular development mode: place the `byebug` statement at the point at which you want execution to halt. Just as it did in development, when you're using breakpoints in tests, byebug presents you with the byebug console as soon as a `byebug` statement is encountered.

Here's an example of a breakpoint in action. I added a breakpoint to the integration test that we built in the previous section (stored in `test/integration/stories_test.rb`):

```
class StoriesTest < ActionController::IntegrationTest
  test "story submission with login"
    get new_story_path
    byebug
    ⋮ test method body…
  end
end
```

 Fixing the Gemfile

Don't forget the Gemfile `platform: "mri"` issue that we ran into earlier in this chapter. Remember, that was in a different folder and so you may have to do it again.

Let's run our suite of integration tests using the command `rails test:integration`. We're presented with the byebug console immediately after the new session has been created—just after the test requests the submission form for the first time. At this point, we're free to explore the environment; below are examples of the characteristics of our code that can be revealed using the console.

First, let's look at the cookies that have been set for the user that the test is impersonating:

```
(byebug) cookies
 => #<Rack::Test::CookieJar:0x007fb6b2cfa880
↳ @default_host="www.example.com",
↳ @cookies=[#<Rack::Test::Cookie:0x007fb6b1fdd210
↳ @default_host="www.example.com",
↳ @name_value_raw="_readit_session=TWtE...9ba",
```

```
↳ @name="_readit_session", @value="TWtE...9ba",
↳ @options={"path"=>"/", "HttpOnly"=>nil,
↳ "domain"=>"www.example.com"}>]>
```

At the point at which the debugger appears, the user has yet to log in, so no
user_id value has been stored in the user's session:

```
(byebug) session[:user_id]
=> nil
```

We can log in with the same statement used by our test a few lines down; the
return value shown here is the numeric HTTP response code for a redirect (which
happens to be 302). Enter this all on one line:

```
(byebug) post session_path, params: { email:
↳ 'glenn.goodrich@sitepoint.com', password: 'sekrit' }
=> 302
```

The user's session now contains a user_id value, as this code and Figure 11-13
show:

```
irb> session[:user_id]
=> 885306178
```

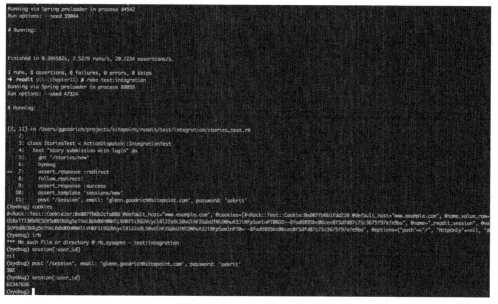

11-13. A breakpoint used in a test

Once again, byebug can be a great time saver if you need to explore the environment surrounding an action in order to write better and more comprehensive tests. Without using breakpoints, exploring the environment would only be possible in a limited fashion; for example, by placing lots of `puts` statements in your tests to output debugging messages and rerunning them countless times for the information you need. Yes, it is every bit as laborious as it sounds.

With the breakpoints provided by byebug, however, you can interact with your models as your application is being run without modifying huge chunks of code. This process couldn't be easier, which means the barriers to writing tests are reduced even further.

Revisiting the Rails Console

We've used the `rails console` command frequently in previous chapters, mainly to explore features as they were being introduced.

The console can also be used to play with your application in **headless mode**. "Headless", in this context, means you can interact with your application from the console just as a browser would interact with it. Using headless mode, you can issue requests like a browser and see the response, including status codes (200, 404,and so on) and the rendered view. In conjunction with breakpoints in tests (covered in the last section), this technique can be a good way to explore your application, in the anticipation of creating a new integration test once you've worked out what you want to do.

When the integration test was introduced to Rails, it came with a new object available by default in the console: the **app** object. This object can be thought of as providing you with access to an empty integration test. You're able to GET and POSTto URLs, and you have access to the session and cookies containers, routing helpers, and so on—just like a regular integration test.

Let's try using the **app** object from the console. You should recognize a lot of the methods we're using here from the integration test that we built earlier in this chapter.

Go ahead and open the Rails console (**rails c**). Initially, we're interested to know what kind of object **app** really is:

```
>> app.class
=> ActionDispatch::Integration::Session
```

Next, let's fetch the front page of our application using the **get** action:

```
>> app.get '/'
...Lots of output...
=> 200
```

The return value is the HTTP response code that indicates a successful page request. We've been using the **:success** symbol in its place in most of our tests until now.

Now we'll check to see what the current controller is:

```
>> app.controller
=> StoriesController
```

Cool! That's what we'd expect. So can we dig around and see if the controller assigned our stories to the view? We can! Granted, I had to dig around to find the right method, but here it is:

```
>> app.controller.view_assigns["stories"].size
=> 2
```

If we try to fetch the story submission form, we receive a redirect (HTTP code 302), as we're yet to be logged in:

```
>> app.get '/stories/new'
=> 302
```

When we receive the redirect, we can look at the URL that the redirect is pointing to by using the following construct:

```
>> app.response.redirect_url
=> "http://www.example.com/session/new"
```

It's easy to follow the redirect that was just issued using the `follow_redirect!` method:

```
>> app.follow_redirect!
=> 200
```

We can also use the `post` method to log in with an email and password, and follow the resulting redirect; however, Rails imposes security-related restrictions on who can talk to your application, even in the development environment. For that reason, we need to explicitly switch off a feature called "request forgery protection," in order to allow the following statement to succeed:[6]

```
>> ApplicationController.allow_forgery_protection =
↳ false
=> false
```

Now it's time to log ourselves in:

```
>> app.post '/session', params: { email:
↳ 'glenn.goodrich@sitepoint.com',
↳    password: => 'sekrit'}
=> 302
>> app.follow_redirect!
=> 200
```

Note that we didn't look at the `app.response.redirect_url` before we accepted the redirection. Here's how you can check the last URL you requested:

```
>> app.request.original_fullpath
=> "/stories/new"
```

As it's an integration test, after all, headless mode also provides you with access to the `session` and `cookies` variables:

```
>> app.cookies
 => #<Rack::Test::CookieJar:0x007ff5680f2548
↳ @default_host="www.example.com",
↳ @cookies=[#<Rack::Test::Cookie:0x007ff56187fb50
↳ @default_host="www.example.com",
↳ @name_value_raw="_readit_session=WmJIV...707",
↳ @name="_readit_session", @value="WmJIV...707",
```

[6.] See https://en.wikipedia.org/wiki/Cross-site_request_forgery for more information about this security issue.

```
↳ @options={"path"=>"/", "HttpOnly"=>nil,
↳ "domain"=>"www.example.com"}>,
↳ #<Rack::Test::Cookie:0x007ff56183d020
↳ @default_host="www.example.com",
↳ @name_value_raw="request_method=", @name="request_method",
↳ @value="", @options={"path"=>"/", "max-age"=>"0",
↳ "expires"=>"Thu, 01 Jan 1970 00:00:00 -0000",
↳ "domain"=>"www.example.com"}>]>
>> app.session[:user_id]
=> 1
```

As you can see, headless mode is a great tool for checking out the possible ways
in which you might develop an integration test. Once you're satisfied with your
findings, open up your text editor and transform your console results into an
automated test. Easy!

A Brief Introduction to Pry

The debugging and introspection tools that come "out of the box" with Rails are
great. I remember when I was first using Rails and realized I could open up the
Rails console and execute my application code–it was a game changer. The Rails
console is incredible, and I can't imagine writing an application without it;
however, there is always room for improvement. Enter Pry.

Pry[7] is "a powerful alternative to the standard IRB shell". It takes introspection to
the next level, and then keeps going. When using Pry, you can:

- change the current context as if you are changing a directory at a command
  prompt
- search your command history
- edit Ruby files in place, and have those changes loaded automatically
- list the methods and constants for a given object or class very easily

---

[7.] http://pryrepl.org/

That's just the very beginning of what Pry can do. Furthermore, it has a robust plugin architecture resulting in numerous plugins that make Pry even better. One of those plugins, pry-rails, replaces the current Rails console with a Pry REPL.

 Nerd Words

REPL stands for read–eval–print loop, which is the nerd name for items such as irb, the Rails console, and Pry.

Let's add pry-rails to Readit and play around with some of the basic features of Pry. Add `gem 'pry-rails'` to the block in the `Gemfile` that also contains byebug:

```
group :development, :test do
  gem 'byebug'
  gem 'pry-rails'
end
```

Run `bundle install` to add pry-rails to the bundle. That's it—now we're cooking with Pry.

The pry-rails gem replaces the Rails console with a Pry console. If you fire up a Rails console using `rails c`, you'll see a new prompt:

```
$ rails c
[1] pry(main)>
```

All of the commands that work in the standard Rails console still work in Pry. But now we have even more awesome toys! Grab the first story, and we'll use some of Pry's tools to navigate around and through the object:

```
[1] pry(main)> s = Story.first
=> #<Story:0x007fd72a3df6e0
 id: 2,
 name: "SitePoint Forums",
 link: "http://community.sitepoint.com",
 created_at: Sun, 13 Mar 2016 14:47:48 UTC +00:00,
```

```
updated_at: Wed, 27 Apr 2016 16:48:55 UTC +00:00,
user_id: 1,
votes_count: 8,
description: nil>
```

Right off the bat, we see Pry making life a bit better. Our story is formatted much more cleanly than in the Rails console and it includes some nice color-formatted text. Let's change the current scope to that story:

```
[2] pry(main)> cd s
[3] pry(#<Story>):1>
```

So what just happened? Well, the prompt changed to indicate that our current scope is a Story object. The `cd` command went *into* the story. I can prove it by typing the name of a Story attribute:

```
[3] pry(#<Story>):1> link
=> "http://community.sitepoint.com"
```

See, I didn't have to type `s.link`, just `link`. That's because the current scope is `s`, the variable holding our story. Watch this:

```
[4] pry(#<Story>):1> ls
      ActiveRecord::Core#methods:
 <=>  ==  connection_handler  encode_with  eql?  freeze
↳ frozen?  hash  init_with  inspect  pretty_print  readonly!
↳ readonly?  slice
    ActiveRecord::Persistence#methods:
 becomes  decrement  delete  destroyed?  increment!
↳ persisted?  toggle!  update!           update_attributes
↳ update_column
 becomes!  decrement!  destroy!  increment  new_record?
↳ toggle      update  update_attribute  update_attributes!
↳ update_columns
```

```
 ActiveRecord::Scoping#methods: initialize_internals_callback
↳   populate_with_current_scope_attributes
    ActiveRecord::Sanitization#methods: quoted_id
 ActiveRecord::AttributeAssignment#methods: assign_attributes
↳   attributes=
    ActiveModel::Conversion#methods: to_model  to_partial_path
    ActiveRecord::Integration#methods: cache_key
 ActiveModel::Validations#methods: errors  invalid?
↳ read_attribute_for_validation  validates_with
    ActiveSupport::Callbacks#methods: run_callbacks
    ActiveModel::Validations::HelperMethods#methods:
 validates_absence_of      validates_confirmation_of
↳ validates_format_of      validates_length_of
↳ validates_presence_of
 validates_acceptance_of  validates_exclusion_of
↳ validates_inclusion_of  validates_numericality_of
↳ validates_size_of

        ...
```

Whoa! That was a *ton* of stuff for such a little command. As you may have
guessed, ls lists the methods and variables for the current scope that is our story.
I bet you had no idea that our little story had so many methods. Obviously, most
of these methods are inherited from ActiveRecord. The ls command takes flags
to help pare down the output. For example, if you just want the instance and
class variables for the current object, use ls -i:

```
[5] pry(#<Story>):1> ls -i
instance variables:
 @_start_transaction_state  @association_cache  @destroyed
↳               @marked_for_destruction  @readonly
↳ @txn
 @aggregation_cache          @attributes
↳ @destroyed_by_association  @new_record
↳ @transaction_state
class variables:
 @@configurations                @@logger
↳ @@raise_in_transactional_callbacks  @@timestamped_migrations
```

```
 @@default_timezone              @@maintain_test_schema
↳ @@schema_format
 @@dump_schema_after_migration   @@primary_key_prefix_type
↳ @@time_zone_aware_attributes
```

If you want to learn about an object and its methods and variables, using Pry in this way is invaluable. We can even see the source of the methods. Remember how we changed the to_param method to make our URLs more friendlier? Type show-method to_param to see exactly what we did:

```
[6] pry(#<Story>):1> show-method to_param
 From:
↳ /Users/ggoodrich/projects/sitepoint/readit/app/models/story.rb
↳ @ line 13:
Owner: Story
Visibility: public
Number of lines: 3

def to_param
  "#{id}-#{name.gsub(/\W/, '-').downcase}"
end
```

To return to the main context, simply type cd ... If you've ever used a command prompt, cd should make perfect sense to you.

I could spend all day going through the features of Pry but, alas, we must move on. I will show you one more trick. You can easily access the ri documentation from Pry:

```
[6] pry(main):1> ri Array
Array < Object


------------------------------------------------------------------
↳ ----------------Includes:
Enumerable (from ruby site)
```

```
(from ruby site)
--------------------------------------------------------------
↳ ---------------- Arrays are ordered, integer-indexed
collections of any
↳ object.
...
```

If you've loaded the ri documentation, it's super easy to read it from Pry.

That's some of what Pry offers, but there's so much more. You know what that means …

Exploring Pry

There are some great screencasts on the Pry website, as well as articles on using Pry with Ruby[8] and Pry with Rails[9] at SitePoint. Check them out, and you'll be very glad you did.

If you want to go back to the standard Rails console (but I'd have to ask: why would you?), simply remove `pry-rails` from the Gemfile and run `bundle install`.

Benchmarking Your Application

As software developers, it's our job to know which part of our application is doing what. That way, when an error arises, we can jump right in and fix it. On the other hand, knowing *how long* each part of our application is taking to perform its job is a completely different scenario.

Benchmarking in software terms is the process of measuring an application's performance, and taking steps to improve it based on that initial measurement. The benchmarking process usually involves profiling the application—monitoring it to determine where bottlenecks are occurring—before any changes are made to improve the application's performance.

---

8. http://www.sitepoint.com/rubyists-time-pry-irb/
9. http://www.sitepoint.com/pry-friends-rails/

While I won't cover the profiling and benchmarking of a Rails application in every gory detail (it's a topic to which an entire book could easily be devoted), I'll give you an introduction to the tools that are available for the job. Keep in mind that your first Rails application is unlikely to have performance problems in its early stages. The objective with your first application (or at least the first *version* of your application) should be to get the functionality right the first time; *then* you can worry about making it fast.

Taking Benchmarks from Log Files

When it's running in development and testing modes, Rails provides a variety of benchmarking information in its log files, as we saw briefly in Chapter 6. For each request that's served by the application, Rails notes all of the templates rendered, database queries performed, and total time taken to serve the request.

Let's examine a sample request to understand what each of the log entries mean. This example deals with a request for the Readit home page:

```
Started GET "/stories" for 127.0.0.1 at 2016-05-06 08:11:11
↪ -0400
Processing by StoriesController#index as HTML
```

These lines represent the start of the block of logging for a single page request. It includes the:

- names of the controller and action
- IP address of the client requesting the page (127.0.0.1 being the equivalent of localhost)
- time of the request
- request method used (GET in this case)
- format requested (HTML)

The next entries in our sample log file correspond to database queries issued by the application. Each entry lists the time (in seconds) that the application took to execute the query, as well as the SQL used. Here's a snippet

```
 User Load (0.3ms)  SELECT  "users".* FROM "users" WHERE (1)
↳ ORDER BY "users"."id" ASC LIMIT 1
 (0.3ms)  SELECT COUNT(*) FROM "stories" WHERE (votes_count
↳ >= 5)
 Story Load (0.1ms)  SELECT "stories".* FROM "stories" WHERE
↳ (votes_count >= 5)  ORDER BY id ASC
 User Load (0.2ms)  SELECT  "users".* FROM "users" WHERE
↳ "users"."id" = ? LIMIT 1  [["id", 1]]
 ActsAsTaggableOn::Tag Load (1.2ms)  SELECT "tags".* FROM
↳ "tags" INNER JOIN "taggings" ON "tags"."id" =
↳ "taggings"."tag_id" WHERE "taggings"."taggable_id" = ? AND
↳ "taggings"."taggable_type" = ? AND (taggings.context = 'tags'
↳ AND taggings.tagger_id IS NULL)  [["taggable_id", 2],
↳ ["taggable_type", "Story"]]
 CACHE (0.0ms)  SELECT  "users".* FROM "users" WHERE
↳ "users"."id" = ? LIMIT 1  [["id", 1]]
 ActsAsTaggableOn::Tag Load (0.1ms)  SELECT "tags".* FROM
↳ "tags" INNER JOIN "taggings" ON "tags"."id" =
↳ "taggings"."tag_id" WHERE "taggings"."taggable_id" = ? AND
↳ "taggings"."taggable_type" = ? AND (taggings.context = 'tags'
↳ AND taggings.tagger_id IS NULL)  [["taggable_id", 3],
↳ ["taggable_type", "Story"]]
```

In the first of these log entries, Rails has asked the database for stories (and their users) to display on the front page. The last few queries represent requests made by the `acts_as_taggable_on` plugin to retrieve all tags for a particular story.

Each of the following lines correspond to a rendered template; when Rails renders a layout template, it explicitly says so by logging `within`:

```
Rendered stories/_story.html.erb (52.8ms)
 Rendered stories/index.html.erb within layouts/application
↳ (63.4ms)
```

A summary entry appears at the end of each page request:

```
Completed 200 OK in 325ms (Views: 278.9ms | ActiveRecord:
↳ 3.1ms)
```

This summary contains totals for the time spent by each of the areas of the application responsible for serving the request. Rails tells us the amount of time that was spent rendering templates and talking to the database (both listed in milliseconds).

You don't need to be a mathematician to figure out that a whopping 43 milliseconds is missing from these numbers. One reason for this difference is that serving the request took only a couple of milliseconds. These numbers come from my version of Readit, which is quite a small application, and the benchmark calculation struggles when calculating time information using such small numbers. In the meantime, Figure 11-14 shows the log file from a complete page request.

For all the comfort and speed that Rails provides developers, it does have its drawbacks. The framework certainly requires a large amount of CPU time in order to make your life easy, which is another explanation for the missing milliseconds in the previous timing calculation; however, the good news is that your framework's overhead won't necessarily increase as your code becomes more complicated. With larger applications, these numbers do become more accurate.

11-14. Benchmarking information in the log file

In any case, it's important to look at your log files every now and then to assess how your application is performing. As I cautioned, take these numbers with a grain of salt—learn to interpret them by changing your code and comparing the new numbers with previous incarnations of the code. This will help you develop a feel for how your changes affect the speed of your application. You should not, however, use them as absolute measures.

Manual Benchmarking

While the default information presented by the Rails log files is great for an overview of how long a certain action takes, the log files cannot provide timing information for a specific group of code statements. For this purpose, Ruby provides the `Benchmark` module, which can be wrapped around any block of code that you'd like to benchmark.

As an example, let's add benchmarking information for the story fetcher implemented in the `fetch_stories` method of our `StoriesController` class. It's located in `app/controllers/stories_controller.rb`:

```ruby
class StoriesController < ApplicationController
  : class methods…
  def fetch_stories(conditions)
    results = Benchmark.measure do
      @stories = Story.where(conditions).order("id ASC")
    end
    Rails.logger.info results
  end
end
```

As you can see, the `Benchmark` class includes a class method called `measure` that simply wraps around the `Story.where` statement:

```ruby
results = Benchmark.measure do
  : code being benchmarked…
end
```

The result of the `measure` method is saved in a `results` variable that we then write to the log file:

```ruby
Rails.logger.info results
```

When you request Readit's front page or upcoming stories queue now (both pages make use of the `fetch_stories` method we just modified), you should find that the corresponding benchmark entries are added to the log file at `log/development.log`:

```
Started GET "/stories" for 127.0.0.1 at 2016-05-06 08:39:05
↳ -0400
Processing by StoriesController#index as HTML
  User Load (0.1ms)  SELECT  "users".* FROM "users" WHERE (1)
↳ ORDER BY "users"."id" ASC LIMIT 1
   0.010000   0.000000   0.010000 (  0.005202)
 . . .
```

Using manual benchmarks in this way gives you an idea of the amount of time required to execute certain parts of your code. Additionally, `Benchmark` has several methods for measuring blocks of code, which leads to ...

EXTRA CREDIT: Master the Art of Benchmarking

Take a look at the Benchmark module in the Ruby documentation[10]. Use one of its other methods to measure code in Readit. Become a benchmarking wizard.

Summary

In this chapter, we've dealt with some of the less glamorous—but very helpful—aspects of software development. We used `debug` statements to inspect certain objects in our views, created a web console on the page to execute Ruby commands in the application, utilized the log files written by Rails to document certain occurrences in Readit, and looked at how the byebug tool can be employed to set breakpoints and explore our application at runtime.

We also covered the topic of integration tests—broad scenario-based tests that have the ability to go beyond the isolated testing of models and controllers.

[10] http://ruby-doc.org/stdlib-2.2.0/libdoc/benchmark/rdoc/Benchmark.html

Finally, we talked briefly about the benchmarks that Rails provides by default, and explored a manual approach to benchmarking a specific group of statements.

In the next and final chapter, we'll take Readit into production mode and discuss the options available for deploying a Rails application for the whole world to use!

Chapter 12

Deployment and Production Use

When Rails applications start to fledge, as their guardian you have to take extra care to make sure they can fly. Admittedly, though, the term "roll" would be more appropriate in the Rails context!

In this final chapter, we'll review the variety of components involved in the process of deploying a Rails application to a production system. Following that, we'll look at fine-tuning an application's deployment so that it's able to cope with a moderate amount of traffic.

The Implications of "Production"

Back in <u>Chapter 4</u>, we discussed the different environments Rails provides for each stage of an application's life cycle. Yet we barely scratched the surface of what it means to flip the switch between the development and production environments.

In a nutshell, moving to the production environment results in four major changes to the way in which our application is run:

- **The Ruby classes that make up your application are no longer reloaded *on each request*.** This means that Ruby's reloading of each class on each request is a nice feature of the development environment because it allows you to make rapid changes to your application code and see the effects immediately; however, when your application's in production mode, the primary requirement is that it is *fast*, which is impossible to accomplish when reloading Ruby classes over and over again. To gain the effects of any changes you make to code while the application's in production mode, you need to restart the application.

- **Your application's users receive short, helpful error messages; they're not presented with the stack trace.** Obviously, the beautifully detailed stack trace that you investigate when you find an error in your code is not what you want users of your application to see. Fear not! Rails never throws stack traces at users while it's in production mode. Instead, you can use the Exception Notification gem to dispatch an email to the system's administrators, notifying them of a potential problem in the code[1]. The email includes the same detailed stack trace you'd see in your browser if you were still in development. In fact, the Exception Notification gem has many notifiers, including HipChat, Slack, and Webhooks in addition to email. With the error notification dealt with, you can simply use a generic error page within your application informing users that an error has occurred and the administrators have been notified.

EXTRA CREDIT: Utilizing External Gems

Using the procedure to pull in an external gem—as we did in Chapter 10—add the Exception Notification gem to Readit and configure it for your needs

- **Caching is available for pages, actions, and page fragments.** To improve the performance of your application, you can cache its pages, actions, and even

---

[1.] https://github.com/smartinez87/exception_notification

fragments of pages. This means that the fully rendered page (or fragment) is written to the file system, as well as being displayed in the user's browser. The next request that's responded to by this page, action, or fragment is served without the data that it contains needing to be recalculated. Rails' caching features are especially useful in situations in which your pages have no user-specific content, and everyone sees the same pages.

Rails expects your static assets to be "precompiled". Rails expects you to be smart about your static assets (JavaScript, CSS files, and so on) and compile them into single files per resource type. For example, all of the JavaScript files referenced in the `app/assets/javascripts/application.js` manifest file should be available as a *single* file in production. Otherwise, the browser will make a call per file, which is expensive. It's the same for the CSS files and `applicaion.css`. Additionally, Rails wants you to digest the single JavaScript and CSS files, which makes them much more cachable. We'll cover more on this process later in the chapter, but remember it's all about performance and best practices.

In the following sections, we'll talk about the server software components that are well-suited for production use, and look at what we can do to make Readit happy and healthy in a production environment.

Choosing a Production Environment

In simple terms, a production deployment of Rails (or any server-side framework or language) boils down to two major components: the web server and the application server. Web servers have always been very good at delivering static content, such as HTML pages, images, JavaScript and CSS files, and so on; however, they are ill-equipped to handle dynamic content, such as that generated by a Rails application. As such, we also need an application server that can accept requests, forward them to our Rails application, and return a response that web servers and browsers will understand.

To put it differently, you want these items to do what they're good at: a web server to serve static files and an application server to talk to Rails. The web server will be on the front lines of our production application, which means it will forward any request for non-static content to the application server. The following figure displays this procedure.

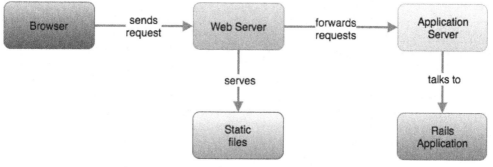

12-1. The Production Environment

For years, setting up a production environment was a difficult, frustrating task. Quite often, developers would have to turn to an army of system administrators for help. But as the software that powers a production website became standardized and the environments more reproducible, smart people commoditized the offering. You've heard of the term "Software-as-a-Service" (SaaS), no doubt. The Internet is rife with companies offering various packaged services and, luckily for us, a production environment for Rails applications is one of them. These offerings use terms such as "Platform-as-a-Service" (PaaS) or "Infrastructure-as-a-Service" (IaaS), riding the SaaS wave and making our lives much easier.

So, while it's important for you as a Rails developer to understand the high-level components involved in serving a Rails application, we'll be opting for the easy road. I'll explain the major components that are used, but we'll use a SaaS offering to deploy the site.

With that said, let's look at two web server software packages that are available to use with Rails applications under the terms of various free software licenses. Several commercial web servers that support Rails applications are also available, but for the sake of simplicity and relevance, we'll only look at open-source options.

Web Servers

Apache

With more than 30% market share, the free Apache web server written and maintained by the Apache Software Foundation is certainly the de facto standard on the web server software market[2]. Apache is a good all-purpose cross-platform web server. It's used by many web hosting providers.

Apache has many strengths, one of which is the huge number of extensions that are available to expand its feature set. It also has a robust interface for back-end services, a useful URL rewriter, and extensive logging capabilities. It's available as free software under the Apache license.

Nginx

Another player in this market is nginx (pronounced "engine x")[3], a high-performance HTTP and proxy server that was originally developed by Igor Sysoev to power several high-traffic sites in Russia.

Many performance evaluations have revealed that nginx is the leader of the pack in terms of raw speed, with Apache scoring second. Apart from outstanding performance, nginx also offers excellent proxy and caching capabilities, SSL support, and flexible configuration options. Nginx is available under the BSD license.

Application Servers

We've briefly covered web servers, so it's time to move on to the next player in our production game: application servers. As mentioned, application servers take in requests and transform them into something Rails can handle. Rails ships with an application server called Puma, by default. You may have noticed it whenever you fire up Readit with `rails s`; for example:

```
$ rails s
 > Booting Puma
```

[2.] http://httpd.apache.org/
[3.] http://nginx.net/

```
 => Rails 5.0.0 application starting in development on
 ↳ http://localhost:3000
 => Run `rails server -h` for more startup options
 Puma starting in single mode...
 * Version 3.4.0 (ruby 2.3.0-p0), codename: Owl Bowl Brawl
 * Min threads: 5, max threads: 5
 * Environment: development
 * Listening on tcp://localhost:3000
 Use Ctrl-C to stop
```

Puma starts up Readit on port 3000, and we're in business. Obviously, Puma is capable of taking a standard HTTP request and providing it to our Rails application, since we haven't used a web server in development. In fact, most Rails developers feel there's no need to use a classic web server in development, as Puma (or another app server) is good enough. To drive this point home, all the application servers we'll discuss in this book are *also* web servers.

As you might imagine, there are many application server options out there today, each with their own strengths and weaknesses. Because Rails is awesome, it's very easy to switch between them. Puma is a perfectly reasonable–if not preferred–option for a production application server, so we'll use it; however, before we do that, let's talk about *why* we can switch app servers so easily.

Rack

The need to easily switch out application servers for Rails applications has been around as long as Rails itself. In the days of yore, switching to a new application server could be tedious and only for the technically experienced. As a result, a gentleman named Christian Neukirchen decided to make a universal handler for connecting web servers to web frameworks (such as Rails) and called it **Rack**[4]. Rack is now the standard way that web frameworks expose themselves to web servers in Ruby.

By complying with the Rack interface, web/application servers can now presume they are communicating with a Rack-based application. Rails is Rack-based, as

---

[4.] http://rack.github.io/

are most of the other Ruby-based web frameworks. Thanks to Rack, developers can write application servers galore without worrying if it will work with Rails. The Ruby community is incredible.

> **EXTRA CREDIT: Racking Up Your Know-how**
>
> It is very much worth your while to read up on Rack. As well as being everywhere in the Ruby web landscape, its design is dead simple. You can learn a lot about HTTP by looking at how Rack works.

So, Puma talks to Rack and Rails is a Rack-compliant web framework. This means that all the application servers we discuss also talk to Rack. But Rack integration is just one part of what application servers do. Each application server takes a different approach to *how* it handles web requests. Let's talk about a couple of pieces of terminology that will help you understand the *how* of each application server before we discuss the servers themselves.

Terminology

Concurrency

When you start to read about web application servers, you'll see a lot about concurrency. **Concurrency** is the ability to *manage* many tasks simultaneously. Think of cooking a big meal. If you had the chicken, the rice and the green beans all going on the stove, you are cooking them concurrently, even if you aren't actively interacting with each all the time. Concurrency, as you can surmise, is a boon for a web server. Handling multiple requests allows a web server to be more performant, and better performance is what we want of our applications.

> **Note: Concurrency ≠ Parallelism**
>
> void confusing concurrency with parallelism. **Parallelism** is doing multiple tasks at exactly the same time. In the meal analogy, it means there's another chef making a salad while you cook the rest of the meal. It's a subtle but important difference.

Threads

If you've been around computing for a bit, you're bound to know (at least, at a high level) what threads are. A **thread** is an execution context with a set of instructions. In other words, when you ask Ruby to perform a task, those instructions are executed on a thread. A process can own multiple threads, which affects concurrency and parallelism.

If an application server is **multi-threaded**, it spawns a thread for each request (or has a pool of threads from which it draws.) Threads are very light, so a single instance of the Rails application can handle many requests.

When you start dealing with threads, it can become complicated. There are fearsome-sounding terms such as **deadlocks** and **race conditions**, which mean your application is either frozen, or has corrupted the data. When an application is **thread-safe**, it can work in a multi-threaded environment without any of those haunting side effects. Unfortunately, since Ruby has never had *real* threading, many Ruby gems fall short of being thread-safe, which means running a Rails app in a truly multi-threaded environment can be challenging.

Threading in Ruby is a massive topic and well beyond the scope of this book. MRI, which stands for Matz's Ruby Interpreter—Ruby's default interpreter, has a global interpreter lock (GIL) that ensures only one thread is executing at any given moment. Ruby switches between threads as needed, but only one is being executed. This avoids a lot of the issues with multi-threading, but has its limitations when it comes to scalability. Again, this is a big topic, so I'm going to suggest you do some ...

 EXTRA CREDIT: Avoid Losing the Thread

While MRI Ruby has the GIL, there are Ruby interpreters with "true" threads, such as JRuby and Rubinius. Needless to say, there's a lot to know about threads. Jesse Storimer has written a wonderful book on it called *Working with Ruby Threads*[5], which I can't recommend highly enough.

[5.] http://www.jstorimer.com/products/working-with-ruby-threads

Multi-process

Concurrent programming and threading are hard. Really hard. In fact, the first rule of concurrent programming is "Don't." If that's the case, what is another option? Well, one is to run multiple processes, each with its own copy of the application. Web servers that run in this manner are called **multi-process**, and they run an instance of the Rails application in each process they spawn. As you can imagine, this requires a much larger footprint than a multi-threaded server, but it avoids the issues of concurrent programming.

Evented Programming

Yet another way to approach concurrency is with **evented programming**. In evented programming, the server fires an event for each request, supplying a callback function to the event that will be executed when the request completes. This is how Node.js works. The main process can then handle other requests while the events are doing work. If your mom told you to go to the store to get eggs, and to call her when you are back home, she has fired off a "GET EGGS" event and the phone call is the callback function. This, in essence, is how evented programming works.

Application Servers for Rails

Now that you have a basic idea of some of the terminology, let's cover one application server per concurrency approach.

Puma

Puma[6] is "A Modern, Concurrent Web Server for Ruby." It is classified as multi-threaded, which means Puma uses a pool of threads to handle web requests. Puma supports *true concurrency* due to the way it uses threads. This translates as Puma having a small footprint but still being able to handle a true multi-threaded environment. In essence, Puma has the potential to be the most efficient server of the bunch, especially if you employ a Ruby interpreter that uses real threads, such as JRuby.

[6.] http://puma.io/

Puma can also be run as a multi-process server, so you don't have to have a thread-safe Rails app to use it. Even in its multi-process form, Puma is still the favorite of many a Rails developer.

Thin

Thin[7] is an evented web server, meaning that it fires events for HTTP requests that are handled by a pool of application instances. The main process then handles the callbacks from the applications and responds to the client. It does this with the "event loop", which accepts requests, fires events, and responds to callbacks. In actuality, thin can handle requests in chunks, enabling efficient handling of streaming requests.

Because of its evented nature, thi excels at handling slow clients and large file uploads without blocking the Rails app. When a user wants to upload a 1080i HD cat video, thin will hand that request off to a worker and return to accept more requests in the meantime.

Unicorn

Unicorn[8] is a multi-process server, so thread safety is not an issue. Unicorn has a master process that monitors "workers", which are essentially instances of your Rails application. Unicorn is designed to handle "fast clients" on high bandwidth connections and it will only work on operating systems that support `fork()` (which excludes Windows, sorry.)

Unicorn was once the belle of the application server ball, but the Internet is not always full of high-bandwidth fast clients. Still, if your use case matches Unicorn's strengths, it's a great piece of software.

Proxying Requests

In the vanilla production environment that consists of a web server and an application server, requests must be proxied from the former to the latter. This is

---

[7.] http://code.macournoyer.com/thin/
[8.] http://unicorn.bogomips.org/

often accomplished in the web server configuration files. Each web server, obviously, has a different way to configure itself as a proxy server. What's important to understand is that the proxying must happen, and it's usually a simple configuration step.

We'll be skipping that configuration in this book, as we're going to leverage a SaaS provider for our production needs instead. If you are curious about how, for example, Nginx is configured to proxy requests, then you have some more ... EXTRA CREDIT.

Software as a Service

As has been mentioned, the creation of a production environment has evolved to the point that companies can offer it as a service. As a result, we can use the tools offered by these companies to easily get Readit on the Internet.

Furthermore, these companies package the production environments with other bells and whistles, such as add-ons for various databases, analytics services, and more. Obviously, there is a cost associated with these services; however, there is also a free plan that allows you to get started without burning a hole in your wallet.

Let's take a look at one of the most popular IaaS services on the Internet: Heroku.

Heroku

Heroku[9] is an Infrastructure-as-a-Service offering that enables developers to create sophisticated deployments for their applications. Apps are deployed using Git, which we discussed in Chapter 2. Revisiting the Git basics we discussed then, when you install Heroku's tools and use them to create a Heroku application for Readit, a Git remote called "heroku" is created. Pushing code to this remote will deploy the application. Here, let me show you ...

[9.] https://www.heroku.com/

Sign Up for a Heroku Account

Visit Heroku's sign-up page[10] and create a free account. You can choose "Ruby" as
your primary language.

Once you've confirmed your account, sign in to Heroku.

Install the Heroku Toolbelt

In order to deploy to Heroku, we need the Heroku toolbelt. Visit the download
page[11] and install the Heroku tools, which is a simple download and executable.
Once installed, you should have a `heroku` command available on the command
line:

```
$ heroku --version
heroku-toolbelt/3.43.2 (x86_64-darwin10.8.0) ruby/1.9.3
heroku-cli/5.1.7-0de2607 (darwin-amd64) go1.6.2
```

Log in to Heroku using the `heroku login` command:

```
$ heroku login
Enter your Heroku credentials.
Email: glenn.goodrich@sitepoint.com
Password (typing will be hidden):
Logged in as glenn.goodrich@sitepoint.com
```

Awesome.

Prepare Readit for Heroku

We have to make some small changes to our application so that it can be
deployed to Heroku. Heroku requires us to use some gems and change the

---

[10.] https://signup.heroku.com/?c=70130000001x9jFAAQ
[11.] https://toolbelt.heroku.com/

database we use in production. Heroku does not support SQLite and requires that we use PostgreSQL[12], a very popular open-source database.

Open up the `Gemfile` in our Readit application and add the following:

```
                                                12-2. Gemfile (excerpt)

... rest of gems ...
gem 'rails_12factor'
group :production do
  gem 'pg'
end
```

We also need to move our `gem "sqlite3"` line into the `group :test, :development` block:

```
                                                12-3. Gemfile (excerpt)

group :development, :test do
  gem 'byebug'
  gem 'pry-rails'
  gem 'sqlite3'
end
```

The database configuration for production has to reflect our need to use PostgreSQL. Open up `config/database.yml` and change the `production` key to:

```
                                            12-4. config/database.yml (excerpt)

production:
  adapter: postgresql
  database: readit_production
  encoding: unicode
```

Finally, we add all of our changes to our local Git repository:

[12.] http://www.postgresql.org/

```
$ git add .
$ git commit -m "Changes for Heroku"
[chapter12 469d64f] Changes for Heroku
3 files changed, 17 insertions(+), 6 deletions(-)
```

Okay, now we're ready to create our application on Heroku.

Create and Deploy the Heroku Application

Using the Heroku tools, create an application on Heroku:

```
$ heroku create
Creating app... done, safe-temple-15085
 https://safe-temple-15085.herokuapp.com/ |
↳ https://git.heroku.com/safe-temple-15085.git
```

Here, Heroku just created an application called "safe-temple-15085" on the Heroku platform for my Readit application. You can see that Heroku tells me where the app will live on the Internet (`https://safe-temple-15085.herokuapp.com/`), as well as the address of the Git remote on Heroku (`https://git.heroku.com/safe-temple-15085.git`).

 Heroku Naming

> The name of your Heroku app will be different, as it's randomly generated for each `heroku create`.

And now, the moment of truth. Let's push Readit to Heroku:

```
$ git push heroku master
Total 0 (delta 0), reused 0 (delta 0)
remote: Compressing source files... done.
... lots of output ...
remote: -----> Launching...
remote:        Released v5
```

```
remote:            https://safe-temple-15085.herokuapp.com/
↳ deployed to Heroku
remote:
remote: Verifying deploy.... done.
To https://git.heroku.com/safe-temple-15085.git
```

Boom! Readit is now on the Internet. If you look through all the output, you can see that Heroku installed our bundle, ran the assets precompile task, and launched our site; however, our database still needs to be migrated, so run the following:

```
$ heroku run rails db:migrate
 Running rails db:migrate on safe-temple-15085... up,
↳ run.8163
 (10.7ms)  CREATE TABLE "schema_migrations" ("version"
↳ character varying NOT NULL)
 (4.5ms)  CREATE UNIQUE INDEX  "unique_schema_migrations" ON
↳ "schema_migrations"  ("version")
 ActiveRecord::SchemaMigration Load (1.5ms)  SELECT
↳ "schema_migrations".* FROM "schema_migrations"
 ... the rest of the migrations ...
```

Heroku opens up a session on the platform and runs our migrations. Now we're ready:

```
$ heroku open
```

This command will open your Heroku application in a web browser.

12-5. Readit on the Internet

How cool is that? The answer is: really darn cool!

I know. You're sitting there wondering how you can use it without having a login. We never implemented a sign-up page, did we? (I smell EXTRA CREDIT!) Well, we can create a user the same way we did locally–by using a Rails console:

```
$ heroku run rails console
Running rails console on safe-temple-15085... up, run.6215
Loading production environment (Rails 4.2.5.1)
 irb(main):001:0> User.create(email:
↳ "glenn.goodrich@sitepoint.com", name: "Glenn Goodrich",
↳ password: "password", password_confirmation: "password")
 => #<User id: 1, password_digest:
↳ "$2a$10$FOuQ8.OH/Tm9tZ7NWSO9KuWJvyqQ7PEe25NqF9cq/er...", na
```

Now you can log in as that user and submit stories to your heart's content.

Services such as Heroku are invaluable to programmers such as us. We can work the way we work ("code, add, commit, push") and our applications are deployed to the Internet without fuss.

Obviously, there is much more that Heroku offers, as well as which there are many other considerations around deploying an app to the world. This chapter was to get you started and give you a quick win. Now it's up to you to take the world by storm.

 Free Plan Limitations

The free plan on Heroku, which is what we're using, constrains your application in a few ways. It only allows you to have a single application process, and it requires your application to "sleep" for six out of every 24 hours. So, if your app is unresponsive, or you are receiving messages about upgrading your plan, that's why.

EXTRA CREDIT: Explore More of Heroku

Heroku has a massive offering. You can append logging or analytics add-ons to your app with just a few mouse clicks. Explore the Heroku Dashboard[13] and the various add-ons that Heroku offers. You'll be amazed.

Alternatives for Session Storage

Once your application is deployed, you'll probably start thinking about ways to improve performance and security. Some low-hanging fruit here are how Rails stores sessions.

As we discussed in Chapter 9, Rails creates a new session for every visitor–logged in or not–by default. Each session is stored in a cookie by default, which is contained in the user's browser. Cookies are not the best way to store session data, as they have size limits (4KB), are insecure, and bloat the requests to and responses from your server.

[13.] https://dashboard.heroku.com/

As a result, when you either want to store additional information in the session (or the flash) or when you need to create more advanced features such as user online statistics or server-side session expiration, the situation becomes a bit dicey with cookie-based sessions.

For this reason, Rails supports alternative session storage containers,one of which we'll look at in this section.

 The Nitty Gritty on Rails Sessions

Justin Weiss, a well-known Rubyist and blogger, wrote a fantastic post on how sessions in Rails work[14]. I recommend you read it.

The `ActiveRecord Store` Session Container

One of the most popular options after the cookie-based default is the `ActiveRecord Store` session container, which stores all session data within a table in your database. While this is not as fast as other options, using `ActiveRecord Store` allows sessions to be accessed from multiple machines—an essential feature for applications large enough to require multiple servers. It's also straightforward to configure. These abilities make `ActiveRecord Store` the preferred option for applications that attract low-to-medium levels of traffic, so let's configure Readit to use it now.

The `ActiveRecord Store` used to be a part of core Rails, but it's been moved to a separate gem, so we'll need to add it to our app. Adding gems to your Rails app should be second nature by now, so add the following to the `Gemfile` and run `bundle install`:

```
gem 'activerecord-session_store'
```

Now we need to make room in our database for the session data. The `activerecord-session_store` gem provides a shortcut for this job in the form of a generator to create a sessions table migration:

[14.] http://www.justinweiss.com/articles/how-rails-sessions-work

```
$ rails generate active_record:session_migration
Running via Spring preloader in process 10919
    create  db/migrate/20160515161105_add_sessions_table.rb
```

This command will create a new migration file that contains the Ruby code necessary to create an appropriate `sessions` table to hold our session data. The migration can then be applied using the regular migration task `db:migrate`:

```
$ rails db:migrate
```

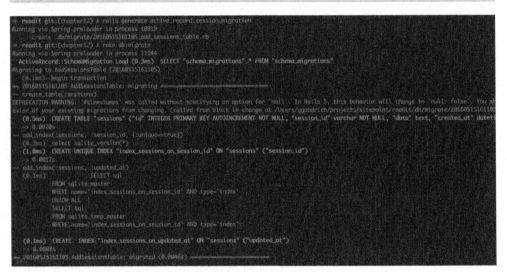

12-6. Migrational output

The figure above shows the output of these migrations being applied.

Next, we tell Rails that we want to use the `ActiveRecord Store` instead of the default file-based session container. We can relay the good news via the `config/initializers/session_store.rb` file; simply change the `cookie_store` value to `active_record_store`:

```
# Change
  Rails.application.config.session_store :cookie_store, key:
↳ '_readit_session'
```

```
#to
 Rails.application.config.session_store :active_record_store,
 ↪ key: '_readit_session'
```

As soon as you restart the application (using `rails s`), sessions will be stored in the SQL database.

We'll need to push that change to our Heroku application so that it's picked up in production. In the root of your Readit source, commit the changes:

```
$ git add .
$ git commit -m "Use ActiveRecord Session Store"
$ git push heroku master
... redeploys site ...
```

Once the site is deployed, run the migration on our Heroku database to create the new sessions table:

```
$ heroku run rails db:migrate
```

The result is shown below.

12-7. Creating the new sessions table

Now we're using the ActiveRecord Session Store in production. It's worth noting that there are other session storage options (such as the `Cache Store`), as well as many authored by the community.

Further Reading

We've done it! Our application is ready for initial public consumption, and the hands-on parts of this book have come to an end. I would still, however, like to alert you to a few additional Rails features and extensions that may come in handy in your future encounters with Rails applications. Think of this as an entire section of EXTRA CREDIT.

Caching

Depending on the project budget and the availability of hardware, every Rails application can only serve so many dynamic pages at any given time. If your app happens to receive traffic numbers that exceed these limits, you'll have to consider options for tackling this problem. One such option is to add caching. **Caching** is a way to store previously generated content that remains unchanged so it can quickly be served again. If you are looking at the list of upcoming stories, and it's the same as it was when you last looked, it's better to see the *same* rendered view than to re-render the view *again*. Caching allows this to happen.

Rails' built-in caching options vary in their levels of granularity. The simplest of all possibilities is to cache whole pages in the form of HTML files. What Rails does in such cases is to take the output that's sent to the browser, and store it in a file on the server's hard disk. This file can then be served directly by the web server without even bothering Puma, provided your setup is configured appropriately. This saves Rails from regenerating page content over and over again, even though the content may not have changed between successive requests for the same page. Another option allows you to cache the outputs of single actions and even fragments of views (a sidebar, for example).

Caching can do wonders to improve your application's performance; however, take care to ensure that the relevant sections of the cache are flushed when pages change, otherwise your users will receive outdated content. Additionally, using cached pages may not be feasible if your application depends on a lot of user-specific content—for instance, in an application whose page content changes depending on who's using it.

The Rails documentation for the caching feature is available online[15].

ActionCable

One of the more exciting changes to the latest version of Rails (version 5) is the addition of **ActionCable**. ActionCable brings WebSockets into your Rails application. What are WebSockets, you ask? WebSockets, effectively, open a two-way communication channel between the browser and the server. Traditionally, the only way the client and server interact in a web application is when the browser posts data to or requests data from the server. With the advent of AJAX (which we discussed in Chapter 7), a one-way, asynchronous channel *from* the browser *to* the server is possible. Using AJAX, if the browser wanted to know when events happen on the server, it can poll in the background and it feels like it's real time. By "poll" I mean that the browser has an infinite loop that runs at a certain interval (maybe, every 10 seconds) and makes a request to the server. Polling for server-side changes is expensive, error-prone, and ties up resources. It would be nice if the server could simply send events to the browser when they happen, without the browser having to poll.

WebSockets does just that. A two-way communications channel is opened between the server and client, and data can be sent in both directions. This opens up the realm of real-time applications. A good example is a chat application, where you have a browser-based client that subscribes to a WebSocket-based channel and the server sends new chat data on the channel as your fellow chatters chat. It feels like a "real" (meaning, not web-based) application. ActionCable takes the convention-based approach of Rails to incorporate WebSockets into your application. The use cases are endless.

When you're ready to look into WebSockets and ActionCable, check out these two articles on SitePoint:

- ActionCable and WebSockets[16]
- Creating a Chat Application in Rails 5[17]

Those posts will get you well on your way to real-time application fun.

[15.] http://api.rubyonrails.org/classes/ActionController/Caching.html
[16.] https://www.sitepoint.com/action-cable-and-websockets-an-in-depth-tutorial/
[17.] https://www.sitepoint.com/create-a-chat-app-with-rails-5-actioncable-and-devise/

Rails API

Another trend in current web application development is the proliferation of the Application Programming Interface, or API. An API is an application that exposes its data and functionality for *other* applications, as opposed to users. An API is meant to be a building block for a larger application, providing functionality to make up the whole. Almost all the services you use on the internet today expose an API, including Twitter, Facebook, Google Maps, and the list goes on and on (and on.)

Before Rails 5, in order to build an API with Rails you had to include some external gems, remove all the view libraries, and go through some custom configuration to get your Rails app into an API-friendly state. Since the Rails Core team is always looking to make Rails useful for today's developers solving today's problems with today's approaches, they made creating an Rails-based API application much easier.

You'll be happy to know that an API application uses many of the things we've already discussed in this book (RESTful routes, JSON) so when you're ready for Shovell to expose an API-only set of endpoints, you won't have much new to learn. Basically, you just start a new Rails app with `rails new readit-api --api` and you're cooking with gas.

We've talked briefly about how Rails will never annoy your users with extensive stack traces if an error occurs in your application. Instead, it will display a polite message to the user that the request couldn't be processed successfully. The default templates for these messages can be found in `public/404.html` and `public/500.html`.

But what if you want to *fix* such errors instead of silently ignoring them? You could certainly comb through your log files every day, checking for unusual activity. Better yet, you could install the `exception_notification` gem, which hooks into your application and sends you an email whenever some unusual activity happens.

The gem can be installed using Bundler; that is, by adding it to the `Gemfile` and running `bundle install`. Documentation that explains how to customize its behavior is available online[18].

Performance

Inevitably as a developer, you will need to optimize your application for performance. Most of the time, performance optimizations focus on single bits in the larger framework of your application. Sometimes it's about making a SQL query run faster, other times it's about caching, and still other times it might be a change in the Javascript. I'll give you a nudge on one potential, and very common, optimization. Back in Chapter 10, we added stories to the `User` model, and in the `Story` show view, we called:

```
Submitted by: <%= story.user.name %>
```

Since `story.user` walks down an association, it must access a *second* table (the `users` table.) This requires a second SQL query. In technical terms, this is what's known as an "N+1 Query" and it's a very, very common source of performances issues. Ideally, since we know that we want to display the user, we'd include the Story's user in the *first* call to the database, along with the stories. That saves us one round trip/story, which can be significant when Readit is huge and has millions of stories.

That is just one example of a performance optimization. There are many, many others, so you know what's coming. But, before we get to that, here are a couple of rules of thumb for performance work:

1. Never optimize too early. Or, more commonly: Performance Optimization is the Root of All Evil. This means that you should not optimize unless you **know** it's going to have an effect. This leads us to...
2. Never optimize something you can't measure. If you can't take before and after measurements around an optimization, then you're probably wasting your time. Refer back to our section on Benchmarking for how to get these numbers.

 EXTRA CREDIT: Getting Rid of the Query

Use Google to figure out how to get rid of our N+1 query in the story show view.

[18.] https://github.com/smartinez87/exception_notification

Summary

In this final chapter, we've plowed through the variety of options available for deploying Rails applications to production systems.

We opted to use Heroku and its service offering to deploy Readit. We took the Readit application code to the production system, initialized the production database, and started serving requests. It doesn't get much easier than that!

Once Readit was running happily in its new environment, we looked at some alternative session storage containers. We found that the `ActiveRecord Store` suited our needs by storing session data in our SQL database.

Finally, I provided a few pointers to more advanced information on some relevant aspects of Rails application development and deployment.

I hope you've found value in the time you've spent with this book, and that you're now able to go forth and build upon what you've learned. Now's the time to get out there and use your knowledge to build an application that changes the Internet! Well, once you finish all your EXTRA CREDIT, that is ...

CPSIA information can be obtained at www.ICGtesting.com
Printed in the USA
BVOW04s0853191016

465445BV00003B/4/P